COME LET US ADORE HIM

Dealing With the Struggle Over Style of Worship

COME LET US ADORE HIM

Dealing With the Struggle Over Style of Worship

DAN DOZIER

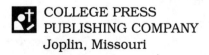
COLLEGE PRESS
PUBLISHING COMPANY
Joplin, Missouri

ISBN 0-89900-749-X (Pbk)

Library of Congress cataloged the hard-cover edition of this as follows:

Dozier, Dan 1952–
    Come let us adore Him: dealing with the struggle over style of
worship in Christian Churches and Churches of Christ/Dan Dozier.
       p.   cm.
    Includes bibliographical references.
    ISBN 0-89900-687-6.
    1. Public worship—Christian Churches and Churches of Christ.
    2. Christian Churches and Churches of Christ—Doctrines.
    3. Music in Churches. I. Title.
BX6799.C25D69 1994
264'.066—dc20
                                       94-38401
                                           CIP

DEDICATION

To JaneLee, my wife of 22 years
and the love of my life,
and to our children, MaryAnn, Amy, and Wesley,
the joys of my life:
Thanks for your love, for your support,
and for your patience,
without which I could never have completed this book.

Table of Contents

Acknowledgments

One might expect to see an acknowledgment page in a book like this. After all, they are customary. What follows is my acknowledgment page; however, it is far more than merely a *customary* feature. After approximately four years of study and work, this book has become a reality, but I did not do it by myself. Scores of individuals contributed to its completion. Many contributed with their prayers, and, although I am unable to name them, I am deeply grateful.

Although I run the risk of overlooking someone's efforts, I dare to mention the names of those who made special contributions. This book actually began as a project/thesis for the completion of my Doctor of Ministry Degree from Abilene Christian University in Abilene, Texas in 1992. Sincere appreciation goes to Drs. Jack Reece and Charles Siburt who served as my primary and secondary advisors for that project. Their counsel steered me in the right direction. Their encouragement kept me going when I felt like stopping. Their enthusiasm for the project made me believe I was doing something that might be genuinely worthwhile to many people.

In its earliest stages, the project/thesis involved a task force of individuals from the Madison Church of Christ who assisted me in the study of worship. They were my first "guinea pigs." They read countless articles, traced down hundreds of Bible verses, and discussed worship for 14 weeks.

Words are inadequate to thank these precious people who gave up their Sunday afternoons for more than three months. The value of their participation was beyond measure. Thanks to Nick Boone, Larry and Linda Bridgesmith, Ronnie Cook, JaneLee Dozier, Bobby Hudson, Billie Jean Marcin, Cliff Mundy, Gerald Parish, Norma Ragan, Margaret Roberts, Mike and Betty Ann Santi, Nila Sherrill, Lorna Shipp, Beverly Smith, Ernie and Mary Taylor, and Marquitta Thomas.

Extra special thanks to Larry Bridgesmith, who not only served as a task force member and my on-site project/thesis monitor, but also as my personal friend and Christian brother who believed in this project and spent more hours helping me than any other individual.

What a staff at the Madison Church! Thank you for your encouragement and for covering for me when I was working so many hours on this project. And what an eldership! I thank them for allowing me the time to do the study and for the opportunity to "field test" this material on them before it was presented to the Madison congregation. Thanks to Steve Flatt, the pulpit minister and my co-worker at Madison. His support meant the world to me, and his assistance in presenting this material to the Madison family was invaluable.

Three cheers for Tammie Flatt and LuAnn Lowe for their outstanding work as proofreaders and to Lyn Rose and Lynn Anderson for their suggestions on improvements in the manuscript.

I would display the height of arrogance if I did not express appreciation for the scores of writers and students of worship whose efforts have enlightened me. Obviously, I have not been able to read all that has been written on worship, but the bibliography at the end of this book acknowledges my indebtedness to authors who have enriched my understanding and magnified my love for the worship of God.

My father and my late mother also contributed to this book — not in direct ways, but in indirect ways. They modeled worship for me during the formative years of my life. Not only did they make certain I was always in worship services, but more importantly, they modeled what the Apostle Paul wrote in Romans 12:1. They offered themselves as living sacrifices. Their holy lives of dedication to the Lord and their unselfish service to others was a demonstration of spiritual worship lived out daily before my eyes. I will be eternally grateful to them for what they taught me.

My children, MaryAnn, Amy, and Wesley, have sacrificed far more time with their daddy than they should have been asked to give in order for me to complete this book. Thanks, kiddos! You're great! I love you, and pray that worship will become as much a passion for you as it is for me.

And last, but certainly not least, thanks to my wife, JaneLee. If it wouldn't embarrass her, I'd write a love letter to her right here, for I want the whole world to know how much I love her. With the gentle push that only a wife can give, she stayed after me relentlessly until this book was completed. Without her support and encouragement I would never have written this book. Thanks, honey! You are my queen!

Above all, I thank the Father in heaven for allowing me to learn more about worship. My prayer is that all who read this book will want to worship Him more fully. He is worthy! So, come, let us adore Him together!

INTRODUCTION
Why Study Worship?

"Bor-ing, bor-ing, bor-ing," they chanted from the bleachers in a listless display of unenthusiastic disgust. Since high school teams do not have to play with a shot clock as college and professional teams must do, the opposing high school basketball team was running a four-corner stall offense, trying to run down the clock and slow up our team's quick and high-powered offense. I refrained from joining in the cheer with the students, but I felt the same way they did — it was boring. Besides, their slow down tactics did not work. They lost the game. Although we won, I did not enjoy the game. It simply moved too slowly. I am glad that few teams play that old slow down game anymore.

What is the most boring thing to you? That is exactly the question producers posed to the audience of the popular television game show, *Family Feud*. The most frequently given answer was "church." Sadly, many Christians have the same response. Public worship elicits little more than disinterested yawns for many Christians who stay up too late on Saturday night to get excited about Sunday morning. Most would rather stay in bed, and many do!

Something is terribly wrong when Christians are not thoroughly absorbed in the worship of God. Robert E. Webber writes:

There is a cancer at the heart of many churches — the failure to understand and practice public worship. There is only one remedy. It is not an easy one and may therefore be shunned by those who are caught up in the instant gratification cult of our modern age. The remedy consists of repentance, . . .a turning away from all shallow and uninformed approaches to worship. It means we must renew our understanding and practice of worship.[1]

Why study the worship of God? Because nothing is more worthy of our attention! The sixteenth century reformer John Calvin spoke of the worship of God as the most exalted form of human activity, observing that nothing else approaches it in dignity and sublimity of experience.[2] C.F.D. Moule exclaimed, "Ultimately, life has no meaning at all unless it is all for God or unless its whole aim is worship."[3] Karl Barth announced, "Christian worship is the most momentous, the most urgent, the most glorious action that can take place in human life."[4] William Nicholls declared that worship is "the supreme and only indispensable activity of the Christian church. It alone will endure. . . into heaven, when all other activities of the church will have passed away."[5]

Although a lot of people would scratch their heads at such marvelous claims for something they consider so uninteresting and unrelated to life, many others would find these same claims intriguing. There is a groundswell of interest in worship these days among people from practically every religious persuasion. That interest is causing many to ask questions which they have never asked before: Are we worshiping as God would have us

[1]Robert E. Webber, *Worship: Old and New* (Grand Rapids: The Zondervan Corp., 1982), p. 20.

[2]M. Eugene Osterhaven, "The Lord's Supper and the Theology and Practice of Calvin," *The Reformed Review* 37 no. 2 (1984): p. 83.

[3]C.F.D. Moule, *Worship in the New Testament* (Richmond, VA: John Knox Press, 1961), p. 85.

[4]Ralph P. Martin, *The Worship of God: Some Theological, Pastoral, and Practical Reflections* (Grand Rapids: William B. Eerdmans Publishing Co., 1982), p. 1.

[5]*Ibid.*, p. 209.

worship? Are our traditional forms of worship pleasing to God? Is it possible to sense God's presence in worship? Can worship touch our emotions and still be biblical? Is there some way to make worship more contemporary and more alive?

Not surprisingly, a storm of controversy swirls around the issue of worship. While one group of Christians is asking the above questions, another group is asking: What's wrong with our worship the way it is? Why all the clamoring for something new? Who are these people instigating all this change? Why do they want to sing all those new songs, and what's all this talk about emotions? Don't they know where all this will lead?

Obviously, everyone's interest in worship is not the same. Some want to re-plow old ground to see what they will dig up; others feel compelled to dig in their heels and resist any notion of change. This alone might be reason enough to study worship, but it is not my principal purpose. It would take the wisdom of Solomon to sort out all the issues surrounding worship, and, even then, there probably still would not be unanimous agreement.

My primary purpose is much simpler: I want to discover how God wants me to express the adoration I have for Him. I have a deep longing — a yearning — to know God and to be in His presence. I want to tell Him how wonderful He is. I want to show Him how grateful I am for His goodness and how thankful I am for His mercy and love. I hunger for more meaningful ways to express those feelings both privately and in the assembly with others who also love the Lord. And, I want to do so with great freedom and joy.

Many others thirst for that same kind of worship. I have not experienced that type of worship nearly as often as I want to. Far too often I have gone to the assembly to worship, only to leave wondering if I had connected with God that day. Too many times I have gone through all the right motions but left my heart somewhere else. On too many occasions, I have left the assembly feeling emotionally cold and spiritually dry.

Most of those times my lack of fulfillment was no one's fault but my own. I came with wrong expectations or, worse yet, with no expectations at all. I came looking to receive something rather than to give something. I left frustrated and with a burden of guilt at the boredom I had felt that day. And there have been times when I have tried to lay the blame for my lack of fulfillment on worship leaders, or traditions, or anything other than myself. Every time I have done that, I have been wrong.

Ultimately, worship depends not on what others do in the assembly but on what *I* do. Whether I truly worship or not depends on what I bring to worship. Therefore I take responsibility for the times I have failed to worship, even though I have gone through the acts of worship. If you feel bored with worship where you assemble, resist the temptation to blame it on those who lead you. Even if the singing is poor and the sermon wanders, or the prayers are rote and the ushers seem to be attempting to set a new speed record for serving the Lord's Supper, *you* have the responsibility to make your heart right before the Lord. You must overcome the hindrances to worship so that you can praise Him anyway!

Yes, each of us is responsible to worship God regardless of how well or poorly those who lead us do their job. However, it is sad when individuals *have to work so hard* week after week to feel that they have worshiped acceptably. Do there have to be so many hindrances to worship? No! Why should we tolerate services that demonstrate no planning week after week? We should insist on better! Is there any excuse for poorly selected songs or ill-prepared sermons? None! Is it good that the congregation be subjected to an order that is so routine that people can go through it half asleep and never miss a beat?

We must not be afraid to explore ways to improve worship. Some people feel threatened when someone suggests a need to restudy their doctrinal beliefs and religious practices. However, if we are unwilling to open the Scriptures and study them with an open mind, we may be guilty of merely defending the opinions of those who have studied the issues before us. That is a rather lazy and irresponsible way to approach our understanding of and relationship with the Lord. This was not the manner with which the forefathers of the Restoration Movement pursued their understanding of God's will. They explored the Bible's teachings with a critical eye, as if they were investigating it for the first time. It was their critical and exploratory thinking that eventually led them to leave their denominational ties and many of their former ways of worship for biblical patterns of worship. Today, they are praised for their open-mindedness and willingness to study the Bible for themselves. Their approach has made them heroes in the Restoration Movement.

However, the open mind and the spirit of inquiry that characterized men like Barton W. Stone, Thomas Campbell, and Alexander Campbell has, in many circles, been replaced with something of a fortress mentality in our own generation. The "critical exploratory thinking" of the early Restoration Movement has been replaced, among some, with the notion that they have fully arrived at the truth and that further examination is unnecessary. Such a mistaken perspective leaves the impression that one is a heretic (or at least a *liberal*) for even raising the questions again. This assessment is an overgeneralization, of course; not everyone among us holds such a defensive mentality toward their biblical understandings. However, many influential leaders have so forcefully and dogmatically defended some "official position" that new thinking about worship, and many other issues, has been discouraged. If we are to enjoy a renewal in worship, we must be willing to critique our current understanding and practice of worship.

We must not only allow one another the privilege of thinking for ourselves, but we must encourage an open atmosphere where individuals can raise questions and express their thoughts. Many people do not feel free to explore and raise questions that seem to challenge established positions. In many cases intolerant believers have, at best, tolerated, and at worst, fostered, a climate that crushes those whose sincere questions and Restoration-like thinking seems to challenge the *party line*. A number of bright and godly people have had their hearts broken and their reputations destroyed by the unloving and caustic pens of those who consider themselves *defenders of the faith*. Such use of fear and intimidation is malicious.

I do not oppose debate and honest exchanges of ideas. It is often in the midst of controversy that we arrive at a better understanding of the truth. What sickens my heart and grieves my soul is the venomous spirit and the inflammatory language used by some who would *straighten out* those with whom they disagree without ever having approached those individuals privately. God forbid that this kind of devilish spirit should prevail among us!

It is long past time to restore the exploratory spirit of the Restoration forefathers! Challenges and questions that arise from a rebellious spirit are motivated and generated in an ungodly heart. I want none of that. However, we have nothing to fear from an honest study of any topic. Rather, we have much to gain. Sadly, many Christians have only an inherited faith — a handed down understanding of what they believe and practice in their own congregations. Many people cannot give a reasoned explanation for why they do the things they do (and leave undone the things they don't do) in worship. "That's just the way we've always done things around here," they may say. "That's the way Daddy and Momma and their parents before them believed. If it's good enough for them, then it's good enough for me." "That's what brother 'So and So' said. If he says it's so, it must be so."

That kind of thinking (or lack of thinking) is tragic because it discourages people from arriving at and *owning* their own faith. It assumes that those courageous souls who have gone before did all the studying and thinking for them. It shows that they have grown too comfortable with their traditions. If currently held positions are truly biblical, they will stand up to the most intense scrutiny, and we will be stronger for the search. If they are not fully accurate, then intense scrutiny will reveal the weaknesses so that we can move toward a truly biblical position.

The responsibility for acceptable worship lies, then, on two fronts — with each worshiper and with those who plan and lead worship. In this book, I am calling for a serious reflection on the way we conduct worship. I am asking you to explore the Scriptures with a fresh look — all with the intent that each of us will become better worshipers and leaders of worship. I pray that you will greet this challenge with a joyful spirit, an open heart, and an eager mind.

Ready? Let's go!

DISCUSSION QUESTIONS
ON INTRODUCTION

1. Why do so many people find worship boring?
2. Why do you think the topic of worship is controversial in many churches these days?
3. Are you satisfied with the worship services where you attend? Why? Why not?
4. What do you expect to gain and to give when you assemble with other Christians to worship?
5. Whose responsibility is it that your worship is both acceptable to God and fulfilling to you?
6. What could make your worship better?
7. Does it frighten you to think that some of the ideas in this book might challenge what you have always believed about worship? Why? Why not?

1

We Need a Sense of Wonder

Our generation is at a distinct advantage over the generations who have preceded us. Science and technology have enabled us to live longer, go farther, travel faster, and live more conveniently than any people before us. We live in an information age. Knowledge continues to explode at such a rapid pace that no one can begin to keep up with it. We are exploring the outer reaches of space, and simultaneously we are investigating the smallest particles of earth. We know and understand more about our universe every day. There probably are very few people who would return to pre-modern times even if they could.

Although we hold a scientific and technological edge over our ancestors, we are also at a distinct disadvantage to them. Pride in our human achievement and a feeling of self-sufficiency have blinded us, in large measure, to the majesty of God. People used to have a greater sense of mystery than most advanced societies do today. Almost all people believed in God (or at least in some divine being) who was *out there* somewhere. God was in heaven — high and holy, all-powerful, all-knowing, and present everywhere. There was a sense of awe and reverence before a God who everyone agreed was too big to understand fully. No one even claimed to understand the mysteries of God — people simply accepted the wonder of God by faith. They marveled at God, were amazed at the Lord, and maintained a healthy fear and respect for the Almighty. It is not that way anymore for countless millions of educated, sophisticated, secularized Westerners. We have grown too smart for all that, or so we think.

Secular people downplay the reality of God, either *out there* in His transcendence or *down here* among us in His immanence. In our scientific age, many people have either reasoned God out of existence altogether or have so reduced Him that the sense of mystery and wonder has disappeared. Modern, humanistic people either attempt to explain Him intellectually and verify Him scientifically, or they lightly approach Him as their good buddy and pal.[1] Cut loose from God, modern people have become pragmatic; if they do not perceive something as being useful, they discard it. They have an attitude of consumerism that asks, "What do I get out of this?," as if getting something out of it expresses an appropriate response to life. When applied to worship, such an attitude pridefully devalues the Lord and treats Him as if He exists to meet our needs.[2]

God Won't Fit in a Box

God is not our servant; He is Almighty God. We must serve Him simply and purely because He is God. We worship Him because He is worthy of worship whether we get anything out of it or not. When we praise and glorify God, we are not conferring anything on God; we are simply recognizing His glory and goodness which are His and always have been His and always will be His. It is only because of God's goodness that we are not consumed when we come into His presence. In His clas-

---

[1] Robert E. Webber, *Worship is a Verb* (Dallas: Word Publishing, 1985), p. 30.
   [2] John E. Burkhart, *Worship: A Searching Examination of the Liturgical Experience* (Philadelphia: The Westminster Press, 1982), pp. 15-16.

sic work, *The Idea of the Holy,* Rudolph Otto describes God as a mystery both terrifying and appealing. In response to those two poles, worship couples a sense of incredible awe with a desire to run toward Him with open arms. There is both a sense of fear and a surge of love filled with a passion to draw near to Him. It is like what Moses experienced when he heard the Lord speak to him from within the burning bush. He wanted to see that incredible sight, but he was afraid to look at God (Exod. 3:1-6). It is the recognition of God's greatness and our frailty that leads us to humble ourselves before Him. When we think too highly of ourselves, we become self-centered. Pride is the greatest enemy of true worship. Humility and reverence are the beginning of the worship of God.

As Isaiah witnessed the awesomeness of the Lord (Isa. 6), so we need to recapture a glimpse of God's majesty, splendor, and glory. Otherwise, in our learning and wisdom, we will become foolish, trading the truth of God for a lie (1 Cor. 1:20-21; Rom. 1:21-22). The truth is that human beings cannot verify God scientifically. We cannot explain His fullness. The Apostle Paul wrote, "For the foolishness of God is wiser than man's wisdom, and the weakness of God is stronger than man's strength" (1 Cor. 1:25).

There are many realities that we cannot detect with any of our five senses. There is what Paul calls "God's secret wisdom" which remains "hidden" to worldly people, but which "God has revealed to us by his Spirit" (1 Cor. 2:7-10). It is only by the Spirit of God that a person is able to understand the realities of the unseen (1 Cor. 2:11-16). Some things are too deep for fleshly minds to comprehend, but "the Spirit searches all things, even the deep things of God" (1 Cor. 2:10). By faith and through the Spirit, Christians are granted insight into the realm of the spiritual which unbelievers cannot see (1 Cor. 1:21, 27-28). However, even Christians see only a small portion of all that God is.

God does show Himself to us, but He also conceals Himself from us. He has revealed Himself to us, yet there is much more of Him that we do not know. God must conceal Himself, for, if He fully showed Himself to us, we could not stand the sight of His majesty. God is too mighty for us to contain or comprehend. We cannot wrap God up in a neat little box where we have Him all figured out and under our control. God's thoughts and ways are higher than our thoughts and ways. Any god which we can explain and control is too small to be God. God is not God unless He remains above us, is more powerful than we are, and is in control of all that exists.

God is Transcendent

This is the meaning of *transcendence*. When we say that God is transcendent, we are admitting that He is above us in every way. Nothing and no one compares to God in His excellence and power and knowledge, or in any other dimension. God is higher than we are. He is beyond our universe and anything we have experienced in this world. The word *transcend* comes from the Latin *transcendere* which literally means *to surmount*. Broken into its parts, *trans* means *beyond* or *over*, and *scandere* means *to climb*. God is so far above us that we cannot climb high enough to reach Him. He is utterly and completely holy — wholly other than us. Therefore, He is deserving of more than all the reverence and awe we can offer Him. God's majesty and holiness demand that we approach Him with reverence.

God is Immanent

Not only is God transcendent, but He is also *imma-*

nent. When we say that God is *immanent* we are saying that He is present with us. He abides with us; even more, He abides *in* us. Herein lies the essence of mystery. The transcendent God, the One who by His very nature is above and beyond us, is also the ever-present God who lives and abides in His people. He dwells among us.

The Apostle John declared that Jesus, the Word, who was with God in the beginning is the One who "became flesh and made his dwelling among us." And, John wrote, "We have seen his glory, the glory of the One and Only, who came from the Father, full of grace and truth (John 1:14).

An angel appeared to Joseph in a dream, explaining that the baby conceived by the Holy Spirit in Mary would be called *Immanuel,* a Hebrew word meaning "God with us" (Matt. 1:23). God with us — imagine that, if you can! As hard as one might try to grasp the concept, it is actually impossible to comprehend fully. Nonetheless, it is true.

Franklin Segler believes that human beings respond on a *superconscious level* in which the worshiper experiences a raised *awareness of God's presence.* Sometimes a person will say, "I *felt* the presence of God." Segler writes, "This aspect of worship cannot be formalized nor carefully defined theologically. Indeed, man should acknowledge a mysterious beyondness in worship which is accepted by faith and needs not to be explained by creeds and formulas."[3] There are many things which cannot be explained but can, nonetheless, be experienced. Is that not true, for example, when a young man falls in love? Some intellectual might try to explain it scientifically, or some philosopher might try to define it, but no words can ever describe what that young man

---

[3]Franklin M. Segler, *Christian Worship: Its Theology and Practice* (Nashville: Broadman Press, 1967), p. 80.

feels and experiences when he is near his beloved.

So it often is with those who love the Lord. God's people cannot live on explanations alone; we live by faith. The Hebrew writer proclaimed, "Now faith is being sure of what we hope for and certain of what we do not see. . . . And without faith it is impossible to please God" (Heb. 11:1, 6). If we insist on being able to explain everything in scientific, rational terms, we will never be able to worship God acceptably. True worshipers agree with Paul: "Oh, the *depth* of the riches of the wisdom and knowledge of God! How *unsearchable* his judgments, and *his paths beyond tracing out!*" (Rom. 11:33, emphasis added). Paul prayed that he might "know this love that *surpasses* knowledge" (Eph. 3:19).

Doubts About Things Mysterious

Due to Alexander Campbell's views, many people in the Restoration Movement have been suspicious of the nonrational and emotional aspects of religion. There were influential Restoration leaders such as Barton W. Stone and Walter Scott who disagreed with Campbell's emphasis on rationalism. Stone and Scott and many of their contemporaries gave a significant place to the non-rational and emotional dimensions of faith. They understood the need to experience a sense of awe in worship. However, through the years, many of Campbell's views became dominant in the movement. The entire Restoration Movement eventually became ambivalent, if not openly antagonistic, toward mysterious aspects of religion. Campbell talked about the need for a personal relationship with Jesus as the Son of God. However, it was said of him that he had a religion that trusted more in the reasons of his head than in the reasons of his heart.

Campbell lived during the period of the Enlightenment which was profoundly influenced by the thinking of such men as the English philosopher John Locke. It was an age which emphasized what was reasonable, rational, and scientific. Campbell keenly distrusted mysticism and the display of emotions in worship, stressing, instead, the ability of human reason to encounter God. On one hand, this message helped many people on the frontier dispense with superstition and human creeds and encouraged them to use their minds in studying the Bible for themselves. On the other hand, Campbell's emphasis on the rational and his open distrust of the mysterious has led many people to view religious experience as all but totally invalid.[4]

There are, however, religious experiences that transcend the realm of human explanation — experiences that are spiritual and not fleshly. Religious experience must always be tested by the truth of Scripture. Admittedly, one may have an emotional experience of such a nature that it is out of line with biblical truth and principles. If I tell you the Lord appeared to me and told me I was an apostle equal to the Apostle Paul or that it was now His will for me to take two wives, you would be altogether right in denying the truthfulness of those "experiences." Neither one can possibly square with Scripture. However, if I tell you that, during times of personal and public worship, I often sense the closeness of the Lord, you would find it impossible to demonstrate from Scripture that such an experience is unbiblical. If I tell you that I have often felt God's presence as I have walked in the mountains and pondered the majesty of His marvelous creation, you would be wrong to say my experience is out of step with the experiences of men and women we read about in Scripture. I cannot put

---

[4]Bruce Epperley, "Exploring the New Frontiers of Disciples of Christ Spirituality," *Mid-Stream* 28 no. 3 (1989): pp. 276-77.

into words adequately what those experiences are like, but I know that they are real, and I believe that they are biblical.

When David, as a young shepherd, gazed into the heavens, he met God. He wrote, "The heavens declare the glory of God; the skies proclaim the work of his hands" (Ps. 19:1). While I believe the promise, "Draw near to God and He will draw near to you" (Jas. 4:8, NASB), I cannot explain exactly how God does that. I cannot put it in a test tube and verify it scientifically. I cannot put it in a syllogism and prove God's method or process. It can be explained by words of faith, but it cannot be explained from a totally rational perspective. Yet, it is true. I have personally experienced God's nearness many times as I have drawn near to Him. I accept it by faith, and I know it by experience. William F. Sherwin's song, "Break Thou the Bread of Life," communicates what I am trying to describe. It conveys an emotion, a longing, and a yearning for closeness and relationship that defies rational explanation. The first verse says:

Break Thou the bread of life,
Dear Lord to me,
As Thou didst break the loaves
Beside the sea;
Beyond the sacred page
I seek Thee, Lord;
My spirit pants for Thee,
O living Word!

The word *beyond* in this song does not indicate an experience or a relationship that adds to the Word or that is out of harmony with Scripture. The word *beyond* tries to get at the nonrational (not irrational, which is altogether different), emotive aspects of worship. Distrust of this type of experience is evidenced in several song books in which editors have changed the words "*beyond* the sacred page" to "*within* the sacred page."

There is a terrible lack of the sense of mystery and wonder in many of our worship assemblies today. Our movement has been careful to practice the correct *acts* and *forms* of worship; we have not been nearly as concerned about the *spirit* and *experience* of worship. True servants of God are always aware that it is the spirit of worship that gives meaning to the rituals and that the spirit is more important than the acts. It is not that the ritual acts of worship are unimportant. It is that God has always been more concerned with the heart than with mere ritual accuracy. David wrote, "The sacrifices of God are a broken spirit" (Ps. 51:17). The broken spirit and contrite heart is something we continue to offer to God. The animal sacrificial system has ceased, but we continue to bring before God a heart of penitence and submission. Through Christ, we offer up a sacrifice of praise (Heb. 13:15).

Jesus taught that we must worship "the Father in spirit and truth" (John 4:23-24). From the beginning of the Restoration Movement, the dominant emphasis has been on worshiping in truth, with relatively little discussion about worshiping in spirit. This lack of emphasis on "spirit" has left a deep emotional void in the hearts of many people. Too many congregations have turned worship into a virtual lecture. They see worship as the time to debate some theological issue or to prove the existence of God. Many people long for a worship that touches their inner beings, not just their heads.

Longing For a Sense of Wonder

Over the last 25 to 30 years, a lot of Christians have left their churches for the charismatic experience. There are many young adults of varying religious backgrounds in America who have been turned off by traditional religion but have turned to alternative sources of religious experience such as Unity, religious science, transpersonal psychology, Asian religions, and the New Age Movement. Many of these people have abandoned traditional religion because they have found its worship to be regimented, cold, lifeless, routine, and empty. They have not found anything in their secular lives to satisfy their deep yearnings for meaning. Nor have they found anything in the worship of their traditional churches which touches their hearts. So, they go after false religious experiences because they seem to promise a way to fill the vacuum.[5] A typical reaction is to preach against counterfeit religions and to try to build defenses to keep people from being attracted to them. But this approach of merely condemning bogus experiences does not entirely solve the problem unless we offer a genuine alternative.[6]

In his book, *Signs of Wonder*, Robert Webber shares insights which are both perceptive and helpful in the analysis of our situation. Webber says that we are living in what C.S. Lewis called *the post-Christian era*. It is a time not unlike the first century when people are pagan, and are looking for answers in such sources as astrology, occultism, and Satanism. People want supernatural answers. They want a God who breaks into their world. Many of them have given up the rationalistic, scientific mindset that has characterized western culture since the days of Sir Isaac Newton in the 17th century. The Enlightenment philosophy of that period offered an anti-supernatural and rationalistic perspective on life. Sadly, many Christians developed a faith and worship which accommodated this worldview, relegating God to

---

[5]Epperley, p. 275.
[6]Daryl Tippins, "Called to Worship: The Assembly as Encounter." Lectures delivered at Abilene Christian University, Abilene, TX. Audiocassette, 1991.

the heavens and rejecting an active presence of God in daily life and worship.[7]

Christians did not let this false worldview go unchallenged, but responded to it by using the very tools of the Enlightenment itself: reason, evidence, and science. Liberals *demythologized* the gospel, stripping it of its content and power. They dealt with the supernatural by trying to explain it away. Conservative scholars vigorously opposed this liberal rejection of the accuracy and reliability of Scripture, but they were unable to maintain a unified approach of their own.

Conservative reactions went in two different directions. One group of conservatives followed the intellectual route, trying to prove Christian faith to be true by using scientific, rationalistic methods. Their schools became bastions for Christian faith, and their periodicals became workshops to hammer out accurate theology. Their pulpits became the place to proclaim the evidence of faith and to dispute with unbelievers. Many of their preachers turned worship almost totally into a period of teaching. Churches growing out of the Restoration Movement have largely followed this approach.[8]

Another group of conservatives traveled a different direction. These were the "emotionalists." They said that Christianity was not something you debated, but rather something you experienced. They wanted a Christianity that touched the heart, moved the will, and resulted in holy living. They wanted commitment and passion. They wanted to feel the presence of Christ and experience the power of the Holy Spirit.[9]

It is sad that conservatives split into two distinctively

[7]Robert Webber, *Signs of Wonder* (Nashville: Abbott Martyn, 1992), pp. 15-17.
[8]*Ibid.*, pp. 18-20.
[9]*Ibid.*, pp. 20-21.

different camps in their battle against the anti-supernatural and rationalistic philosophy of the Enlightenment. It is sad because each approach touches on a necessary element of worship. It is sad because it points out the tendency we seem to have for going to extremes. Balance is hard to maintain, but balance is what we desperately need. We must use our intellect as we ground our worship in the truths of Scripture. As a balance to a purely intellectual approach, we also must engage our hearts and emotions as we attempt to lift up our voices in worship to God.[10]

We need to return to the Bible to recover a sense of wonder in worship. Several writers have stressed the importance of wonder. William Quayle said, "When wonder is dead the soul becomes a dry bone."[11] Albert Einstein said, "The scientist's religious feeling takes the form of rapturous amazement at the harmony of natural law which reveals an Intelligence of such superiority that compared with it all the systematic thinking and acting of human beings is an utter insignificant reflection . . . ."[12] Einstein also said, "The fairest thing we can experience is the mysterious. He who knows it not, can no longer wonder, no longer feel amazement, is as good as dead, a snuffed-out candle."[13] Walter Percy said, "Life is a mystery. Love is a delight. Therefore I take it as axiomatic that one should settle for nothing less than the infinite mystery and infinite delight that is God. I demand it. I refuse to settle for anything less."[14] G.K. Chesterton said, "The world will never starve for want of

---

[10]*Ibid.*

[11]Warren W. Wiersbe, *Real Worship* (Nashville: Oliver/Nelson Books, 1986), p. 41.

[12]Prentice Meador, "Keep Silent Before Him," in *Harding College Lectures* (Austin, TX: Firm Foundation Publishing House, 1978), p. 94.

[13]Wiersbe, p. 45.

[14]Tippins, "Called to Worship."

wonders, but only from want of wonder."[15] Geoffrey Wainwright wrote,

> As to transcendence, for my part I can do no more than purpose the living experience of worship as evidence of the rootage of creative reality in a creative Reality and declare that I remain unpersuaded by reductionist interpretations which allow psychology or sociology to explain away that irreductible experience.[16]

In other words, no human explanation is going to take away one's own personal experience of God's transcendence in his own life. Perhaps Thomas Carlyle said it most concisely, "Wonder is the basis of worship."[17]

Carlyle's words about the importance of wonder come to life in several New Testament passages. When the shepherds returned from seeing the newborn Jesus, they were "glorifying and praising God for all the things they had heard and seen" (Luke 2:20). Years later during Jesus' ministry, some men brought a paralytic to Jesus. Unable to get through the crowd, they climbed on the roof of the house in which Jesus was teaching, cut a hole in the roof, and let the man down through it in front of the Lord. When Jesus saw their faith, he forgave the man his sins and healed him on the spot. When the people saw the man walking, the scripture says, "Everyone was *amazed* and gave praise to God. They were filled with *awe* and said, 'We have seen remarkable things today'" (Luke 5:26; see also Matt. 9:8; Mark 2:12). On another occasion Jesus was healing many people. Matthew says, "The people were *amazed* when they saw the mute speaking, the crippled made well, the lame walking and the blind seeing. And they praised the God

---

[15]Wiersbe, p. 43.

[16]Geoffrey Wainwright, *Doxology* (New York: Oxford University Press, 1980), p. 2.

[17]Wiersbe, p. 43.

of Israel" (Matt. 15:31). On yet another occasion Jesus raised to life the dead son of a widow from the city of Nain. Luke reports that the people "were all filled with *awe* and praised God" (Luke 7:16).

The point is that a sense of awe and amazement and wonder naturally leads us to worship. It is hard to amaze people anymore. With heart-lung transplants, space walks, and *Star Wars* special effects, we have become somewhat callous in the amazement department. We have seen a lot of things that would have shocked our ancestors beyond belief. It takes a lot to fill us with a sense of wonder these days. Unless we continually encounter the amazing God in His Word, we may also discover that we are not too impressed with Him anymore either. That is a horrifying thought, but it has become a reality in the lives of countless millions of people. There are even a surprising number of Christians who rarely feel a sense of amazement at what God has done and what He is still doing.

Please read the following sentence several times and meditate on its implications: **The church will never renew its worship until we rediscover a sense of awe and reverence and amazement and wonder at who God is and what He has done and what He continues to do.**

A Hunger For Relationship With God

The hunger in many people's hearts is for a personal relationship with God. They want more than to know *about* God; they want to *know* Him. The prophet Jeremiah wrote:

> This is what the LORD says:
> "Let not the wise man boast of his wisdom
>   or the strong man boast of his strength
>   or the rich man boast of his riches,
>   but let him who boasts boast about this:

WE NEED A SENSE OF WONDER

that he understands and knows me,
  that I am the LORD, who exercises kindness,
    justice and righteousness on earth,
      for in these I delight,
        declares the LORD" (Jer. 9:23-24).

The Apostle Paul had such a longing. He also prayed that he might "know Christ" (Phil. 3:10). Moses had such a relationship with God. The Bible says, "The Lord would speak to Moses face to face, as a man speaks with his friend" (Exod. 33:11). However, Moses wanted to know who God was going to send with him to lead the Israelites to the promised land. God assured him, "My Presence will go with you" (v. 14).

Most men would have been satisfied to have God's Presence with them, but Moses wanted more than God's Presence — he wanted to see the fullness of God's glory (v. 18). God did not allow Moses to see His face, but the Lord agreed to hide Moses in a cleft of a rock and allowed Moses to see His back as He passed by (vv. 19-23). Moses' yearning to encounter the Lord is the yearning of all God's children. We want to see God's face, to be in His presence, and to enjoy fellowship with Him. The full intimacy of such knowledge will not come until heaven, but we long for it even now as we express our heartfelt adoration and worship.

Human beings communicate on at least three levels. First, there is the level of intimacy and relationship. This involves the kind of language that lovers use between themselves. It is the kind of language shared between a parent and child. It is language that builds and is reflective of trust, hope, and understanding. Many of the Old Testament Psalms are written in this intimate level. Second, there is the level of information, facts, and cognition. This involves the language we use to explore the world. It is the language of business, science, and rationality. This second level of communication is concerned very little with emotional involvement or human relationships. Third, there is the level of motivation and persuasion. This type of language is used in advertisements, politics, and sermons to try to get people to do something.

All three levels of communication are essential to public worship. However, true worship is primarily level one communication, employing the language of intimacy and relationship. It is the level of communication that says, "Father, I love you. I adore you. I need you. Thank you." It is obvious in many congregations that we are uncomfortable with worship that utilizes level one language. Instead we have gone to level two language which talks a lot about God and gives the facts about Him but which seldom talks and relates to God on a warm, personal level.

We simply must get back to a level of intimate relationship in our worship of God. We see that intimate level of communication in words like these of the Psalmist: "As the deer pants for streams of water, so my soul pants for you, O God. My soul thirsts for God, for the living God. When can I go and meet with God?" (Ps. 42:1-2). "O God, you are my God, earnestly I seek you; my soul thirsts for you, my body longs for you, in a dry and weary land where there is no water" (Ps. 63:1). "How lovely is your dwelling place, O Lord Almighty! My soul yearns, even faints, for the courts of the Lord; my heart and my flesh cry out for the living God" (Ps. 84:1-2).

Public worship must be more than ceremony and going through the right forms. Worship must be a time when worshipers encounter God, when we actually meet with God Who graciously comes into our midst. H.H. Rowley wrote, "the greatest gift of God is Himself, and the supreme end of worship is to be lifted into the spirit of God, to share His life, His thought, His purpose."[18] Think what it will be like when we actually see God face to face. I doubt we will coolly and rationally analyze the situation. That encounter will overwhelm us in every conceivable way. It will touch our hearts and emotions like nothing else ever has.

The Place of Emotion in Worship

When we deal with the matters of wonder, reverence, and awe before the Holy One among us, we also must deal with the issue of emotion in worship. What we do in public worship should occur somewhere between the extremes of total passivity and unbridled enthusiasm. It has been suggested that in worship we need to intellectualize our emotions and to emotionalize our intellect.[19] There needs to be a balance between the intellectual and the emotional. Many churches ignore or even oppose personal spiritual experience that involves the emotions. Leonard Allen has brought to light the writings of lesser known Restoration brethren who were contemporaries of Alexander Campbell. One was Dr. Robert Richardson who stressed the need to enter into a spiritual union with God. Concerning Dr. Richardson, Allen writes:

> In a time when doctrinal, polemical, and organizational matters preoccupied the movement, he remained a persistent — at times almost solitary — advocate of a deeper, richer spirituality. It was here, he felt, that the movement was most lacking. . . . A few other voices had raised such concerns before him. John Rogers of Carlisle, Kentucky, for example, had written to Campbell in 1834, noting that 'many of us in running away from the extreme of enthusiasm, have on the other hand, passed the temperate zone, and gone far into the frozen regions.' 'There is, in too many churches,' he added, 'a cold-

---

[18]H.H. Rowley, *Worship in Ancient Israel* (Philadelphia: Fortress Press, 1967), p. 264).

[19]Segler, p. 79.

hearted, lifeless formality, that freezes the energies.'

And Campbell himself, on a few occasions,' could raise such concerns. Religion certainly was an intellectual matter, he wrote in 1837, 'but religion dwelling in the heart, rooted in the feelings and affections, is living, active, and real existence.' This is what fills the soul with divine life. 'This is religion,' he concluded; 'all the rest is machinery.'[20]

We do not base our theology on emotions or on experience, but we make a great mistake if we completely divorce our theology from our emotions and experience. If worship is a response of the whole person to God, then we cannot ignore emotions. We express emotions at practically every other event in life. Why should our worship be devoid of such expressions? It does not make sense, and it is not biblical. Many saints are introverted in their expression of worship, in much the same way that many husbands are reserved in their expressions of love toward their wives. Yet those same saints will jump up and down, yell, applaud, and act in otherwise uninhibited fashion as they declare their love and support for their favorite ball team. They will praise their favorite player with great enthusiasm and animation.

It is true that some people are reserved and quiet in the expression of their ideas and emotions. It would be out of character for them to be demonstrative in any setting at any time. For them to demonstrate a great deal of emotion in worship would be out of character with their true nature. However, when a person who says, "It's not my nature to show my emotions in worship" demonstrates unrestrained enthusiasm in other activities, it probably has nothing at all to do with their *nature*. Inhibited praise for God may have something to do with fleshly pride. Reserved worship may stem from a heart

---

[20]Leonard C. Allen, "Holy Mysteries," *Wineskins* 1 no. 5 (1992): pp. 10-11.

that is ashamed of Christ. It may even result from incorrect or poor teaching on how we are to declare our praise. Our dominant rationalistic heritage has caused us to fear our emotions. If we feel our emotions stirring, we almost instinctively sit on our hands, keep a straight face, and fight back the tears. Paul's instructions to do things decently and in order (1 Cor. 14:40) has ceased to be a guard against chaos (as it was intended); instead it has become a ball and chain that shackles our spirits and chokes our worship to death.

Walt Disney was a master movie maker. He learned from experience that to be successful, every animated film had to have two ingredients: laughter and tears. Disney's philosophy was that his movies had to touch a full range of people's emotions. The same is true of worship.

Obviously, there must be doctrinal truth at the heart of worship. Unless enthusiasm and emotion are inseparably linked to the truth, they are meaningless. The perfect blend is emotion regulated by understanding and enthusiasm directed by the Word of God. It is wrong to manipulate people's emotions artificially. But it is just as wrong to make a conscious effort not to touch people's emotions. If there is never laughter, never a sigh, never a tear, never a smile, never a joyful "amen," never a burden or a release from some burden — if there is only stone-faced, passionless exercise of the routines and rituals of worship, then spiritual rigor mortis has overtaken the entire process.

Scripture is written for the heart as well as the head, and we must balance both. Scripture and worship appeal to both our objective and subjective sides. Lawrence Richards and Gib Martin write:

> Each believer is responsible to listen to the voice of God speaking to him in a personal, directing, or instructing way. The objective Word without the living voice has often led to a dead orthodoxy, just as the concept of a living voice apart

from Scripture has led to a subjective mysticism. In the church of Christ, Scripture and voice are both essential . . . ."[21]

Ilion T. Jones writes:

It is open to question whether worship can be fully Christian in the New Testament sense of that term unless it calls the emotions into play. . . . There is no way to redeem man without affecting his emotions. A man does not believe anything until he feels it. Everything creative in human life has to be charged with emotion to succeed. Worship is not complete until the worshiper's emotions are moved. . . . If worship is to be made fully Christian, fully alive, in the New Testament sense, it must provide an open channel for the incoming of the Holy Spirit, "who works when and where and how he pleases."[22]

Emotionalism is the tendency to overindulge the emotions or to be too much affected by them. However, *emotionalism* is different from the genuine expression of true *emotion*. I deplore religious emotionalism which is devoid of a biblical foundation. However, I agree with Handley Moule who said that he would rather tone down a fanatic than resurrect a corpse. It would be better not to have either extreme, but if I have to make a choice, give me the fanatic.[23] One reason it's so hard to bring about worship renewal in some places is that some churches are full of emotional corpses. We simply must take our emotions out of the freezer and expose them to the warm glow of God's passionate love.

Human beings experience many emotions: happiness and sadness, elation and depression, security and fear. Practically every emotion is expressed in Scripture, espe-

---

[21]Lawrence Richards and Gib Martin, *A Personal Theology of Ministry* (Grand Rapids: Zondervan Publishing House, 1981), p. 98.

[22]Ilion T. Jones, *A Historical Approach to Evangelical Worship* (New York: Abingdon Press, 1954), pp. 77, 85.

[23]Wiersbe, p. 24.

cially in the Psalms. There we read of people who worshiped God even when they felt depressed about the struggles of life (Ps. 73). They did not wait to praise the Lord until they felt good emotionally. We must not allow bad moods and feelings to hinder us from praising God. Michael Coleman and Ed Lindquist write:

> A sacrifice of praise is a deliberate act of faith in God's Word, an outward manifestation of trust in Him — regardless of what is going on at the moment. Praise is a decision, an act of the will, not the emotions. Whether you've had a good day or a bad day doesn't really matter.[24]

If we praise the Lord during those times when we feel down, we will discover that our emotional state improves almost every time. Praise has the ability to lift us out of the depths of despair onto a higher plane. Coleman and Lindquist add, "If we can praise God in the midst of our circumstances, then the circumstances will no longer have control over us; we'll have the key to spiritual victory."[25]

Joy in Worship

The characteristic note of Old Testament worship is exhilaration. Israel rejoiced to praise God in several areas of life. The greatest celebration surrounded the annual Passover, which was a time to remember the deliverance God provided for them out of Egyptian bondage. They also celebrated the covenant which God gave Israel at Mt. Sinai (Exod. 24; 34; Ps. 106). God was always steadfast to His covenant even when His people were fickle, and they praised God for His faithfulness. The Feast of Booths was also a time of joyous celebration (Neh. 8:10, 12, 17).

---

[24]Michael Coleman and Ed Lindquist, *Come and Worship* (Old Tappan, NJ: Fleming H. Revell Co., 1989), p. 37.
[25]Coleman and Lindquist, p. 29.

David wrote, "I was glad when they said to me, 'Let us go to the house of the LORD'" (Ps. 122:1, NASB). "Let the heart of those who seek the LORD be glad" (1 Chron. 16:10, NASB). "Shout joyfully to the LORD . . . Come before Him with joyful singing . . . Enter His gates with thanksgiving, and His courts with praise" (Ps. 100:1, 2, 4, NASB). "Blessed are those who have learned to acclaim you, who walk in the light of your presence, O LORD. They rejoice in your name all day long; they exult in your righteousness" (Ps. 89:15-16).

Just as worship under the Old Covenant was celebrative, so also the characteristic note of New Testament worship is celebration (Acts 2:46-47; 5:41; 8:39; 13:48; 15:3, 31). The noun or verb form of *joy* and *rejoice* occurs 125 times in the New Testament. There is no question that joy characterized worship in New Testament times. We must be dead serious about worship, but we must not be *mournful* about it, never smiling, always with long and somber frowns. Somebody needs to remind our hearts and tell our faces that we are saved and that, if we are to rejoice in our hearts, we also are to rejoice in our physical expressions.

Too often people go to the assembly to be scolded rather than to experience the joy of their salvation. Let the words of Hebrews 12:22-23 soak in: "But you have come to Mount Zion, to the heavenly Jerusalem, the city of the living God. You have come to thousands upon thousands of angels in *joyful assembly*, to the church of the firstborn, whose names are written in heaven." John E. Burkhart writes, "True celebration of God is quite festive, sometimes almost playful, and conspicuous in its gladness as it takes delight in what God is about."[26] J. Daniel Baumann writes:

---

[26]Burkhart, p. 29.

Worship frequently degenerates into a formalism that is devoid of vitality and spiritual life. Biblical worship, I contend, is celebration. That is not to say we are to be flippant or careless, nor that we gather in order to exchange emotional highs and get spiritual goose pimples. . . . Worship should both fill the mind with God's truth and the spirit with God's joy.[27]

Worship is not always solemn and lifelessly somber. It must be reverent and orderly — and joyful! The well-known Westminster Confession says: "Man's chief end is to glorify God and to *enjoy* Him forever." In the second century, Clement of Alexandria said, "Accordingly all our life is a festival: being persuaded that God is everywhere present on all sides, we praise him as we till the ground, we sing hymns as we sail the sea, we feel his inspiration in all that we do."[28] The Western values of thrift, industry, and ambition have crowded out much of the festive nature of mirth, play, and merrymaking.[29] We are not sure it is permissible to celebrate in worship. However, the essence of worship is to celebrate what God has done. We exalt Him and sound His praises, we sing joyfully to Him, and we magnify and glorify His name.

Authentic celebration cannot be contrived. It must be rooted in an event. In the Old Testament, that event was the exodus. In the New Covenant, it is the Christ-event: His death, burial, resurrection, and ascension and the giving of the Holy Spirit. Worship can cause us to see our sinfulness. A vision of the holiness of God often results in a healthy sense of guilt that ought to lead us to repentance. However, worship is not meant to leave us locked in the despair of guilt. Worship extends hope of redemption. When judgment is sounded, there also

[27]J. Daniel Baumann, "Worship: The Missing Jewel," *Christianity Today* (1981): p. 29.
[28]Burkhart, p. 14.
[29]Webber, *Worship is a Verb*, p. 14.

must be a way of deliverance described. When guilt is inflicted, the possibility of forgiveness must be assured. God's help must be conveyed. If people consistently leave worship feeling worse than when they came, something is wrong. Someone or something has robbed them of the joy of their salvation. When the joy of our salvation is present, we celebrate the forgiveness we receive in Jesus Christ. We celebrate our rescue from death and the Lord's gift of life. We celebrate our freedom from slavery to sin. Just as God freed Israel from Egyptian bondage, so He has freed us from sin's clutches through Jesus Christ. We celebrate the gift of the Holy Spirit. When we celebrate in worship we do not celebrate our own dedication to God. We celebrate the work of Christ, not what we have done. We celebrate what Christ has done in the past, is doing now, and will do in the future.

One of our most beautiful hymns is Charles Welsey's *Love Divine, All Loves Excelling*. The entire song is a moving prayer. The last two stanzas read:

> Come, Almighty to deliver,
> Let us all Thy life receive;
> Suddenly return, and never,
> Nevermore Thy temples leave;
> Thee we would be always blessing,
> Serve Thee as Thy hosts above,
> Pray, and praise Thee, without ceasing,
> Glory in Thy perfect love.
>
> Finish then Thy new creation,
> Pure unspotted, may we be;
> Let us see our whole salvation
> Perfectly secured by Thee;
> Changed from glory into glory,
> Till in heav'n we take our place,
> Till we cast our crowns before Thee,
> Lost in wonder, love and praise.

In heaven we will be able to pray and praise Him

without ceasing. There we will be able to fully glory in God's perfect love. Then we will realize our whole salvation as we see Him face to face. But until we get there, let us worship with all our hearts. Let us, even now, earthbound though we are, find ourselves "lost in wonder, love and praise!"

DISCUSSION QUESTIONS
ON CHAPTER ONE

1. Do you possess a sense of wonder when you come before God in worship? Why or why not?

2. Can you fully explain God intellectually or verify Him scientifically? Read 1 Corinthians 1:25. How does your answer affect the way you worship?

3. God is both transcendent and immanent. What does each word mean in relation to our worship of Him?

4. What does it mean to worship God in spirit and in truth (John 4:23-24)? Have you placed greater emphasis on truth or on spirit? What difference does it make?

5. Evaluate Thomas Carlyle's statement: "Wonder is the basis of worship."

6. What is the difference between knowing about God and knowing God?

7. Read Psalms 42:1-2; 63:1-5; 84:2. Have you ever felt like this?

8. Someone has said, "We need to intellectualize our emotions and to emotionalize our intellect."

   a. What place does emotion play in worship?

   b. What place does intellect play in worship?

9. Is worship in any way a celebration? How much joy can be expressed in worship?

45

2
What Is Worship?

What, exactly, is worship? It is hard to give a simple definition because the Bible itself does not give one. There are a number of different words which appear in the original languages of Scripture (Hebrew, Aramaic, and Greek), all of which are translated "worship" in our English versions. In order to arrive at a description of worship we have to put together various shades of meaning from these words in the original languages. Unless you are a language scholar, you probably will not be able to pronounce or remember these words. But do not worry — nobody is going to give you an exam. I do hope, however, that their meanings will give you a fuller appreciation for the richness of the concept of worship.

It's All Greek To Me — And Some Hebrew, Too!

Here are the most important Hebrew and Greek words which come into our English translations as "worship":

1) *Hištaḥawah* השתחוה (from the root word *šaḥah* שחה or, more probably, *ḥawah* חוה).

Found 170 times in the Hebrew Bible, this is the most common word in the Old Testament for worship. It means "to bow down" in reverence and humility before another, whether man or God. Bowing down, or prostrating oneself, was the common way of expressing one's unworthiness before a greater person. It showed an awareness of God's splendor and majesty. It is the word

used in Genesis 18:2 where Abraham *bowed low* before
the three strangers who had come his way. It is used in
Exodus 12:27-28, "Then the people *bowed down* and
worshiped." David anticipated a time when all nations
would *bow down* before Yahweh (Ps. 22:27).

2) *Proskuneo* προσκυνεω.

This is the basic Greek equivalent to *hištaḥawah*. It has
the same overtones of submissive lowliness and deep
respect. *Proskuneo* literally means "to kiss toward." It also
means to do obeisance, to prostrate oneself, to reverence, and to show humility. Found 59 times, it is the
primary verb for worship in the New Testament. This is
the word used to describe those who approached Jesus
as worshipers (Matt. 8:2; 9:18; 14:33; 15:25; 20:20; John
9:38), and in many other New Testament passages (Acts
8:27; 10:25; 24:11; 1 Cor. 14:25; Rev. 19:10; 22:9).

In the famous passage in John 4 where Jesus
discussed worship with the Samaritan woman, the Lord
told her that a time had come when true worshipers
would worship the Father in spirit and truth. *Proskunein*
in various forms is used repeatedly throughout the
passage. It is also found in Revelation 5:14, where the
twenty-four elders *fell down* and worshiped (*prosekunesan*)
God.

3) *Abad* אבד

This is the second most frequently used Hebrew word
in the Old Testament to describe worship. It means "to
serve," and that is the way it is often translated in
English. It is from the same root as the term "slave" or
"servant." This is an important point to understand. The
Hebrew could think of no higher privilege than to be
called a servant of God. Unlike the Greek concept of
slavery as servile abasement in captivity, the Israelite
thought of the word "servant" in terms of a relationship
with a kindly master. This is the word found in Exodus
3:12, "When you have brought the people out of Egypt,

you will *worship* God on this mountain" (see also Exod. 4:23; 7:16; 8:1). It is also found in Deuteronomy 10:12-13:

> And now, O Israel, what does the LORD your God ask of you but to fear the LORD your God, to walk in all his ways, to love him, to serve the LORD your God with all your heart and with all your soul, and to observe the LORD's commands and decrees that I am giving you today for your own good?

4) *Latreia* λατρεια or *latreuo* λατρευω.

This is the Greek word that most closely corresponds to *abad*. It, too, means "to serve." It is one of the most common words in the New Testament. Often it is translated "serve" or "service," as in Hebrews 9:14, "How much more, then, will the blood of Christ, who through the eternal Spirit offered himself unblemished to God, cleanse our consciences from acts that lead to death, so that we may serve the living God!" Often it is translated "worship." That is how it is used in passages like Romans 12:1, "Therefore, I urge you, brothers, in view of God's mercy, to offer your bodies as living sacrifices, holy and pleasing to God — this is your spiritual act of worship." (See also Matt. 4:10, Rom. 1:9, 15:16, Heb. 9:9; Rev. 22:3.) It was this approach to worship that gave us such Psalms as Psalms 42, 43, 65, 84, and 122.

A related word to *latreia* is *leitourgos* λειτουργος or *leitourgia* λειτουργια, from which we get the English word "liturgy." The word is composed of the word for "people" (*laos* λαος) and the word for "work" (*ergon* εργον). In ancient Greece, a liturgy was a public work, something performed for the benefit of the city or state. Liturgy is a work performed by the people for the benefit of others. The word came to be used by Christians for the public ministry to God. It is now confined to services of worship. Some churches growing out of the "free church" tradition do not use the word "liturgy." It

49

sounds too "high church" for some — too much like religious bells and smells and incense. Therefore, traditionally, some groups have avoided its use. However, those churches mean exactly the same thing when they use the term "service" in reference to the forms and order of our worship assembly. The terminology is relatively unimportant, but the concept of doing service for God in worship is very important.

There are other Greek words like *eusebeo* ευσεβεω and *sebomai* σεβομαι which convey the ideas of reverence and respect, showing piety toward, fearing, and showing profound awe.

There are at least two clear impressions I get from the meanings of these words. First, they indicate a yielding of the human will to God. No one can worship God acceptably who comes before Him with a prideful heart and a stubborn, unyielding will. We must come in genuine reverence and humility, with our hearts bowed low, our spirits laid prostrate before Him, and our lives given in grateful service to the Majesty on high. Second, these words clearly indicate a physical response. People are not to come to worship like spectators at a concert, watching the preacher and worship leaders do their performance on stage. There is no place in worship to sit passively as an audience who listens and watches but does nothing to participate.

Attempts to Define Worship

You can see now why it is hard to come up with a single, simple definition of worship. The Hebrew and Greek words contain such a wealth of meaning that no one definition can possibly do justice to the glory that belongs to worship. Yet writers have tried. Here are a few of my favorite definitions of worship.

At its heart, worship is the reply of the creature to the Creator. It is the response of the beloved to the Lover. It is the reaction of the ransomed to the Redeemer. Worship is an experience of deliberate focusing on God for the purpose of encounter with him.

Randall Harris & Rubel Shelly
(*The Second Incarnation*, p. 118)

Worship in its broadest sense is a meeting between God and His people in which God becomes present to His people, who respond with praise and thanksgiving.

Robert Webber
(*Worship: Old and New*, p. 12)

Ordinarily it is thought that worship consists of the mechanical acts of singing, praying, giving, expounding God's Word and taking the Lord's Supper. But these external performances are not worship; rather they are the outward expressions of it. Worship . . . is an attitude of the soul. It is a subjective experience of the soul in its adoration of God, which may find expression in overt forms.

Waymon D. Miller
("Worship — A Transcendent Wonder")

The worship of God is not a rule of safety — it is an adventure of the spirit, a flight after the unattainable.

Alfred North Whitehead
(*Science and the Modern World*, p. 12)

What is praise? It is adoration. It involves exaltation. It moves in and out of thanksgiving, bows before the mystery of God, glorifies the revelatory nature of God, magnifies the majesty of God, lauds the love of God, and rejoices in the presence of God.

C. Welton Gaddy
(*The Gift of Worship*, p. 105)

After more than forty years in the ministry, one preacher acknowledged that he could not define worship, but he gave the following description: "If you leave church with your faith stronger, your hope brighter, your love deeper, your sympathies broadened, your heart purer, and with your will more resolute to do the will of God, then you have truly worshiped!"

Franklin Segler
(*Christian Worship*, p. 12)

Worship is the submission of all our nature to God. It is the quickening of conscience by His holiness; the nourishment of mind with His truth; the purifying of imagination by His beauty; the opening of the heart to His love; the surrender of will to His purpose — and all of this gathered up in adoration, the most selfless emotion of which our nature is capable . . . .

William Temple
(*Readings in St. John's Gospel*, p. 68)

Worship celebrates God's saving deed in Jesus Christ.

Robert Webber
(*Signs of Wonder*, p. 33)[1]

Worship Is Central in the Life Of the Church

The church exists to accomplish many different things. The church is to teach and baptize the lost, to educate and train its own in the ways of God, to serve our fellow human beings (especially our brothers and sisters in the Lord), to build up and support fellow believers, and to spur one another on toward love and good deeds — just to name a few.

The most important thing the assembled church does is worship God. Without worship, a congregation ceases to be a church. If worship is not the fundamental activity of the church, every aspect of its ministry will be adversely affected. When the church fails to worship, it ultimately fails in every other area as well. John MacArthur says, "Worship is to the Christian life what the mainspring is to a watch, what the engine is to a car. It is the very core, the most essential element."[2] Worship is the source of the church's power to carry out its mission in the world. It is the foundation of everything else the church is doing. Worship is fundamental.

---

[1]See Bibliography for publisher information on the works quoted here.
[2]John MacArthur, *The Ultimate Priority* (Chicago: Moody Press, 1983), p. 13.

Someone has said that if worship is just one thing we do, everything becomes mundane. If worship is *the* one thing we do, everything takes on eternal significance. Olando Costas said it this way, "Worship is not a mere function of the church, it is her *ultimate* purpose."[3] If the church does not worship, it does not live.

Years ago, A.W. Tozer called worship "the missing jewel of the evangelical church."[4] Praise God that there are some bright rays of hope these days that more and more churches are wanting to learn to worship. Many churches are trying to improve their worship and, as they do, are finding that the worship of God is the life-blood of the congregation and the dynamic behind every other area of service. It is easy to get things turned around. Some of us are so driven to be active in the Lord's service that we seldom take time to do what God instructed us to do: "Be still, and know that I am God" (Ps. 46:10). Adoration too often comes in a distant second to busy-ness in the Kingdom.

Ann Ortlund, in her excellent little book, *Up With Worship*, uses a rather startling illustration that's right on target. She says that worship plays a similar role in our relationship with God to the role that sexual intercourse does in a relationship between a husband and a wife. A wife may insist that she loves her husband and offer as proof the fact that she cooks his meals, washes his clothes, and manages his household. But if she seldom makes time to have sexual intercourse with him, if she seldom stops from her busy schedule to look him tenderly in the eyes and tell him how precious he is to her, he will soon begin to wonder if she really loves him

---

[3]Orlando E. Costas, *The Church and its Mission: A Shattering Critique from the Third World* (Harrisburg, PA: Christian Productions, Inc., n.d., pamphlet).

[4]A.W. Tozer, *Worship: The Missing Jewel of the Evangelical Church* (Harrisburg, PA: Christian Productions, Inc., n.d., pamphlet).

at all. Without that intimate bond, the relationship becomes sterile, dry, and unsatisfying. God ordained intercourse in marriage as a ritual that bonds two partners together, and He says, "Do not deprive each other" (1 Cor. 7:5).

We may teach a Bible school class, visit the sick and imprisoned, and provide shelter for the homeless. We may exclaim that we are busy doing any number of good things in God's Kingdom, but if we seldom give full attention to worship, God may wonder if we really love Him. If we seldom seek God's face to tell Him, "Dearest Father, I adore you more than life itself, and you are truly precious to me," then our relationship with Him becomes dry and lifeless. Worship, both private and corporate, is a ritual which God ordained, too — to bind us experientially to Him — and He says, "[do] not give up meeting together" (Heb. 10:25).

Worship: The Ultimate Priority of Heaven

The closest picture we have of what heaven will be like is in the book of Revelation. On practically every page there are scenes of saints and angels and creatures offering up their praises to the Father and the Lamb.

Let me challenge you to do something before you go to the next chapter. Read Revelation, at one sitting if possible. Do not get bogged down in all the symbols. This time, look for only one theme. Find a colored pen or highlighter and mark every passage you read that has anything to say about worship. Note the way in which praises are offered, not only in the beautiful choice of words but also in the physical postures and volumes with which worship is expressed. Allow those scenes to touch your heart. Permit those words to become your own as you offer them up to God. Read them out loud. Don't merely call words. Read them with feeling. Express them with genuineness and sincerity of heart. Address them to the Father, Almighty God. You will not be the same afterward as you were before!

John's record of what he witnessed and experienced sends chills of joyful anticipation up and down my body. I cannot read those words without profound emotion. I cannot meditate on those words without longing to join that throng which surrounds the glorified throne. I, too, want to see His face. I want to hear the creatures cry out:

> Holy, holy, holy
> is the Lord God Almighty
> who was, and is, and is to come.
> Revelation 4:8

I hunger to see the twenty-four elders fall down before Him who sits on the throne, to see them lay their crowns before God's throne and say:

> You are worthy, our Lord and God,
> to receive glory and honor and power,
> for you created all things,
> and by your will they were created
> and have their being.
> Revelation 4:9-11

I thirst to hear the numberless chorus of angels who surround the throne singing in a loud voice:

> Worthy is the Lamb, who was slain,
> to receive power and wealth and wisdom and strength
> and honor and glory and praise!
> Revelation 5:11-12

I long to hear every creature sing:

> To him who sits on the throne and to the Lamb
> be praise and honor and glory and power,
> for ever and ever!
> Revelation 5:13

Not only do I hunger to see it — not only do I thirst to hear it — I also long to unite with all the inhabitants of heaven as I lift my hands and my voice in praise to our loving Father and to His precious Son. To bow before Him — that will be glory!

Yes, that is what heaven will be. My spirit yearns to know more of heaven right here, right now. Perhaps yours does also. But we must be patient, for at best, our worship here is but a foretaste of what it will be then.

Did you see the last four words of Revelation 5:13?: "For ever and ever!" Worship is not something we do until Jesus comes again. When Christ comes, He will take us to heaven where we will continue to worship — only there we will worship as we have never worshiped before. Until He comes, let us praise Him as best we can, even with the human limitations that hinder us. That is what this book is all about — searching for a better understanding of worship and for ways to praise Him more fully.

DISCUSSION QUESTIONS
ON CHAPTER TWO

1. Discuss the meanings and implications of the Hebrew word *hištaḥawah* and the Greek word *proskuneo*.

2. Discuss the meanings and implications of the Hebrew word *abad* and the Greek word *latreuo*.

3. Why are humility and reverence essential characteristics when we worship God?

4. In what way does worship require a physical response?

5. Respond to the statement: "The most important thing the assembled church does is worship God."

6. Why do you think worship is such a vital part of heaven?

3
Let's Talk Theology

"Theology." That is one of those words many of us do not use in everyday conversation. To some people, "theology" sounds heavy, even scary, and they are not sure they even like the word. But, do not be afraid of theology. The word simply refers to teachings about God. We cannot study worship without talking about God.

Hang in there with me through this chapter. At first glance it may seem like you are traveling through some deep waters, but resist the temptation to jump ship. What we are about to consider is bedrock. You will make a big mistake if you try to build an understanding of worship without a solid foundation on which to erect it.

A Theology of Worship is Important

Theologians have written a great deal about many aspects of the Christian faith, but there has been far less written about a theology of worship. This has resulted in what Ralph Martin calls "a veritable kaleidoscope of patterns and forms of worship throughout Christendom."[1] This does not mean, however, that people have no theology of worship. Every Christian and every congregation has a theology, even if they are unaware of it or unable to articulate it clearly. This is why we must examine our views and biases in light of what Scripture says about worship.

---

[1]Ralph Martin, *The Worship of God*, p. 2.

We do not come to our study of Scripture in a vacuum. We cannot separate our views of the Bible from our experiences, culture, human reason, and traditions. We have *glasses* through which we *see* worship. Therefore, we must investigate our biases as well as explore the Bible anew. The truths of Scripture never change, but there are always social, economic, political, and cultural changes which require the church to adapt if it is going to meet modern challenges with the unchanging message of reconciliation.

Let's Avoid Two Extremes

We must avoid two extremes in our study. One extreme seeks after worship that is based almost totally in the desire for an experience that gives us a warm and exciting emotional feeling. Such worship is sentimental and weak. It may not be founded on biblical truth at all. We must be sure that we worship God in truth (John 4:24). Christian worship is based on the truth that God has revealed about Himself in the Bible. The other extreme turns Bible study into a purely intellectual endeavor. Such an approach is not only cold and lifeless, but it is also false and harmful. Emotions and knowledge must meet in proper balance in a strong faith and fruitful Christian life. A sound theology will correct a tendency toward emotionalism in worship, and heart-felt worship will keep theology from becoming a cold, intellectual game.

A Theology of God

A theology of worship begins with theology in its root sense — a study of God. What we believe about God will determine the nature of our worship. If our view of God is incorrect, our worship of God will also be misguided.

If we believe God is a vengeful, angry being who is anxious to punish, we will try either to avoid Him or to placate Him. If we see Him as a permissive, sleepy old grandfather, we will not take Him seriously. If we view Him as a rule-giver who demands perfect obedience, we will approach Him legalistically and without joy. If we think of Him only as an idea, we will approach Him as a philosophical pursuit. But, if we understand Him as Father and a personal God who loves us and longs to enjoy fellowship with us, we will seek to know Him in personal relationship.

Let us consider a few truths about God that influence the way we worship Him. The first truth about God is that He exists. The Bible assumes His existence (Gen. 1:1). "The fool says in his heart, 'There is no God'" (Ps. 14:1). ". . .anyone who comes to him must believe that he exists and that he rewards those who earnestly seek him," (Heb. 11:6). Worship makes no sense unless God exists.

The second truth about God is that from the beginning He has revealed Himself. He has done so primarily through the written word and through His Son, Jesus Christ (John 1:14; Heb. 1:1-3; John 14:9). He reveals Himself as majestic in holiness. He is completely pure, totally righteous, entirely perfect, and wholly unlike any thing or anyone else that exists. In contrast, we are unholy, impure, unrighteous, imperfect, and common. When we become aware of God's holiness and our sinfulness, everything in us prompts us to fall on our faces crying "Holy, holy, holy is the Lord God Almighty" (Rev. 4:8; also Isa. 6:3). God's holiness prohibits us from approaching Him flippantly (Heb. 12:28-29).

The third truth about God is the greatest paradox in the universe: the all-holy God is also the all-gracious God whose love is so incomparably great toward us in Christ Jesus that we may come into His presence with confidence (Heb. 4:14-16). He permits us to call Him "Abba, Father" (Rom. 8:15; Gal. 4:6). He allows us to participate in His divine nature (2 Pet. 1:4). Through the Holy Spirit, we have access to the Father (Eph. 2:18; Rom. 5:2). Through Jesus' death and the precious blood He shed to pay the penalty for our sins, we can come before God with full assurance of faith (Heb. 7:25; 10:19-22; 1 Pet. 3:18). God made this possible by taking the initiative. God is seeking worshipers (John 4:23). That means that God is active in worship. He loved us first (Rom. 5:6-8; 1 John 4:10-19), and we respond with adoring worship. Because of His unspeakable love, He saved us by His grace (Eph. 2:4-5). The gospel brings reconciliation, and reconciliation is at the heart of all true worship.

All this compels us to worship. Worship fulfills the purpose for which we were created. Made in God's image, we long to be in fellowship with Him. We yearn to worship. Our hearts beat in rhythm with the Psalmist who wrote, "As the deer pants for streams of water, so my soul pants for you, O God. My soul thirsts for God, for the living God. When can I go and meet with God?" (Ps. 42:1-2).

The fourth truth about God is that He is the only true God, and He demands our exclusive worship (Exod. 20:5; Isa. 42:8). Yahweh is a jealous God. Jesus taught us to love the Lord God with all our heart and soul and mind and strength (Mark 12:29-30). God is to be loved and worshiped because He deserves it. God is worthy of our praise and adoration.

Worship Must Be God-Centered

God is the primary focus of worship. Although we are to edify one another in worship, people are not the primary focus of worship. People are not worthy of praise, but God is. Sometimes we forget that God is to be at the center of our worship. Suppose you take a friend to a big football game. The stadium is packed with screaming fans, the game is unbelievably exciting, and the score is neck and neck. However, all your friend wants to do is talk about the crowd and the size of the stadium. He could care less about what's going on down on the field. He's just enjoying the chit-chat with you and the fellowship with thousands of sports fans. It is nice for him to enjoy the crowd, but the important thing is happening down on the field. After all, how many people would show up if the football teams were not going to be there?

So it is with the assembly. The important matter is the Father and what He is doing for His people. When we come together, we must not be so preoccupied with one another that we forget that it is God whom we have come to praise. The chief aim of worship is to please God, to adore and praise Him.

This means we must not come to worship with a "me-centered" agenda. It must offend the Father when we are more concerned about what we want, what we would like to do in worship, or what makes us feel good than we are about what God wants, what would honor Him the most, and what would give Him the most pleasure in worship. We are to seek to glorify God before we seek to gain anything for ourselves. Jesus taught that finding oneself requires losing oneself. That's also true in worship.

Rubel Shelly and Randall Harris write in their book, *The Second Incarnation*:

> We are probably most worshipful when we are the least conscious of the worship itself. To say the least, when worship becomes self-conscious rather than God-conscious, its purpose has been defeated. . . .Only when an encounter with the Living God is fostered — with whatever 'feelings' may accompany that

encounter (e.g., celebration, melancholy, tears, laughter, judgment, etc.) — has worship transpired.

To create settings that deliberately manipulate emotions and tantalize participants is cheap theater rather than worship. Or, if one insists on calling it worship, it is self-worship rather than the worship of God. True worship does not call attention to itself; it serves instead as a means for focusing attention on God. As with any spiritual sign, worship points to a greater reality that lies behind the immediate experience. It points beyond itself to the Living God who is the object of worship.[2]

Sometimes we use the worship service to soothe, titillate, anger, convict, motivate, or evoke some other noble response in the worshipers, but, if we have not been helped to praise God, our time together cannot properly be called worship. The purpose of worship is not to entertain, to meet the budget, to recruit volunteers for ministry, to promote programs, to reach attendance goals, or to receive a blessing. Worship must be directed to God.

It is easy to get worship off focus even when we have the best of motives. For example, think about the invitation which is extended at the conclusion of the sermon. No one questions the importance of people making a public response to the gospel. However, if we leave the impression that everything which we have done during the worship hour is primarily to get people to walk down the aisles, we have taken the primary focus off God and placed it on human response. It is not unusual to hear someone ask, "Did we have any responses today?" meaning "Did anyone walk down the aisles?" When is the last time you heard someone ask, "Was God glorified today in worship?" Our questions betray our mistaken concepts of worship.

When worship is centered around people rather than

[2]Rubel Shelly and Randall J. Harris, *The Second Incarnation* (West Monroe, LA: Howard Publishing Co., 1992), pp. 120-121.

God, it is a perversion. It may be education or manipulation or harassment or a pep rally for the latest church program, but it is not true worship. It is common to hear people talk about a *worship experience*. This phrase tends to suggest that worship is important because it induces feelings. It is appropriate and important for worship to touch the emotions, but if worship is focused more on the worshiper's feelings than upon God Himself, that worship is off target. We must worship God whether we feel like it or not. True worship is dependent not on feelings but on giving God the praise He deserves.

Worship Must Be Christ-Centered

Not only is Christian worship focused on God, but it is also centered on Jesus Christ. The New Testament, in keeping with the Old Testament, teaches that we are to worship God alone (Matt. 4:10; Luke 4:8; 24:53; John 4:23-24). However, the New Testament also talks of worship to Jesus. At His birth wise men bowed down and worshiped Him (Matt. 2:11). Throughout His earthly ministry, people continually bowed down in homage to Jesus (Matt. 8:2; 9:18; 15:25; 20:20; 28:9; Mark 5:6). He was worshiped by the twelve whom He chose as His apostles (Matt. 14:33; 28:17; Luke 24:52). The multitudes and individuals cried out His praise (Mark 11:9-10; John 9:38).

Jesus never declined to accept this worship, nor did He see it as incompatible with the worship due to God alone. Thomas, upon seeing the resurrected Jesus, exclaimed, "My Lord and my God!" (John 20:28). Jesus claimed that the Father had committed all judgment to the Son and that all believers should honor the Son as they honor the Father (John 5:22-23).

Worship is centered in Christ because it is only

through Him that we have access to God. The work of Jesus on our behalf goes all the way back to creation, where Christ was with God and the Holy Spirit (Gen. 1:26-27; John 1:1-3). After humanity's sin and fall Jesus entered the creation He had made. He became flesh and lived among us (John 1:14). He died to redeem lost humanity. By His death Jesus secured the death of death. God did not leave Jesus in the grave, but raised Him.

In worship we not only remember the saving acts of God in the past, but we also anticipate the renewal of all things in the future. We are saved now in Christ, yet we are not all that we will be after His second coming. We will be changed into the very likeness of Christ (1 Cor. 15:35-54). One thing, however, will not change — worship will never end.

The Holy Spirit Helps Us In Worship

We are faced with a tremendous paradox. Ralph Martin writes, "God is holy, yet He seeks our communion; God is great, yet in some way he is enriched by our praise; God is love, yet He desires His love to be acknowledged and enjoyed and shared by us."[3] How can we offer worship to God which is pleasing to Him when we are so unholy? How can we confess our sin and at the same time celebrate God's presence? Humanly, we cannot bring these two things together. It is exactly at this point that we need the Holy Spirit to help us. The Holy Spirit fills an indispensable role in worship, accomplishing several vital functions on our behalf:
  1) He enables us to confess Jesus as Lord (1 Cor. 12:3).
     Charles Wesley captured this idea in his noble stanza addressed to the Holy Spirit:

---

[3]Ralph Martin, *The Worship of God* (Grand Rapids: William B. Eerdmans Publishing Company, 1982), p. 173.

No man can truly say
That Jesus is the Lord,
Unless Thou take the veil away,
And breathe the living word;
Then, only then, we feel
Our interest in His blood,
And cry, with joy unspeakable,
Thou art my Lord, my God!

2) The Spirit checks any tendency toward erroneous worship which seeks to offer to God what is unacceptable to Him (1 Cor. 12:3; 14:32ff).
3) He inspires prayer. We are to "pray in the Holy Spirit" (Eph. 6:18; Jude 20). As we pray, "The Spirit himself intercedes for us with groans that words cannot express" (Rom. 8:26).
4) Through Christ and by the Spirit we have access to the Father's love (Eph. 2:18; Rom. 5:5).
5) He leads us into the deep truths of God's Word (1 Cor. 2:10-16; John 16:13-15).
6) He convicts people of sin and leads them to acknowledge the presence of God (John 16:8; 1 Cor. 14:25).
7) He gives new birth into Christ (John 3:5-6; 6:63).
8) The Holy Spirit transforms us into the likeness of Christ (2 Cor. 3:17-18).
9) The Spirit enables us to live the life of Christ (Gal. 5:22-25).

These things we cannot do for ourselves, but the Holy Spirit works them in us if we belong to Christ. This is why the apostle Paul warned the church in Philippi not to trust in the flesh and why he wrote, "We . . . worship by the Spirit of God" (Phil. 3:3). Worship is our way of responding to the love that God has shown us. It is kindled within us when the Holy Spirit touches our human spirit. Richard Foster writes:

Forms and rituals do not produce worship, nor does the formal disuse of forms and rituals. We can use all the right techniques and methods, we can have the best possible liturgy, but we have not worshiped the Lord until Spirit touches spirit.[4]

Not What?, But Why?

Far too much of the discussion about worship centers on the elements and styles of worship. The emphasis tends to be on answering the question, "*What* should we do or not do in worship?" Such discussions often end up centering on matters of personal taste, of what we like and do not like. However, this misses the point of worship. The question of "what" is an important issue, but it is not as fundamental as the question of "why." Darryl Tippins said:

> Why do we come together? Until we address this most basic question, discussions of music or responsive readings, or three songs and a prayer are trivial and beside the point. Who cares if we sing a German anthem or "Bringing in the Sheaves" if we don't know why we are there. Even if our style and form are correct they become idol and idolatrous if we don't know the point. Without a point we are a bewildered, impoverished, and estranged people.[5]

We worship because we want God, we want to meet with Him. "Oh God, you are my God, earnestly I seek you; my soul thirsts for you, my body longs for you, in a dry and weary land where there is no water" (Ps. 63:1).

The primary purpose of life is to adore God. True worship can get lost amidst all the activity of our churches. Too often our churches major on ministry and minor on adoration. Like Martha, we can become so deeply entrenched in activity that we miss the real priority of life, which is kneeling at the feet of our Lord

---

[4]Richard J. Foster, *Celebration of Discipline* (San Francisco: Harper & Row, Publisher, 1978), p. 138.

[5]Tippins, "Called to Worship." Audiocassette.

in genuine praise (Luke 10:38-42). The well known shorter catechism of the Westminster Assembly states: "The true end of man is to glorify God and enjoy Him forever."

Paul also informs us that we have been chosen in Christ and destined to live for the praise of His glory (Eph. 1:4-6). Our bodies are temples of the Holy Spirit, and we, therefore, are to glorify God even in our bodies (1 Cor. 6:9-20). The apostle Peter tells us that we "are being built into a spiritual house to be a holy priesthood, offering spiritual sacrifices acceptable to God through Jesus Christ" (1 Pet. 2:5). Peter also wrote, "But you are a chosen people, a royal priesthood, a holy nation, a people belonging to God, that you may *declare the praises* of him who called you out of darkness into his wonderful light" (1 Pet. 2:9).

The word *worship* comes from the Anglo-Saxon *weorth-scipe*, which was later developed into *worthship* and then into *worship*. It means to attribute worth and honor and dignity to an object. Why do we worship God? Because He deserves it and because we long to honor Him. As we worship God we ascribe to Him supreme worth. He alone is worthy. "Ascribe to the LORD, O families of nations, ascribe to the LORD glory and strength. Ascribe to the LORD the glory due his name; bring an offering and come into his courts" (Ps. 96:7-8). "Worthy is the Lamb that was slain to receive power and riches and wisdom and might and honor and glory and blessing" (Rev. 5:12, NASB).

Too often we attend public worship with a "What's in it for me?" attitude, as if God exists merely to meet our needs, to fill us up and to give us blessings. The philosophy of our day is that unless something has a use, it has no intrinsic value. When we approach worship this way, we treat God as if He is our servant. Make no mistake about it — God is not our servant. He is our God, and we are His servants. We worship God because of who He is, not because of what He can do for us. It is appropriate to ask things of God, but not until we first offer Him a sincere heart and life of praise. We must worship God with a "What can I offer up to the Lord?" attitude. Paul urged Christians "to offer your bodies as living sacrifices, holy and pleasing to God — this is your spiritual act of worship" (Rom. 12:1).

Christians do not offer animal sacrifices as did the Hebrews under the Old Covenant. We offer the spiritual sacrifice of ourselves, and God expects our best. King David said that he would not offer God anything which cost him nothing (2 Sam. 24:24). There is no place in worship for a slipshod, flippant, or frivolous approach to God's presence. Although we are not to worship God for what we can get out of Him, that does not mean that we get nothing out of worship. True worship will transform us (Rom. 12:1). As we worship God over time, we find in Him refuge and strength, companionship and belongingness, peace and joy, meaning and fulfillment, and healing and security.

Think of Worship as a Response

What should be our answer to all that God has done and continues to do for us? The only adequate responses are worship and adoration and a life which strives to bring honor and glory to God. The key word is "response." God is the initiator, and we are the responders. "We love because God *first* loved us" (1 John 4:19). We do not worship God in order to be loved by God. He already loves us. Our worship of God takes place within God's love. Worship is not an effort to get God's attention. Rather, it is a response to the God who has already invited us to worship Him, who, indeed, is seeking us to worship Him (John 4:23).

C. Welton Gaddy says that worship is a gift between lovers. Our worship is a love gift to the love-giving God. Worship is a gift between lovers who keep on giving to each other. This is the kind of giving and receiving that forms a circular pattern between God and His people which defies comprehension and lasts forever.[6] Gaddy writes, "Worship is not a tactic calculated to win God's grace. Worship occurs because of God's grace. Worshipers gather within God's grace. Worship is a celebration of God's grace."[7] God wants us to worship Him not because He is narcissistic, but because He knows we need to worship so that we will be like Him. He gives. In worship we give back, thus becoming like God in His giving nature.

There are commands present in worship: repent, believe, go, do. But, the commands never come first. The New Testament teaches that God's gifts always precede demands. So many of our churches get these backwards in worship. We push demands and try to create a sense of guilt in people for all they do that is wrong. We hope this approach will lead people to love and serve and worship God. It seldom works that way. What we need to do first is what God does first — tell people of God's love and what He has done for them. Then, allow God's love to be the motivating force that leads them to respond in obedient faith.

God would have us respond with our minds, our emotions, and our wills. Ronald Allen and Gordon Borror write: "Worship is an active response to God whereby we declare His worth. Worship is not passive, but is participative. Worship is not simply a mood; it is a response."[8] John E. Burkhart says, "Worship is the

---

[6]Gaddy, pp. xi, xv-xviii.

[7]*Ibid.*, p. 98.

[8]Ronald Allen and Gordon Borror, *Worship: Rediscovering the Missing Jewel* (Portland: Multnomah Press, 1982), p. 16.

celebrated response to what God has done, is doing, and promises to do."[9] The question in worship is not "What can I give to someone who *has* everything?" Rather, it is "What can I give to someone who *gives* everything?" God will still be God even if we never worship Him. But if we do not worship Him, we are the ones who lose. It is unnatural (sinful) for us not to respond with worship.

Worship Engages the Heart

We cannot worship God acceptably unless our response wholly captures our attitudes and engages our hearts. There is a great difference between institutional worship and worship as a natural response to what God has done. Institutional worship is a system in which people worship because they feel forced to or in which they merely go through the motions. They think if they carry out certain rituals and follow a prescribed set of forms, they have worshiped. However, we can worship this way without ever engaging our hearts. We can go through all the right motions and carry out all the right forms and be as cold and lifeless as a corpse.

The early chapters of Isaiah describe how God's people had a correct form of worship but were displeasing to Him because their lives were full of injustice and their hearts were not right (Isa. 1:11-17; see also Amos 5:21-24). They went through the proper motions, but those motions were without meaning. In Matthew 15:1-9 we read how Jesus condemned some Pharisees and teachers of the law because they were careful to practice their traditions of worship while not fulfilling the moral obligations which God had clearly laid upon them. To that group of hypocrites Jesus applied the words of the prophet Isaiah:

---

[9]Burkhart, p. 99.

These people honor me with their lips, but their hearts are far from me. They worship me in vain; their teachings are but rules taught by men.   Mark 7:6-7.

God wants in worship what He has always wanted — submissive lives and genuine hearts. King David's words ring as true today as they did 1,000 years before Jesus:

You do not delight in sacrifice, or I would bring it; you do not take pleasure in burnt offerings. The sacrifices of God are a broken spirit; a broken and contrite heart, O God, you will not despise.   Ps. 51:16-17.

It is not that God did not want Israel's sacrifices. God had commanded the Israelites to make sacrifice in worship. God did not want their worship unless their lives reflected godliness and their hearts were given to Him. That is true of our worship still. Going through the motions without engagement of heart and a life of discipleship is completely unacceptable to God — a sheer waste of His time and ours!

Norman Bales writes:

Worship renewal requires us to focus more on the internal condition of our hearts than the external structure of the service. The corporate worship of the church will never be a satisfactory experience until we develop a quality relationship with God in the privacy of our closets. . . .Little doubt exists as to the need for worship renewal in most churches, but the renewal we need involves inward change more than it does outward modification.[10]

The deepest joys of worship come only to those who throw all their hearts and energies into it, never to those who leave their hearts behind, no matter how many prayers they pray or songs they sing.

---

[10]Norman Bales, "How to Initiate Worship Renewal," *Image Magazine* 9 no. 2 (March/April 1993), pp. 18-19.

When people finally comprehend how marvelously God has blessed them, no one will have to coerce them into worship. The problem will be how to contain worship. Where hearts and attitudes are right, worship will break out everywhere.

Worship Involves All of Life

In one sense, worship encompasses all of life. We tend to divide life into secular and sacred. This is a false dichotomy. In the total life of Israel there was a fusion between the spheres of secular and religious. Israel was to be "a kingdom of priests and a holy nation" (Exod. 19:6). Their total life was a service (worship) before the Lord. Paul wrote, "And whatever you do, whether in word or deed, do it all in the name of the Lord Jesus, giving thanks to God the Father through him" (Col. 3:17). If we take that verse seriously, we cannot restrict worship to the sacred. Everything we do is to be dedicated to the glory of God. As Christians we are God's priests, and our bodies are His temple. As such, our entire lives — not merely certain days and hours in the week — are to offer glory to God.

Technically, it is not biblical to say we are "going to worship," since all we do, both in and outside the assembly, is to be done to the glory of God (1 Cor. 10:31). Our whole lives should offer up glory and praise to the Father. Our Sunday assembly is to be the corporate overflow of that daily worship. The assembly also is the congregational celebration of our mutual victory in Christ and joint dependence on God.

The Lord's Day Is Special

While it is true that worship involves all of life, it is also true that something unique happens when God's people assemble in public worship. In the assembly we can see the face and presence of God in each other.

The Lord's Day assembly is vital to our existence as Christians. Although there is immense value in personal, individual worship, the church is not an unconnected collection of individuals. The church is the body, one body, of which Christ is the head (1 Cor. 12:12-31). We worship as a group of people who have much in common. The basic word for assembly in the New Testament is *ekklesia* εκκλησια. The New Testament uses the word more than 100 times to refer to gatherings of Christians. The idea of Christians living isolated from other Christians was an unknown idea in New Testament times. The individualism of modern western cultures has invaded the mindset of many Christians, but it is foreign to the New Testament concept of the church. Jesus promised, "For where two or three come together in my name, there am I with them" (Matt. 18:20).

Worship Edifies Christians

Another great purpose of worship is edification (1 Cor. 14:3-5, 26). A focus on God is primary, but a proper God-focus leads to a genuine concern for other people, especially for fellow believers. In the New Testament there are no accounts of disciples assembling just to praise God. From the very birth of the church, believers assembled not only to praise God but also to study, to fellowship, to break bread, to pray, to share, and to eat together (Acts 2:42-47). Christians are to build up one another (1 Cor. 14:12).

This concern and edification are predicated on the truth that people need each other. Congregational worship can be enhanced by private worship, but corporate worship can never be replaced by private worship.

The two are complementary. If we try to separate worship and fellowship, we do damage to both. From other people we gain strength, encouragement, comfort, and courage to live for Jesus. The assembly allows us to interrelate with others of like faith as we sing together, pray together, and study together. We can exhort, rebuke, and admonish each other. As we gather around the Lord's Table, we recall together all that our Lord has accomplished on our behalf. The world tries to pull Christians away from the Lord and each other. Assembling for worship with other Christians "spur(s) one another on toward love and good deeds" (Heb. 10:24-25). If we give up assembling together we give up that essential encouragement.

The two most important purposes of the assembly are to encounter God in worship and to edify one another in fellowship. Some people have tried to pit encounter against edification. It is not a matter of either/or; it is a matter of both/and. Jack Reese insists:

> It is possible to have edification without encounter with God. It happens all the time. There are all kinds of people all the time encouraging each other. It is not possible to have true encounter with God without edification. When God is in our midst we are constantly encouraging each other. We are not sitting in an audience offering a vertical worship to God. We are sharing and encouraging each other. If we believe we actually encounter God in our midst, it makes encouragement more important, not less important. So we are constantly encouraging each other to look Godward, Who is not up, but in, among, and in the midst of His people.[11]

---

[11]Jack Reese, "Called to Worship." Audiocassette.

DISCUSSION QUESTIONS
ON CHAPTER THREE

1. How do you see God? How does your view affect your worship?

2. How do you explain a God Who is completely holy, and yet is all-gracious?

3. Evaluate the statement, "Reconciliation is at the heart of all true worship."

4. Is your worship focused on God or on your own desires?

5. Is there a conflict between the worship of God and the worship of Jesus?

6. In what ways is the Holy Spirit involved in worship?

7. Why do we worship?

8. What does it mean to say that worship is a response to God?

9. Why is it dangerous to worship without engaging one's heart in worship?

10. Is worship something you do only when Christians assemble for a worship service? Explain.

11. Why is the Lord's Day special?

12. How is the worship service edifying to worshipers?

4

Biblical Backgrounds of Worship

We are the products of our past. This is also true of
the church which Jesus established almost twenty
centuries ago. Although the Church was new, it was built
on the foundation which God had already laid down
under the Old Covenant (Acts 3:25). The Christian
movement did not come into existence without a
heritage. Although Jesus knew that He was establishing a
new covenant, in no way did He ever try to cut Himself
off from His Jewish roots or His Hebrew faith. Jesus
insisted that He had not come to abolish the Law and
the Prophets but to fulfill them (Matt. 5:17). If we are
going to understand worship as the first Christians practiced it, we must understand the Old Testament roots of
Christian worship.

Worship From The Beginning

Human beings have always felt a need to worship.
Cain and Abel offered sacrifices to God. Throughout
those dawning centuries of the human race, people like
Enoch, Noah and his sons, and other patriarchs and
their families worshiped the Lord. Their forms of
worship were simple but sincere.

The turning point in worship seems to have come
with God's calling of a man named Abram, whose name
was later changed to Abraham (meaning "Father of
many nations," or "Father of the faithful"). Abram was a
good, moral man but one who did not know God, one

who worshiped false gods in his homeland, Ur of the Chaldees. However, God called Abram to leave his home, his family, and his country to go to an unknown land where God would lead him. Abram was a man of integrity and faith, willing to obey this God who had called him to follow. God took the initiative in calling Abram. It is important to see that. It was not Abram who sought God first. God sought fellowship and worship from Abram. Abram's obedience was a response to God's initiative. Worship is still a response to God's initiative.

God has always desired to walk with His people and to dwell among them (Gen. 3:8; Exod. 25:8; 29:45-46; 30:36; Lev. 26:11-12; 1 Kings 6:13; Ezek. 37:26-28; Zech. 2:10-11; John 14:17; 2 Cor. 6:16; Rev. 21:3). That desire is apparent in the names He gave the Tabernacle: the dwelling place, the tent of meeting, the Holy Place. The tent of "meeting" did not refer to a place of assembly, but to the "meeting" of God with His people. Again, we see that it was God who made the provision and appointed the time and terms of this meeting.

The names God gave the Tabernacle indicate His desire to meet with His people. However, "the Holy Place" insists that the God who met with them was a God to be feared and held in reverent awe. God, who is entirely perfect, absolutely holy, and completely righteous, chose to meet His sinful people in worship. To say that God is holy is to emphasize the otherness, the mystery, the transcendence, the inaccessibility, and the unapproachableness of God. Yet God chose to dwell in the midst of an imperfect people whom He had called to praise Him. It was only because the Holy One was in their midst that Israel was made a holy people (Exod. 19:6).

Holiness is a divine characteristic, not a human one. Therein lies one of the greatest paradoxes of all the ages. God, Who is "the Holy One of Israel" (2 Kings 19:22; Ps. 89:18; Isa. 5:24; 12:6), chose to dwell in the midst of a sinful people. He is often called "the Holy One among you" (Deut. 7:21; Isa. 12:6; Hos. 11:9). He chose to dwell in their midst not because they were worthy of His presence, nor because He was obligated to them in any way, but simply because He loved them and longed to have their affection and praise. Throughout all the generations, that desire on God's part has remained constant.

God's desire for His people's worship is also evident in Moses' encounter with Pharaoh (Exod. 5-12). Repeatedly, God instructed Moses to say to Pharaoh, "let my people go that they may worship me." After the Israelites left Egypt and arrived at the foot of the mountain in the Sinai, once again it was God who initiated the relationship with the freed slaves.

Exodus 24:1-8 contains five basic structural elements for this meeting between God and His people. First, God called his people to meet with Him. "Come up to the Lord . . . You are to worship" (Exod. 24:1). God was the one Who initiated worship. Second, God expected His people to participate in this encounter with Him. Although Moses and Aaron were God's designated leaders, all the people had a participatory role to play. The people offered sacrifices to the Lord (Exod. 24:5). Third, God proclaimed His Word to them. Worship is not complete without hearing from the Lord. Fourth, worship involved a continuous renewal of commitment to the relationship God initiated with them. "They responded with one voice, 'Everything the LORD has said we will do'" (Exod. 24:3, 7). By giving assent to God's words, the Hebrews showed that they accepted the conditions of God's covenant with them. Fifth, God ratified the covenant with His people. God sealed it by having Moses sprinkle the blood of the sacrifice of young bulls on the people (Exod. 24:8). Man's meeting with God was climaxed by this dramatic symbol of ratification.[1]

Although God revealed these principles more than 3,500 years ago, they remain valid today. God still calls us to meet Him, to participate in the encounter, to listen to His Word, and to renew our commitment to Him continuously. It is the blood of the new covenant, the precious blood of Jesus Christ, which ratifies our covenant relationship with God. When we understand the implications of God's holiness and our own sinfulness, it can be frightening to know that Holy God comes into our midst when we assemble to worship. Yet it is even more frightening to think that God might separate Himself from us. David expressed that horrible thought when he penned Psalm 51:11, "Do not cast me from your presence or take your Holy Spirit from me." How reassuring it is to hear the words of Jesus who promised "For where two or three come together in my name, there I am with them" (Matt.18:20).

Centralized Worship Around The Temple in Jerusalem

For many years, Israel's worship centered around the Tabernacle and the Ark of the Covenant within it. The tabernacle was a movable tent-like structure which changed locations every time the Israelites moved. With the rise of the Israelite monarchy and King David, worship became centralized in Jerusalem. The centralized nature of Hebrew worship was solidified with the construction of the temple by David's son, Solomon. All the sacrifices were to be done at the temple. This centralized worship helped curb some of the idolatry which had grown common throughout the nation of

---

[1]Webber, *Worship, Old and New*, pp. 24-25.

Israel. However, the construction of the temple in Jerusalem never succeeded in stamping out idolatry.

Worship in the temple was very institutional with several orders of priests conducting services which were highly liturgical. Sacrifices were offered with great ceremony and ritual. Formality marked everything about temple worship. When the Babylonians destroyed the temple in 587 B.C. and most of the nation was forcibly resettled in Babylon, Hebrew worship suffered a severe blow. With no temple or priesthood or sacrifices, the Jews faced a most uncertain spiritual future. How were they to conduct worship without the temple and the rituals which were such an essential part of it?

The Rise of the Synagogue

No one knows for certain when the Jewish synagogue began, but many Old Testament scholars believe it arose sometime during the seventy-year captivity in Babylon. "Synagogue" means "gathering place." This substitute for the temple began for the purpose of helping the Jews keep their faith alive during those difficult decades of exile. The synagogue provided a place and a structure in which to worship God without the temple, without the Levitical priesthood, and without animal sacrifices. When the temple was destroyed, the Jews were not free to invent new forms of worship. They did, however, gather informally for festivals and on the Sabbath to encourage one another in the faith and to share their common hope for a speedy restoration to their homeland and the rebuilding of the temple.

It is not likely that the Jews intended the synagogue to become a new institution. However, it ended up becoming the most influential institution in Jewish life. Abraham Millgram writes, "At the time, . . . no one could possibly have foreseen that from such humble seeds would grow so majestic a tree, under whose shade hundreds of millions of people would find rest, stimulation, and nourishment."[2] Unlike the temple, which was twice rebuilt and twice destroyed following the Babylonian exile, the synagogue thrived without interruption.

Three elements were central in synagogue worship. The first element was praise. The Talmud (the repository of the wisdom and traditions of the Pharisees) says: "Man should always first utter praises, and then pray." The ruler of the synagogue would begin by having someone call the worshipers, "Bless ye the Lord, the One who is blessed." Then the congregation would respond with an appropriate blessing, perhaps modeled after Nehemiah 9:5-37, "May the Lord, the blessed One, be blessed forever and ever."[3]

The second element of synagogue worship was prayer. This included the recitation of the shema and the eighteen benedictions or blessings (Deut. 6:4ff.). The third element of synagogue worship was instruction. There was always the reading of Scripture. This reading came in two parts. First was a reading from the books of the law, which were divided into designated readings to allow the law to be read through completely in three years. Some insist that this is the historical basis for the use of lectionaries. Second, there was a reading from the prophets — a passage selected by the reader (see Luke 4:16-20).[4] This system is believed to go back to the first century B.C. In a later age, it was divided into 54 sections.[5] It was most likely through the synagogue that

---

[2]Abraham Millgram, *Jewish Worship* (Philadelphia: The Jewish Publication Society of America, 1971), p. 64.

[3]Wendell Willis, *Worship: A Definitive Study of the History, Methods and Intent of Christian Worship* (Austin, TX: Sweet Publishing Co., 1973), p. 23.

[4]*Ibid.*, p. 24.

[5]Rowley, p. 235.

Jesus gained his knowledge of the Scriptures. This emphasis on prayer and study of Scripture led the Jews to refer to the synagogue as both a "house of prayer" and a "house of instruction."

While both men and women participated in the congregational response to the worship, they were segregated as to their stance in the building. Women were veiled, and men were bareheaded.[6] Worship in the synagogue was far less structured and more informal than the highly formal ritual and ceremony of the temple. The synagogue was the place where the exiled Jews remembered and recalled God's actions among the people. The emphasis was upon what God had done. The Israelites celebrated God's actions in the reading of their history and Scripture. They also sang their songs, which were the Psalms. In their prayers of praise, they blessed God for His acts on their behalf. Their reflections were their sermons. As they did these things they were reminded of who they were as God's people. James F. White writes:

> Worship thus was a way of transmitting the corporate memories of a people with whom God had convenanted. It was not the remembrance of a dead, detached past, but a means of having God by worshipping Him in the here and now. As past events were recalled they became present reality through which God's saving powers were again and again experienced. Through worship, people could relive the whole history of salvation. Individual lives were changed by sharing in the recital of common memories, just as an adolescent is helped to discover his or her identity as the family together recalls past experiences by looking through their photograph album. Survival through identification with the group's corporate memories of how God had acted for His people is the core of synagogue worship.[7]

---

[6]Lynn Hieronymus, *What the Bible Says About Worship* (Joplin, MO: College Press Publishing Company, 1984), p. 34.

[7]James F. White, *Christian Worship in Transition* (Nashville: Abingdon, 1976), pp. 12-13.

There is a valuable principle of worship here for Christians. Our worship should also include times of remembering what God has done, not only for us but for His people down through the ages. Obviously, this is one of the reasons why the Lord's Supper is indispensable. In it we are to remember Jesus' death, burial, resurrection, and exaltation — the very events that have brought us redemption.

We, too, need to tell the old, old stories of God's workings — stories that shape our identity, stories that build our faith, stories that reassure us that our God is still alive, just as He was so many years ago. We tell the stories in many of our songs. Preachers must be sure to balance their preaching to guarantee that people hear the stories of how God moved among His people of every age. To fail to remember is to cut ourselves off from the faith-building events and heritage that explain who we are and where we are going by God's mighty hand.

Differences Between The Temple And The Synagogue

Synagogue worship was led by laymen, not priests. Leaders were chosen on the basis of ability and piety. Priests were preferred only for pronouncing the prescribed benedictions as required by the law (Num. 6:24-26). The synagogue was the religious, educational, and social center of Jewish life. By the first century, the temple (which had been rebuilt after the Babylonians destroyed it in 587 B.C.) was little more than a symbol for most Jews who did not live in Jerusalem — the city of David was too inaccessible for them. Even in Jerusalem, the synagogue played a much more prominent role in people's lives than did the temple. The Talmud indicates that there were 394 synagogues in Jerusalem alone when the Romans destroyed the temple in A.D. 70. Therefore, corporate Jewish worship continued uninterrupted after the temple fell.

Synagogue worship differed from temple worship in at least five significant ways. One, synagogue worship was less formal, with fewer ceremonies and rituals. Two, the teaching of Scripture was foremost in the synagogue. That was not true of temple worship. In contrast, the most prominent element of temple worship was the animal sacrificial system. Three, because there were no animal sacrifices to offer at the synagogue, there was little need for the priests. Four, the teacher, rather than the priest, was the central figure in the synagogue. The fifth difference has to do with lay participation. In the temple, the priests performed all the functions of worship. However, in the synagogue there was far more lay participation in worship.

Although the services of the temple and the synagogue were radically different, the two institutions coexisted harmoniously. The teachers of the synagogue never denied the authenticity and the centrality of the temple service, and the leaders of the temple never denied the religious importance of the synagogue service. There was no competition between the two institutions. Each performed its own functions with the full approval and support of the other.[8]

Usually, the synagogue building was simple: a raised podium, a seat for the learned teacher, and an ark to contain the sacred scrolls. The offices of the synagogue were lay positions. A president (or ruler) was selected from among the male members because of his age and integrity. He had an assistant (or "minister" but not in a professional sense of "minister").[9]

The order of worship in the synagogue was not strictly fixed in the first century, but it had a fairly traditional structure. The service usually opened with

---

[8]Millgram, p. 76.
[9]Hieronymous, p. 32.

readings from the Psalms (especially popular were Ps. 19, 32, 34, 90, 91, 135, and 136). Next the congregation recited the shema (Deut. 6:4-9; 11:13-21; Num. 15:37-41). This was followed by a main prayer called the eighteen benedictions or the eighteen blessings. After this, various members of the congregation read from the Hebrew text of the law and the prophets. Then the Hebrew was translated into Aramaic, which was the conversational language of the people.

Translating the word of God into the spoken language of the people had its precedent established centuries earlier in Nehemiah 8:8. Often, although not always, a male chosen by the ruler of the synagogue would give an expository address based on the text which had been read earlier. More than likely this lesson would come from the reading from the prophets rather than from the law. This "sermon" was known as the *derashah* דרשה, an act of "searching" for truth.[10] Both Jesus and the Apostle Paul were given the opportunity to give this lesson (Luke 4:21, Acts 13:15). The service sometimes concluded with a doxology. If a priest were present, he would close the service with a benediction or a blessing. There was a certain rigidity in the order of synagogue worship, yet there was flexibility with regard to the content within that order. One could say there was freedom within a somewhat structured framework.[11]

Jesus' Attitude Toward the Temple and the Synagogue

It probably would not be accurate to say that Jesus fully approved of either the temple or the synagogue worship in His day. Jesus began His ministry teaching at the synagogue in Galilee (Mark 1:21-27). He spent the

---

[10]Webber, Worship, *Old and New*, p. 29.
[11]Hieronymous, pp. 32-33.

last week of His earthly life teaching in the precincts of the temple (Mark 14:19). Jesus worshiped in both, but He seems to have had some reservations about the temple. Although He attended the appropriate festivals there and called it His Father's house, the gospel accounts never record His offering a sacrifice at the temple. Jesus' chief concern seems to have been to make sure the temple was kept as a house of prayer for all the people (Mark 11:17). That is why He cleansed the temple when some money-hungry Jews were trading there. Jesus valued the temple primarily for the facilities it offered for communion with God and for prayer. That was more important to Him than the sacrificial apparatus associated with the temple. In His own body Jesus was going to be establishing a new offering. He told a Samaritan woman that there would be a time and place when the temple would not be important (John 4:19-24). Jesus was more closely related to the synagogue than the temple. He frequently worshiped at the synagogue and made it a practice to teach there (Matt. 4:23; Mark 1:21, 38-39; Luke 4:15-32; John 6:59; 18:20). Many of His healings were done at the synagogue, and it was there that He first publicly announced His mission (Luke 4:16-22).[12]

The Influence of the Synagogue on Christian Worship

The synagogue was the Jewish institution which had the greatest impact on the worship of the early Christians. The first Christians were Jewish converts. Therefore, it should not be surprising that they would borrow heavily from their religious roots in the synagogue. The early church looked enough like Judaism that more than once it was confused for a sect of the

---

[12]Willis, pp. 25-26.

Jews (Acts 24:5,14; 28:22). When one studies worship in the synagogue, it is easy to see the origin of many worship practices in the first century church. There was a great emphasis on prayer and the reading and exposition of Scripture.[13] There was also great emphasis upon the retelling of God's saving acts throughout history on behalf of His people.[14] The early church's worship was similar to that of the synagogue in many ways.

Christian Worship Distinct From Synagogue Worship

There were also many ways in which the church's worship was distinct from that of the synagogue. Christians used writings of their own leaders such as the Apostles, Mark, and Luke. The gospel accounts and the epistles took precedence over the law and prophets. Although the Psalms were used to express worship in Christian services, Christians wrote new songs and hymns which reflected their beliefs about Jesus Christ (many scholars believe passages such as Phil. 2:5-11 served as first century hymns). Ephesians 5:18-19 urges Christians to speak to one another in psalms, hymns, and spiritual songs. Baptism and the Lord's supper were distinctive Christian practices.

Oscar Cullmann believes that the Lord's Supper was the basis and goal of every Christian gathering.[15] Christian worship was marked by a consciousness that the Holy Spirit had come to make Jesus known in their midst. Worship became primarily a celebration of the acts of God manifested in Jesus. The resurrection motivated an unshakable hope which was not present in the synagogue. There was a spontaneity about the worship

---

[13]Willis, pp. 23-24; Rowley, p. 235.

[14]White, *Christian Worship in Transition*, pp. 12-13.

[15]Oscar Cullmann, *Early Christian Worship* (London: SCM Press, Ltd., 1953), p. 29.

of the early church that made it dynamic, enthusiastic, intimate, and heartfelt.

Christian worship also occurred on a different day — Sunday, in honor of the day of Jesus' resurrection from the grave. Early Christians also met in a different place for worship. They were not opposed to "church buildings;" they simply did not have any at first. It was not until the third century that Christians began to build buildings for worship.[16] The primary difference between synagogue worship and Christian worship was that Old Testament worship focused on the Exodus-event, while Christian worship focuses on the Christ-event.[17] Christian worship has deep roots in the past — especially in Judaism. Many of the particulars of worship changed in Christian worship, but the "why" of worship has never changed.

Worship as Described in the New Testament

It is considerably more difficult to trace the development of worship in the New Testament than to trace the development of worship in the Old Testament. Robert Webber writes:

> There is no single highly developed statement on worship in the New Testament. Rather, brief descriptions provided by hymns, confessions, benedictions, doxologies, and subtle hints in words descriptive of worship are scattered throughout the New Testament documents.[18]

Unlike Old Testament worship, New Testament worship has no strict pattern, formula, or specified order. Different styles or emphases are evident among

---

[16]Segler, pp. 27-29; Ilion T. Jones, pp. 84-85.
[17]Webber, *Worship, Old and New*, p. 30.
[18]*Ibid.*, p. 33.

different groups in the New Testament. The worship of Palestinian Jewish Christians was more closely tied to the customs and patterns of Jewish worship. It was not unusual for them to worship "in the temple courts" (Acts 2:46). Jewish Christians who lived outside Palestine (Hellenistic Jews) were not attached to the temple and cultic practices of their Palestinian brethren. They had much less interest in preserving continuity with Hebraic religious practices than did Aramaic Jews. They renounced Jewish rituals and reinterpreted them as having been fulfilled in Christ (Matt. 26:26-28; Luke 4:21; 24:25-27, 44-47).

The most extensive example of early Gentile Christian worship is found in Paul's Corinthian correspondence in the mid-first century. Gentile Christians were highly interested in maintaining freedom in worship. With no Jewish background, they needed to be taught how to worship God acceptably. From the letter of 1 Corinthians we get several ideas of liturgical practices in mid-first century Greece: forms of blessing (1 Cor. 1:3; 16:23), worship on Sunday (1 Cor. 16:1-2), possible celebration of Pentecost (1 Cor. 16:8), and Passover (1 Cor. 5:7), the use of the holy kiss (1 Cor. 16:20), and church discipline (1 Cor. 5:5; 16:22). We also learn that keeping order in worship was important (1 Cor. 14:40). Paul does not give us a specified order of service, but he does mention many major aspects of Christian worship, especially in 1 Corinthians 12 and 14: revelation, knowledge, prophecy, instruction, prayer, singing, and giving thanks. There were also preaching and the Lord's Supper.[19]

Several Christian worship practices grew directly out of synagogue worship: Scripture reading (1 Tim. 4:13; 1 Thess. 5:27; Col. 4:16); Psalms and hymns (1 Cor.

---

[19]*Ibid.*, pp. 37-40.

14:26; Eph. 5:19; Col. 3:16); common prayers (Acts 2:42; 1 Tim. 2:1-2); the people's "Amens" (1 Cor. 14:16); a sermon or exposition (1 Cor. 14:26; Acts 20:7); a confession of faith (1 Cor. 15:1-4; 1 Tim. 6:12); and almsgiving (1 Cor. 16:1-2; 2 Cor. 9:10-13; Rom. 15:26). Joined to the above practices was the Lord's Supper (1 Cor. 10:16, 11:23; Matt. 26:26-28; Mark 14:22-24; Luke 22:19-20). The Prayer of Consecration would include thanksgiving (Luke 22:19; 1 Cor. 11:23; 14:16; 1 Tim. 2:1), prayers of intercession (John 17), and perhaps the recitation of the Lord's Prayer (Matt. 6:9-13). Probably, there was singing in this part of the service, and the kiss of peace (Rom. 16:1; 1 Cor. 16:20; 1 Thess. 5:26; 1 Pet. 5:14).

These provide a general idea about the elements included in Christian worship in the first century. However, because the New Testament does not provide a systematic picture of Christian worship, some guidance may be sought regarding worship from the practice of the early church beginning in the second century. That is where we travel next in our exploration of worship.

DISCUSSION QUESTIONS
ON CHAPTER FOUR

1. What is implied when we say that God took the initiative in calling us to worship Him?

2. Why would a holy God want to dwell among a sinful people?

3. What were the differences between worship in the temple and in the synagogue?

4. In what ways is Christian worship indebted to synagogue worship?

5. In what ways is Christian worship different from synagogue worship?

6. Why is it important for Christians to retell the stories of God's great acts in the past? Is God still active today? How?

7. Why do you think there is no strict pattern or formula for worship in the New Testament?

8. In what ways is your worship assembly like worship assemblies in the first century?

9. In what ways is your worship assembly different from worship assemblies in the first century?

10. If you could be transported back in time, how comfortable do you think you would be with the way the first century Christians practiced worship?

5

Indebted to Our Past

Henry Ford did more for us than give us the automobile. He contributed to a lousy attitude that seems to pervade much of our society. He is the one who is purported to have originated the line: "History is bunk!" Sadly, millions of people agree with him. History is viewed as boring and irrelevant. Most people simply do not care about events in the past.

This presents a major problem for us in our study of worship. While most Christians would concede that it is important to survey the historical backgrounds of worship in the Old and New Testaments, many would wonder why anyone should be concerned with what was going on in Christian worship 10, 50, or even 100 years ago. Even more, why would anyone care about what was happening in worship hundreds or even thousands of years ago? This lack of interest in history is a symptom of our modern, secular culture which has little sense of connectedness to the past. The spirit of individualism that pervades our society encourages us to forget the past and to disregard its traditions. This disconnectedness, however, is causing us to lose a sense of our identity.[1]

Leonard Allen is correct when he writes that churches of Christ today face something of an identity crisis partly because we are not familiar with our past as a movement or with our tradition as a people. The same could be said of all churches associated with the Restoration Movement.

[1]C. Leonard Allen, *The Cruciform Church* (Abilene, TX: ACU Press, 1990), pp. 2-3.

With the passage of time, as one generation handed its faith and practices down to the next generation, there were subtle, yet inevitable changes. Restoration churches today are not exactly as they were in the 1940s and 1950s. Those churches of the '40s and '50s were not like the ones that existed at the turn of the twentieth century, and churches of the early 1900s were significantly different from the churches in which Alexander Campbell worshiped before and after the American Civil War. Each of us individually is born with a past; we arrive in this world with a heritage. The same is true for today's churches. We are the products of our past.[2]

History teaches us much about ourselves if we have the wisdom to recognize it. Darryl Tippins tells a most intriguing story:

> Saul Bellow, the prize-winning American novelist, tells of his visit to an Israeli kibbutz, a small farming community near Herod's Caesarea. Bellow was struck by the fact that Roman ruins lay all about the farm. While they were plowing a field one day they turned up an entire Roman street. Pottery fragments lay scattered everywhere. Marble columns rested in the grass. A fallen capital served as a garden seat at one farmer's home.
>
> As I read Bellow's description, I couldn't help thinking of the state of today's Christians who seek to renew Christian worship. Just as those modern citizens of Israel carry out their mundane chores on top of a buried classical culture, today's Christian worshipers live atop a rich spiritual past which they only dimly recognize. How these worshipers would be nourished if only they could get in touch with the resources of their past![3]

We whose roots are in the Restoration Movement are incorrect if we assume that we burst on the scene in the mid-nineteenth century, free of the influence of the religious, social, and philosophical thoughts of the period.

---

[2]Allen, *The Cruciform Church*, pp. 3-4.
[3]Darryl Tippins, "Rediscovering Christian Worship," *21st Century Christian Magazine* (December, 1991): p. 19.

Those who shaped our Movement were impacted by their own culture. Leonard Allen says of Alexander Campbell, probably the most influential of all the nineteenth century Restorationists, "Campbell was a brilliant intellectual and an intensely serious biblical scholar, but he was, like all of us, a child of his time."[4]

Just as our Restoration forefathers were influenced by their own times as well as their past, so the church of today is also impacted by our times and our past. None of us in any period of history can free ourselves from our present or our past. We have a history that helps us understand who we are today. This is precisely the point: to fully understand who we are today (to know our identity), we must know something of our history.

A few years ago, Alex Haley captivated a nation with his study of his own family's roots. Knowing his roots helped Haley know who he was. In our study of worship, it will help us to know our roots as well. Once we acknowledge that churches of Christ stand in a long and rich tradition, we can move on to the next important step: to learn something about our past which will allow us to assess and critique our tradition.

The understanding that we are a part of a tradition also frees us to critique traditions other than our own, "granting them," as Leonard Allen says, "what we ourselves wish to be granted: sincerity and zeal, honesty and intelligence." When we do that, we can learn from both their failures and their successes in trying to take the Bible seriously and to follow God faithfully.[5]

When we reject a historical perspective, worship can be viewed only from its current culture. If we isolate ourselves from the past, we become imprisoned in the present. The present, with all its shortcomings, then

---

[4]Allen, *The Cruciform Church*, p. 25.
[5]*Ibid.*, pp. 9-12.

becomes the norm. Worship renewal requires us to explore beliefs and practices of the past. Therefore the remainder of this chapter explores relevant parts of that history.

Many old forms of worship have not lost their value for today. We must find ways to fit those forms to our own cultural setting. Contemporary worship must be biblically based and culturally appropriate if it is going to connect with people in our modern society. However, contemporary worship should not be drastically out of step with many of the historical forms of worship that have proven helpful through the centuries. Doing so would require us to sever ourselves from much of the heritage that gives us meaning and identity.[6] The old sage was correct who said that those who ignore history are doomed to repeat it. Those who ignore history not only make the mistakes of the past, but they also forfeit the successes and insights of those who have gone before.

Do not be afraid of what you will learn from history — you probably will be amazed. For the first time you may realize where many of our worship beliefs and practices come from. And you may be surprised that some of the things that appear so newfangled today are really so old that we never knew they existed.

Ancient Christian Worship
(second through fourth centuries)

During the first century, the church struggled to define itself in relation to its Jewish origins. In the next two centuries, the church fought to maintain its integrity in a world that was hostile to Christianity. The church was forced to confront the diverse cultures, philoso-

---

[6]Webber, *Worship, Old and New*, pp. 11-12.

phies, and religions of the Greco-Roman world.[7] Following the close of the New Testament, there was a period of at least 50 years about which we have very limited details of the worship of early Christian communities.[8] For that matter, not even the New Testament gives elaborate descriptions of worship services. Webber speculates that little was said about it in those early years of the second century, not because worship was unimportant, but because information was being withheld so as not to cast their pearls before swine. The Lord's Supper in particular was deliberately protected from pagans.[9]

There are only a few important sources of information regarding worship from the close of New Testament days up to A.D. 200. One of those is a letter from Clement of Rome to the Corinthian Church, dated about A.D. 96. Clement's letter is an exhortation, not specifically about worship. However, at the end of the letter is a prayer in which many phrases occur that are similar to those found later in the liturgies of the fourth century. He recorded the expression: "Holy, Holy, Holy, Lord of Hosts, every creature is full of Thy glory." This is quite similar to the wording of what is called the *Sanctus* and may have been its early form. Likely it was a customary part of the Lord's Supper. Clement also referred to the "offering" or "oblations," probably indicating the offering of alms. These words later became a technical expression for the offering of the elements of the Lord's Supper.[10]

---

[7]William H. Willimon, *Word, Water, Wine and Bread* (Valley Forge: Judson Press, 1980), p. 29.

[8]Ilion T. Jones, p. 87.

[9]Webber, Worship, *Old and New*, p. 45.

[10]Ilion T. Jones, pp. 87-88; and William D. Maxwell, *An Outline of Christian Worship: Its Developments and Forms* (London: Oxford University Press, 1936), pp. 7-9.

Between A.D. 110 and 113 the Roman Emperor
Trajan received a series of letters from Pliny, the governor of Bithynia. Pliny was concerned about what he
considered a cult who met secretly within his governmental domain. His letters give some ideas about the
types of things Christians practiced in their assembly in
the early second century. Pliny's investigation revealed
many of the worship practices of the Christians. They
were in the habit of meeting on a fixed day before
daylight and reciting responsively among themselves a
hymn to Christ as a god. They taught moral admonitions
against theft, robbery, and adultery. They were obligated
to keep their word and pay their debts. These followers
of Christ would disband and come together again later
to have a common meal.

Even though Pliny believed that the meal was ordinary and harmless food, he issued an edict banning the
meal, a function which was often associated with "clubs."
Clubs in that period usually had political agendas, and
therefore were a political threat to peace and imperial
authority. Fraternities tended to be stubborn, immoral,
trouble makers. The Christians agreed to discontinue
this meal, probably indicating it to be the agape meal
and not the Lord's Supper. Apparently the agape meal
initially was their customary practice, but Christians did
not consider it essential. That is not the case with the
Lord's Supper. Christians would have faced death rather
than give up the Lord's Supper.[11]

The Teaching of the Twelve Apostles, usually called the
Didache, dates between A.D. 100 and 130. It gives direc-
tions for the agape meal, the celebration of the Lord's
Supper, and baptism. It verifies that Christians met
"every Lord's Day" for the agape meal and the Lord's
Supper, which were still held jointly.[12]

---

[11]Frans Jozef Van Beeck, "The Worship of Christians in Pliny's Letter,"
Studia Liturgica 18 no. 2 (1988): pp. 122-23.
[12]Ilion T. Jones, p. 88.

The *Didache* also records well known eucharistic prayers (prayers of thanksgiving), but the precise place and meaning of many of the prayers is unclear.[13] Early Christian worship, like temple and synagogue worship, also observed daily hours of prayer practiced in the synagogue: the third hour (Acts 2:15), the sixth hour (Acts 10:9), and the ninth hour (Acts 3:1). Tertullian (c. 165-220), a teacher and theologian in Carthage and Hippolytus (died c. 236), a presbyter and teacher in the church in Rome, gives evidence that these hours of prayer were still being observed by Christians in the early third century. According to the *Didache*, the Lord's prayer was repeated three times daily.[14]

In the mid second century, sometime between A.D. 140 and 155, Justin (c. 100-165) wrote his *Apology* to the Emperor Antoninus Pius. This philosopher, teacher, apologist, and martyr from Rome informed the Emperor that on Sundays Christians met in one place to read the memoirs of the apostles or the writings of the prophets as long as time permitted. After the reading, the president gave a discourse urging listeners to imitate what they had heard. Then they stood together and prayed. Afterward, they brought bread and wine and water, for which the president offered prayers, followed by the congregation's "amen." Then the elements were distributed to each person.

Everett Ferguson says that the Lord's Supper was an important time of fellowship for those early Christians. The deacons took the elements, over which thanks were expressed, into the homes of absent members. Thus efforts were made to incorporate even those who could

---

[13]Josef A. Jungmann, *The Early Liturgy to the Time of Gregory the Great* (South Bend: University of Notre Dame Press, 1959), p. 6.

[14]Webber, *Worship, Old and New*, p. 52.

not be present into the unity and fellowship of those who were able to assemble.[15]

It is clear from Justin's Apology that two items were emphasized in Christian worship of his day: the Lord's Supper and attention to the Word of God. This twofold emphasis came to be a major element of structure for Christian worship through the centuries.[16] In Justin's writings it is clear that none but baptized believers were allowed to partake of the Lord's Supper. Sometime after Justin there was a separation of the baptized from the unbaptized at the Lord's Supper. Tertullian was the first to inform us that the unbaptized were sent from the room when the Lord's Supper was served. The first part of the service, consisting of Scripture reading, preaching, singing, and prayers, was attended by everybody, baptized and unbaptized alike. The second part, consisting of the observance of the Lord's Supper, was attended by the baptized only.[17]

Shortly after the close of the second century, Hippolytus wrote his *Apostolic Tradition*. In it he recorded what he considered to be the correct rites and customs so that they would not be destroyed by people whom he described as "mindless innovators." The distinguishing mark of Hippolytus' eucharistic prayer is its brevity and simplicity, unlike the longer, more elaborate prayers of later times.[18]

The Eucharist, which means "thanksgiving," was a vital part of early Christian worship. The Greek word for giving thanks and the Greek word for praise are used without great distinction in the New Testament (Mark 8:6-7). In the prayers recorded by Hippolytus, it is

---

[15]Everett Ferguson, *Early Christians Speak*, Austin, TX: Sweet Publishing House, 1972), p. 101.

[16]Webber, *Worship, Old and New*, p. 49.

[17]Ilion T. Jones, p. 92.

[18]Willimon, *Word, Water, Wine and Bread*, pp. 33-35.

evident that the Lord's Supper was a joyful triumph at the victory of Jesus. The resurrected and ascended Christ was present in the meal and in the breaking of bread. For this reason, the worship of the early church was characterized by a tremendous sense of joy and gladness (Acts 2:46-47).[19] There is no doubt that they were partaking of a resurrection meal, not a wake for a departed hero.[20]

The information we have from the second century is too fragmentary to use as the basis on which to reconstruct a complete order of worship for the period. It seems clear that the worship of the second century was quite simple. The order of worship was still relatively brief. Some prayers were extemporaneous and free. The agape meal and the Lord's Supper were still observed jointly.[21] There did, however, tend to be a standardizing of worship with the passing of time. In the early church, there was no set order of worship, but, by the time the *Didache* was written (between A. D. 100 and 130), there seems to have been an emerging pattern of worship. There were set prayers intended to be used at the table. Since the prophets were fading off the scene and more regular local preachers were appointed by the church, there tended to be more of a development of standardized liturgies. At least by the time of Justin, there was a definite order of worship elements.[22] Still, much remains obscure about the worship of this period.[23]

With the conversion of the Roman Emperor Constantine (c. 274-337) in A.D. 313, the status of Christianity changed dramatically. His conversion was a watershed

---

[19]Webber, *Worship, Old and New*, pp. 53-55.
[20]Willimon, *Word, Water, Wine and Bread*, p. 37.
[21]Ilion T. Jones, pp. 90-91.
[22]Ralph Martin, *Worship in the Early Church* (Westwood, NJ: Fleming H. Revell Co., 1964), pp. 138-39.
[23]Jungmann, p. 7.

event in the history of Christianity.[24] The church grew
rapidly, formed its theology in various creeds, and developed a more fixed form of worship.[25] From the birth of
Christianity until the time of Constantine, the church
suffered periodic times of imperial persecution. Partly
due to that persecution and also due to its own poverty,
the church was a relatively private community. Groups
were small and usually met in houses or in secluded
outdoor places such as quarries and sandpits, or in the
crypts of the catacombs. However, with Constantine, the
church *went public*. In the centuries following, Christian
worship not only transformed paganism, but paganism
also influenced the church. Christianity began to borrow
much from the trappings and procedures of civil government — the basilican building, the clothing, the processions, the lights and the incense.[26]

Constantine built magnificent buildings for worship
in Rome, Constantinople, and Jerusalem. These large
new buildings affected the church's liturgy. The basilica,
a Roman building, was adopted as the primary architectural form for places of Christian worship. These impressive structures were used by the Romans as meeting halls
where people gathered for law courts, markets, and
important governmental functions. Because of the building's associations with dignity, power, and prestige, it
was natural that the basilica was chosen for housing
Christian worship. It had a wide central aisle bordered
by columns and side aisles, with an apse opposite the
main entrance. The apse contained a chair from which
the clergy sat and taught. In front of the apse, closer to
the assembled people, was a small, square table. The
interior was usually covered with mosaics or paintings of

[24]Ilion T. Jones, p. 35.
[25]Webber, *Worship, Old and New*, p. 63.
[26]Ilion T. Jones, p. 35.

Christian scenes. The setting was great for processions, pomp, and drama, but the long buildings tended to turn people into spectators of what was going on *up there* at the other end under the apse. Apparently no one regarded this as a problem, and the Western Church eventually came to view the linear, rectangular basilican plan as the only appropriate architectural arrangement for worship. This architectural design dictated much of the focus and form of the liturgy for centuries to come.[27] The basilican model is a dominate architectural form in church buildings throughout the world even in the twentieth century.

Two centers of worship arose during this period: Rome and Constantinople. Each center developed its own worship style reflecting its theology. Each was influenced by the different cultures from which it arose. Culture played a large part in the development of worship in the Eastern Church. The Eastern worldview was influenced by the Greek love for the aesthetic: for poetry, literature, art, and philosophy. All of this added a sense of imagery and artistic expression to their worship. The Eastern Church (sometimes referred to as the Byzantine Church) made extensive use of ceremonial signs and symbols and stressed a sense of the mystical.

The Western Church, centered in Rome, also reflected its culture. The Roman mindset was considerably different from that of the Byzantine. Romans had a pragmatic approach that was evident even in their buildings and laws. Worship in the Western (Roman) church was not ostentatious or highly ceremonial. Rather, Roman worship was characterized by soberness and simplicity which was obvious in both the order and symbols of their worship. Ceremony was simple. Items that have come to be associated with Roman Catholic

---

[27]Willimon, *Word, Water, Wine and Bread*, pp. 40-41.

worship such as the elevation of the host, the ringing of bells, the use of lights, censing, and genuflections were not in use in the fifth century; they came into use much later.[28]

The church of this period was profoundly affected by what historians call "mystery religions." These religions were based on the worship of foreign gods such as Dionysus (an ecstatic cult from Turkey), Cybele (a goddess from the region of Phrygia whose worship spawned wild, but spectacular processions), Isis (a major Egyptian goddess), and Mithra (a religion based on the old Persian god of light and elements of the Zoroastrian dualism of Good and Evil).

The name "mystery religion" derives from the secret symbols and rites revealed to members only. These mystery religions almost certainly were the "clubs" of which the Roman Governor, Pliny, was fearful in the early second century. In the last few centuries before Christ a plethora of these cults, mostly from the Middle East, began to spread throughout the Greco-Roman world by means of migration, trade, and military service abroad. Their popularity continued well into the Christian era.

These religions promised salvation in the present and bliss hereafter. However, unlike in Judaism and Christianity, members of mystery religions were not required to give up their traditional religions. Initiation into several cults was possible. The widespread popularity of these cults, coupled with the new legal status of Christianity afforded by Emperor Constantine, made it easy for people to blend Christian beliefs with pagan practices of the mystery religions.

Emperor Theodosius, who ruled Rome from A.D. 379 to 395, took Constantine's favor toward Christianity

---

[28]Webber, *Worship, Old and New*, pp. 63-66.

even further than his predecessor. He made Christianity the only legitimate religion of the empire. Before Constantine's conversion, Christians were despised, often persecuted and sometimes executed by official Roman decree. However, after Christianity was legalized and declared the only legitimate religion of the empire, it became a faith of power and prestige. If a person wanted to succeed in any area of Roman life, he or she had to show loyalty to Christianity.

Over the centuries the Roman church grew wealthy and politically powerful, as was evident in the Roman Catholic Church of the Middle Ages.[29] There is no doubt that the blending of Christianity, as it had come to be influenced by official Roman governmental recognition and support, with the mystery religions of the period paved the path which worship traveled into medieval times. As this blending progressed with time, Christianity and the worship of God grew more and more polluted.[30]

Worship During The Middle Ages
(from about A.D. 400 until about 1500)

Starting in the fourth and fifth centuries, there was a steady departure from the faith and worship of the New Testament, which changed the character of New Testament Christianity. By the end of the fourth century, many of the foundation stones upon which the medieval church was erected had already been well laid. Ilion T. Jones writes, "The process of transforming New Testament Christianity to the apostate Christianity of medievalism had already been well begun."[31] By the

---

[29]C. Leonard Allen and Richard T. Hughes, *Discovering Our Roots: The Ancestry of Churches of Christ* (Abilene, TX: ACU Press, 1988), p. 126.
[30]Ilion T. Jones, p. 96.
[31]*Ibid.*, p. 97.

fourth century there were signs that worshipers had lost their confidence in worship and turned instead to a desire to influence and placate God with sacrificial practices. The elements of the Lord's Supper became objects of fear to be handled only by the priests who were consecrated for this holy task. People became increasingly more passive in worship, looking to a holy priesthood to minister God's grace to them. This passivity is seen most clearly in the practice of the priest placing the bread directly on the worshiper's tongue in order that it not be touched by unholy hands.[32]

As worship continued to evolve in medieval times, it grew increasingly more complex. The length and procedures of worship expanded. The emphasis was on the dramatic and symbolical, upon form and ceremony.[33] During the fourth century, the language of worship changed from Greek to Latin. Along with this, the older, more flexible worship patterns gave way to more formalism and less variety. Worship leaders began using books containing fixed prayers rather than the more spontaneous prayers of earlier times.[34] Jones writes, "In many instances the whole procedure was a form of magic, a superstition."[35]

In the Middle Ages, the people were moved away from those who were leading worship. In many religious circles, a screen or wall separated the clergy from the people. This separation encouraged a deepening sense of the *terrifying* nature of the holy mysteries. By the time of the Reformation, elaborate performances and symbolism characterized worship in the Roman church. Ceremonial forms grew steadily more elaborate. These forms

---

[32]David R. Newman, *Worship As Praise and Empowerment* (New York: The Pilgrim Press, 1988), p. 53.

[33]Ilion T. Jones, p. 111.

[34]Willimon, *Word, Water, Wine and Bread*, pp. 41-42.

[35]Ilion T. Jones, p. 111.

became ends in themselves rather than means to help people encounter God. Therefore, they took on a cultic character all their own.[36]

During the late medieval period, there had developed such a segregation of clergy and the people that even the devout people who came to worship were little more than spectators watching something that they could not understand. A growing dissatisfaction existed among many of the common people. Even many of the priests sensed a growing emptiness in their worship. It is not easy to evaluate late-medieval worship. However, many liturgical scholars are rather negative in their assessment of this period of church history.[37]

The Protestant Reformation
(from about 1500 until about 1650)

Dissatisfaction with worship was one major cause of the Protestant Reformation which began fairly early in the sixteenth century. The Reformation was a revolutionary movement of large proportions which, once it started, involved all the major interests of the people — not only religion, but also economics, politics, social arrangements, and education. The medieval period has also been called *The Dark Ages*. With the Reformation, light began to shine.

Reformation Before Martin Luther

Even before what most people call the Protestant Reformation, there were many groups of sincere believers who were trying to free themselves from the corrupted religion of the Catholic Church and to find ways of

---

[36]Webber, *Worship, Old and New*, p. 67.

[37]James F. White, *Protestant Worship: Traditions in Transition* (Nashville: Abingdon, 1976), p. 25.

worshiping God for themselves. One of these groups was the Waldensians in Italy. Largely they were made up of common people who longed for a more simple and vital type of Christianity. They stressed obedience to the gospel, asceticism, and a concern for social renewal. They were critical of priests who lived unworthy lifestyles. They were opposed to the images which decorated the cathedrals. They objected to the hierarchy of the Catholic Church and to all its other practices that were opposed by Scripture. Since their roots extend as far back as the thirteenth century, some church historians have referred to their work as the "first" Reformation and the efforts of Martin Luther and his contemporaries as the "second" Reformation.[38]

John Wycliffe (c. 1329-1384), who has been called "the Morning Star of the Reformation," was another influential reformer who lived prior to the sixteenth century. He attacked the institution of the papacy, repudiated the doctrine of transubstantiation, wished to have religious orders abolished, and opposed the sale of indulgences. Holding to the Bible as the only authoritative guide for faith and practice, he instigated a translation of the Latin Version, known as the Vulgate, into English.[39]

The very rise of such men as Wycliffe was an omen of an approaching revolution. When it came, it affected the whole religious system of the medieval Church, at the heart of which was their method of worship.[40] The Reformation is important because it sought to correct the corruptions that arose during the late medieval period.[41]

---

[38]Peter Toon, "Waldenses," in *The New International Dictionary of the Christian Church*, pp. 1025-26.

[39]Robert G. Clouse, "Wycliffe, John," in *The New International Dictionary of the Christian Church*, pp. 1064-65.

[40]Ilion T. Jones, p. 120.

[41]Webber, *Worship, Old and New*, p. 15.

Great Reformation Leaders

Many church historians credit Martin Luther (1483-1546) with the beginning of the Protestant Reformation. Although the Protestant Reformation principally was a reform of theology, it was inevitable that a reform of worship would result from it.[42]

In 1520, Luther published *The Babylonian Captivity of the Church*, in which he unleashed one of the most radical challenges ever directed to the whole system of late medieval worship and its sacramental system. This treatise was but the first of several which eventually led to Luther's separation from the Catholic Church. Luther sought to free people from captivity to the Catholic mass, the doctrine of transubstantiation, and the burden of human work offered to please and appease God. James F. White contends that no greater shift has ever occurred in Christian worship than that which resulted from this treatise.[43]

Luther's theology of the laity led him to believe that all Christians were called to minister to one another. He maintained that laity should have the same dignity as clergy. The consequences of that understanding were enormous, for Christians no longer had to sit passively but were taught to play a priestly role. Luther taught them to sing and pray, a privilege made easier because he changed the language of worship to the vernacular of the people.

One of Luther's greatest changes came in the realm of music. A fervent lover of music, he relished its use in worship in every possible way. Luther described it as "one of God's greatest gifts." He utilized hymns as a vital tool in shaping people's thinking. They sang songs about

---

[42]*Ibid.*, p. 73.
[43]White, *Protestant Worship: Traditions in Transition*, pp. 36-39.

God's greatness, joyous songs about salvation that helped reshape people's theology. Luther also changed the form and function of preaching in worship. His sermons dealt with biblical texts in a direct and earthy fashion that the people could understand readily. His sermons were folksy and anecdotal, aimed at helping people visualize the biblical story with graphic examples drawn from daily life. Luther made preaching an essential part of Protestant worship.[44]

Another powerful leader in the Reformation was Ulrich Zwingli (1484-1531). Growing out of his influential efforts was what has been called Reformed worship. Zwingli had a passion for the new learning of his day. He was fluent in Greek and, like Luther, was conversant with the scholarship of contemporary humanism. Leonard Allen and Richard Hughes refer to this as "Christian Humanism," a movement to get back to the fountain or the source — back to the wisdom of a purer and nobler age.

This humanism grew from the Renaissance opposition to the highly rationalistic approach of Scholasticism, a plan developed by Thomas Aquinas (1225-1274) as an attempt to form a system of theology based on insights of Aristotle's philosophy. If that sounds confusing, it was. By the end of the Middle Ages, Scholasticism spawned a bureaucracy of churchmen and theologians who knew very little about Scripture but were experts at disputations, traditionalism, arguments based on cleverness, and the creative use of syllogisms.[45]

Erasmus of Rotterdam (1466-1536) was among the greatest Christian Humanists. He and others sought to restore to Christianity the devotion and ethical behavior of Jesus, the Apostles, and the early church. Unlike the

---

[44]*Ibid.*, pp. 40-47.
[45]Allen and Hughes, pp. 12-19.

Restorationists who were to come approximately three centuries later, the humanists were not concerned with restoring the primitive church. They simply wanted to restore the teachings of ancient Christians and to learn how to live authentically and with true spirituality.

Primary to these humanists was the belief that Scripture alone was the authority for faith and practice. The major implication of this belief was a rejection of church tradition which had assumed predominance over Scripture. Although all the Reformers agreed on the principle of "Scripture alone," they did not all agree on exactly what that meant for the life and shape of the church. They did not apply the teachings of Scripture the same way in every case.[46] Their strong emphasis upon "Scripture alone," however, did become a foundational building block in the thinking of nineteenth century Restorationists such as Barton W. Stone, Walter Scott, Thomas Campbell and Alexander Campbell.

Although Zwingli gained much from the Christian Humanism of his time, his own study of Scripture led him to very different conclusions than the conventional learning and practices of his day. Zwingli, whose work centered in Switzerland, reached quite different conclusions than his German contemporary, Martin Luther. Luther's approach is accurately called "reformation." Leonard Allen says Luther "sought to reform and purify the historic, institutional church while at the same time preserving as much of the tradition as possible. Zwingli's approach can more accurately be called "restoration." It sought to restore the essence and form of the primitive church based on biblical precedent and example; tradition received scant respect."[47]

Zwingli believed that the Bible provided "a complete

---

[46]*Ibid.*, pp. 22-23.
[47]*Ibid.*, p. 23.

blueprint for all time, laying out the details of church government, forms of worship, and rules for behavior." Luther, on the other hand, believed that the Bible provided "a central core of saving truth, leaving many of the details to human discretion and the changing circumstances of time and place." Theologians who followed Zwingli's thought emphasized the Bible as a blueprint or pattern for careful imitation. They wanted to get rid of traditional forms and practices of the Catholic Church because they did not believe the Bible supported them. False forms, they taught, should be replaced with forms found in Scripture.[48]

Zwingli went beyond Erasmus' thoughts of going back to the pure sources. Whereas Erasmus wrote of the "philosophy of Christ," Zwingli wrote of the "law of Christ." For Zwingli, God was a lawgiver, and the Scriptures provided specific laws and forms to which the church must adhere strictly. Luther was not concerned about the blueprints, forms and patterns which Zwingli saw in Scripture. He was more concerned with God's saving grace through faith in Christ.

Zwingli's literalism and stress upon biblical forms led him, in the ornate cathedral in which he preached, to strip the structure bare of everything which was not specifically prescribed in Scripture, including the vestments, the paintings (he whitewashed the walls), the images, and the organ. Zwingli did not believe that the New Testament warranted congregational singing, so he eliminated *all* forms of music in worship. Believing Zwingli had missed the point, Luther accused him of turning the gospel into a new legalism.[49] Although his career was shortened by an untimely death, Zwingli brought radical transformation to Christian worship.[50] It

---

[48]*Ibid.*, pp. 23-24.
[49]Allen and Hughes, pp. 27-28.
[50]White, *Protestant Worship: Traditions in Transition*, p. 61.

should be apparent to anyone who is familiar with the theology of the Restoration Movement that many of us stand far closer to Zwingli than to Luther. Zwingli's views concerning biblical forms, patterns, and blueprints have deeply influenced our movement via their impact on the thinking of our Restoration forefathers of the nineteenth century.

John Calvin (1509-1564) was another scholar who made significant contributions to the work of Reformation. On a number of doctrines and practices he assumed a mediating position between Luther and Zwingli. This was especially true concerning both the interpretation of the elements of the Lord's Supper and the frequency with which the Supper was to be observed. Luther wanted the Lord's Supper served daily throughout Christendom. Zwingli believed that a quarterly observance was adequate. Calvin called for observance of the Lord's Supper weekly, attacking the custom of annual communion as "an invention of the devil" and "the abomination of the mass set up by Satan." Zwingli's view eventually held sway throughout most of Protestant Christendom.[51]

Although many of the Reformers believed that the twofold structure of Word and the Lord's Supper should be maintained in worship services, Zwingli insisted that only the Word be maintained weekly. This view continues to dominate the view of those in the Calvinistic or Reformed tradition. That influence extended through the English Puritans to the Baptists, Presbyterians, Congregationalists, and a number of independent groups, and spread through them to most of American Protestant Christianity.[52]

The Reformers had several common concerns. They

---

[51]Wainwright, pp. 327-328.
[52]Webber, *Worship, Old and New*, p. 76.

rejected the Catholic Mass and the medieval view of it as a repetition of the sacrifice of Christ. They also rejected the doctrine of transubstantiation, which said that the elements of the Lord's Supper actually became the body and blood of Jesus when the bread and wine were taken. Underlying this doctrine was the Roman Catholic belief that the mere performance of the Mass brought about the presence of Christ automatically, thus promoting an attitude that the blessings of God would come even if the recipient had no faith.

The Reformers also insisted on the restoration of Scripture to the place it held in ancient Christian worship. The medieval Church had placed so much emphasis on sacraments that preaching and teaching the Word had fallen into a disreputable state. Zwingli went even farther than Luther in insisting that the people were to give ear to the Word of God *alone*. Consequently, as we have already seen, Zwingli abolished vestments, pictures, and anything else that would detract from the centrality of the Scriptures.[53]

Calvin was influenced indirectly by Zwingli through the work of Martin Bucer (1491-1551) of Strasbourg. Bucer combined Zwingli's emphasis with Lutheranism and developed "The Strasbourg Liturgy." Bucer reduced worship to its most simple and basic forms. Most of the parts of worship that called for a response from the people disappeared from worship. Bucer also discarded lectionaries, books which contained portions of Scripture appointed to be read at public worship on particular days of the year. This allowed the minister to pick the text from which he would preach. It was common for sermons to last an hour. This shift in practices placed great emphasis on a highly rational approach to worship. Calvin's liturgy, following Bucer's

---

[53]*Ibid.*, pp. 74-76.

synthesis of Zwingli and Luther, became the major approach to worship in the Reformed Churches.[54]

Zwingli's teachings on Scripture even impacted Puritan worship traditions in England in the 1600s and 1700s. Although Scripture was held up as the only rule of faith and practice, the Old Testament was not valued very much. The New Testament was the source from which the blueprints of worship were to come. Only items of worship that were specifically mentioned in the New Testament were practiced. Musical instruments, which are not *explicitly* mentioned in New Testament assemblies, were regarded as a distraction from "pure" worship. No room was given to innovation or to a sense of a developing tradition. On the contrary, a stifling literalism effectively blocked any notion of creative spontaneity in the forms of worship to be used.[55]

There were differences and disagreements among the Reformers. The basic disagreement occurred over continuity with the Roman Catholic heritage. Although Luther is regarded as the first major reformer, he was also one of the least radical when it came to making changes in many of the worship forms. Lutheran and Anglican traditions retained much of traditional Catholic worship. Zwingli's followers and the Anabaptists made a radical break with the past. The Reformed churches which later became more associated with Calvin, maintained a middle position. Zwingli and the Anabaptists repudiated all ceremonies as pagan and began getting rid of all the traditions and rubrics of the Catholic Church. Anabaptists rejected infant baptism and even the necessity of formal public worship, moving it into private homes.[56]

---

[54]*Ibid.*, pp. 77-78.
[55]Martin, *The Worship of God*, pp. 6-7.
[56]Webber, *Worship, Old and New*, pp. 76-77.

During the first four days of October, 1529, nine Protestant Reformation leaders met at Marburg to discuss their beliefs and practices. They agreed on almost all the major articles of faith, but they could not agree on all matters of worship. From that time until the present, the Protestant Reformation has been characterized by its different traditions of worship.[57]

Positive Contributions Resulting from the Protestant Reformation

The development of Protestant worship from the seventeenth through the twentieth centuries can only be traced through a history of each religious group. However, the leaders of the Reformation achieved many things which are generally characteristic of Protestant worship today. Among the most notable was the abolition of the priesthood. In its place they taught the "priesthood of all believers." They substituted the word "minister" for the word "priest" and eliminated all sacerdotal functions formerly performed by the priests. They elevated preaching and the Word of God to a prominent position in worship, establishing the Protestant hallmark of "Scripture only." They returned the Bible to the people in their own language and insisted that people had the right to read and interpret Scripture for themselves. They stressed the importance of going back to the sources of the Christian faith, back to the fountainhead, back to the pure stream of biblical teaching.

Although Luther was nowhere near as radical concerning the abolition of traditions as many others in the Reformation Movement, all of the Reformers strongly challenged the traditionalism of the Catholic Church. They encouraged people to participate actively

---

[57]White, *Protestant Worship: Traditions in Transition*, pp. 58-59.

in worship, not just to watch as they had done for centuries. They stripped worship of its highly liturgical nature and substituted much simpler forms of worship. They revived extemporaneous prayer. They abandoned symbolism and, in most places, they ceased to follow the church year with its highly prescribed calendar of events and ceremonies. Zwingli adamantly supported a restoration of biblical forms and patterns as a blueprint for the faith and practice of the church — including the practices of worship. Luther strongly disagreed with Zwingli on this point, but it is Zwingli's view that has more profoundly affected the theology of our own Restoration Movement.[58]

There is little doubt that American Restoration leaders in the nineteenth century were deeply influenced by the theology hammered out in the Protestant Reformation. One certainly observes many of the same emphases in the writings, teachings, and practices of leaders within the Restoration Movement in our own generation.

The Rise of English Puritanism

The Protestant Reformation had at least three currents, each with a somewhat different emphasis. Each current had common concerns, but each developed its own distinctive shape. One current centered in Germany with Luther. A second current centered in Switzerland with Zwingli and Calvin. The third major current was in England with the Puritans.[59] English Puritanism arose in the second half of the sixteenth century. The focus on restoring biblical forms and patterns reached its greatest intensity during this period. It was through English

---

[58]Ilion T. Jones, p. 141; Allen and Hughes, pp. 32-33.
[59]Allen and Hughes, p. 21

Puritanism that restorationist thought reached America.[60] Echoing the interpretation of Zwingli and the Swiss Reformers, the English Puritans said that nothing should be done "but that which you have the expresse warrant of God's word for." For the Puritans, the Bible served as a complete pattern of faith and order that must be duplicated.[61]

Thomas Cartwright (1535-1603), a Puritan spokesman, insisted that the very silence of Scripture was prohibitive. In other words, unless Scripture clearly and specifically called for some practice, Christians were not at liberty to innovate their own practices. Anglican Church scholars disagreed with Cartwright, saying that matters of salvation do not change, but that some areas of church affairs needed to be adjusted as time passed. The simplicity of the primitive church's worship and organization were appropriate for their unsophisticated age, the Anglican Church maintained, but different structures and forms were necessary for the modern age.[62]

One illustration of this principle of prohibition based on silence is evidenced in the Puritans' rejection of the prayer books which were used in the Anglican Church. The Puritans believed not only that prayer books hindered them from a more spiritual worship but also that they were unwarranted by Scripture. John Smyth (1565-1612), an early English Baptist who was influenced by the English Puritans, wrote:

> We hold that the worship of the New Testament properly so called is spiritual proceeding originally from the heart: and that reading out of a book (though it is a lawful ecclesiastical action) is no part of spiritual worship, but rather the invention of the man of sin, it being substituted for a part of spiritual worship.[63]

[60]*Ibid.*, p. 35.
[61]*Ibid.*, p. 43.
[62]*Ibid.*, pp. 42-45.
[63]Webber, *Worship, Old and New*, p. 79.

Churches within the Restoration Movement traditionally have accepted this basic view. Not only have they avoided liturgical books, but church members have often criticized men for reading a written prayer rather than praying extemporaneously. The implication is that reading from a prayer book is unscriptural and that a prayer without written notes is somehow more heartfelt and spiritual than one written out, even if far more thought and planning went into the written prayer.

Why draw attention to worship practices of the English Puritans? There are three reasons: One, these practices continued to stress the essentiality of restoring biblical forms and patterns, a theme that is at the heart of Restorationist theology. Two, Cartwright's beliefs about the silence of Scripture influenced the later thinking of Thomas Campbell whose motto, "Where the Scriptures speak, we speak; where they are silent we are silent," became a rallying cry for churches growing out of the American Restoration Movement. Three, most of our nineteenth century ancestors in the Restoration Movement were of British stock and Puritan lineage. Although they differed with major tenets of Puritan theology, they retained many of the same assumptions about the Bible, the church, and the task of restoration.[64] Thomas and Alexander Campbell drew upon English Puritan influence long before they ever reached America.[65]

Puritan influence on the American Restoration did not cease with the Puritanism of England. Beginning in the 1620s English Puritanism was transplanted to America. Under the auspices of the Massachusetts Bay Company, John Winthrop led a fleet of ships carrying more than 400 English Separatist Puritans from England

---

[64]Allen and Hughes, p. 47.
[65]*Ibid.*, p. 60.

to America. By 1640, perhaps as many as 20,000 people, most with Puritan sympathies, immigrated to the Massachusetts Bay Colony. This group was very much in the lineage of restorationist thinking. Many of the New England Puritans became conceited, thinking that they had indeed restored all of God's institutions to their original forms.

The person who perhaps most represented this view was John Cotton (1584-1652), a Puritan minister and Boston preacher. Cotton, who became a dominant figure in the colony, wrote smugly that the New England churches were as close as could be to what "the Lord Jesus [would erect] were he here himselfe in person." Such an exclusive attitude led Cotton and others to try to coerce Baptists, Quakers, and other dissenters to conform to their doctrinal standard. They even imprisoned some and publicly whipped one dissenter. Not everyone in New England agreed with Cotton's views. One dissenter was Roger Williams (1603-1683), the founder of Rhode Island. Williams, himself a seeker of God's will, strongly believed that those who thought they had completed the restoration of God's perfect plan were deluded.[66]

DISCUSSION QUESTIONS
ON CHAPTER FIVE

1. How does learning about our past help us improve our worship in the present?

2. Do you feel that your worship practices and traditions are indebted to others who have gone before you? How?

3. Many Christians in the first and second centuries

---

[66]Allen and Hughes, pp. 49-60.

observed the Lord's Supper in the larger context of a common meal (the Agape meal). Would you feel comfortable doing that today? Why?

4. Why was the "conversion" of Emperor Constantine such a watershed event in Christianity?

5. If mystery religions infiltrated Christianity in the early centuries, are there false religions that are trying to infiltrate Christianity in our own day? Name some. What affect does this have on worship?

6. What did the Reformation leaders of the 15th through 17th centuries accomplish that has influenced the way we worship today?

7. Why are those who challenge others to think and restudy often persecuted?

8. What was the major difference between the theology of Luther and Zwingli?

9. In what ways were Alexander Campbell and other Restoration leaders influenced by the theological discussions of their own day?

10. Do you think your church has restored all the worship of the New Testament church? Support your answer.

11. Which of our worship practices are traditions and which are biblical?

    a. Why is it important to distinguish between the two?

    b. Why is there resistance to changing traditions?

6

Worship's Roots in the Restoration Movement

Several powerful forces were converging that set the stage for the development of Protestant churches in early eighteenth century America. There was the Great Awakening in America in the 1730s and 1740s, with the preaching of men like Jonathan Edwards (1703-1758) and George Whitefield (1714-1770). This coincided with the outbreak of spiritual revival in the colonies usually called "Revivalism." Due to their impact on Whitefield, Pietism and Moravianism also influenced the American church scene.

Revivalism and the Great Awakening

By the early 1700s, churches established in New England by the Puritans had grown staid, formal, and rationalistic. In this atmosphere, Jonathan Edwards, a Congregationalist preacher, protested the churches' coldness and sacramentalism. His preaching, which emphasized humanity's sinfulness and need for salvation, was a breath of fresh air. He stressed personal religious experience, holy living, and the priesthood of all believers. In 1734, mass revivals broke out in New England due to Edwards' preaching.[1]

In 1740, when the English Methodist preacher George Whitefield arrived in America, the Awakening was already widespread. Whitefield came to America

---

[1]Allen and Hughes, *Discovering Our Roots*, p. 65.

from England with a fire that his friend and contemporary, John Wesley (1703-1791), had helped to fan within him. Wesley, who became a leader of the Evangelical Revival and founder of the Methodist Church in Great Britain and America, had a dramatic conversion experience. This experience in which he claimed he found "saving faith" came on May 24, 1738 during a Moravian meeting in Aldersgate Street, London. He reported that his "heart was strangely warmed" as he listened to the reading of the preface of Martin Luther's commentary on the New Testament book of Romans.[2]

As spiritual malaise had afflicted the Puritan churches in America, churches in England were also plagued by a lack of spiritual fervor. In the "Age of Reason" (also called the age of Enlightenment) in which Wesley lived, the Anglican Church had exalted reason and rationality in both its preaching and liturgy. It had become the church of the educated, wealthy, and elite. The people were cultured and orderly but cold and emotionally uninvolved in the life and worship of the church. This distressed Wesley, himself a devoted member of the Church of England. He began preaching to anyone who would listen. His message spoke to the heart, not just to the head. He proclaimed that the blood of Jesus and the grace of God freely justified sinners and that the Holy Spirit gave Christians power to live pure and holy lives.[3]

The Influence of the Moravians and Pietists

Whitefield was influenced by Moravianism and Pietism primarily through his relationship with Wesley, whose own life had been changed by his encounters with these revivalists. The Moravian Church had its beginning in the mid-fifteenth century shortly after the death of the

---

[2]Webber, *Worship, Old and New*, pp. 82-83.
[3]Allen and Hughes, p. 138.

reformer John Huss. The Moravians were essentially missionaries who stressed the sole authority of the Scriptures, simplicity in worship, receiving the Lord's Supper in faith without any human priest or authority to serve or explain it, and disciplined Christian living. They loved to sing in worship. They wrote hymns about Jesus' suffering that touched people at a feeling level. Robert Webber says that their songs were "emotional, imaginative, sensuous, with a minimum of intellectual structure."[4] Wesley first met Moravian believers during his brief failed efforts as a missionary in America among the Indians. He was deeply impressed by their devotion and spirituality. It was at a Moravian meeting, once back in England from America, that Wesley had his conversion experience that turned his life around.[5]

Besides Moravianism, Pietism also was a major factor in the thinking of Wesley and Whitefield. Pietism was a movement that originally started among Protestants in Germany in the early 1600s. Disturbed with the way the European Reformers had synthesized Christian faith, and disgusted with the controversy that constantly seemed to swirl among the Reformers, the Pietists separated themselves from the Reformation. They called on people to live holy lives, to do good works, to gain a better knowledge of Scripture, to avoid controversy, and to evangelize the world.[6]

Revivalism Brought A Rise In Great Hymns

It was also during this period of Revivalism that many of the best known and loved Christian hymns were composed. For quite some time in Reformed Churches

---

[4]Webber, *Worship, Old and New*, p. 82.

[5]J.G.G. Norman, "Moravian Brethren," *The New International Dictionary of the Christian Church*, p. 676.

[6]Robert Clouse, "Pietism," *The New International Dictionary of the Christian Church*, p. 780.

the people had sung songs drawn exclusively from the Old Testament Psalms. John Calvin insisted that the Psalms were the only things worthy to be sung in worship. The Revivalists, however, wrote their own hymns. People like Isaac Watts in Britain were writing personal devotional songs such as "When I Survey The Wondrous Cross" and "Alas! And Did My Savior Bleed?"

John Wesley's brother, Charles, made his greatest contribution to Revivalism by writing hymns. He is credited with composing more than 7,200 hymns and giving musical expression to the evangelical faith.[7] It is no wonder, in this setting, that the powerful preaching of Edwards and Whitefield created such a revival in America. Thousands of people reported conversion experiences in what was interpreted as the dramatic outpouring of God's Spirit.[8]

The Second Great Awakening On The American Frontier

In the late 1700s, brave and adventurous people were moving westward into the great American Frontier. Back on the East Coast people were more educated than the frontier pioneers. The highly trained clergy in the East had become accustomed to instructing the faithful and knew little about converting the unsaved on the frontier. James F. White writes of "the Americanization of Protestant worship" when he talks about the worship practices which developed on the American frontier. This "frontier tradition," as White calls it, includes such groups as Southern Baptists, Disciples of Christ, and Churches of Christ.[9]

Church historians refer to the period between 1790 and 1810 as the Second Great Awakening. The frontier

---

[7]Webber, *Worship, Old and New*, pp. 82-83.
[8]Allen and Hughes, p. 65.
[9]White, *Protestant Worship: Traditions in Transition*, pp. 171-72.

tradition coincided with this awakening. It arose out of a need to convert and minister to the largely unchurched people who were scattered over enormous expanses of rugged frontier. The leaders of this movement hit upon an idea that they gleaned from the Scottish Presbyterians who gathered three or four times a year for communion. Immediately preceding those times was an intensive period of examination of conscience and preparation for the Lord's Supper. This intensive period sometimes lasted for several days.

In 1796, James McGready traveled from North Carolina to serve three small churches in Logan County in south-central Kentucky, just above the Tennessee/ Kentucky border. In the summer of 1800, he staged what is sometimes called the first camp meeting as an outdoor communion service at Gaspar River, Kentucky. In 1801 at Cane Ridge, Kentucky, there was a huge camp meeting with a Presbyterian minister, Barton Warren Stone (1772-1844). This camp meeting, with its estimated attendance from 10,000 to 25,000 people, changed the face of religion in America, influencing churches both in their mission and their worship.

Camp meetings were important social events too. They were ecumenical events with Baptists, Disciples, Presbyterians, and Methodists working together to arrange the meetings where preaching was done at different places on the same grounds. However, for the closing services, the faithful and new converts regrouped along denominational lines.[10]

The Goal of Revivalism: Convert the Unsaved

In this environment, the goal of preaching and worship became the conversion of the unsaved. The early revival preachers never intended for revival

---

[10]*Ibid.*, p. 173.

services to replace worship services. However, in some places that is precisely what happened.[11] Almost overnight a shift occurred in the approach to religion in America to one of pragmatism. In other words, revivalistic preachers would do whatever worked to win converts.

Prior to the rise of pragmatism, the frontier tradition stressed the local autonomy of each congregation. Its leaders also insisted on following only the forms and patterns of worship that they found in the blueprint of the New Testament. Both were principles which they inherited from Separatist and Puritan traditions. Most groups in the frontier tradition continued to hold to the concept of local autonomy. However, with the rise of pragmatism, they became willing to try innovative methods that their strict literalism of the past never allowed. Revival leaders designed music to move people emotionally and physically. During outdoor camp meetings, they laid the sawdust trail, easily marking the way for converts to come forward. They introduced the mourners' bench for those desiring prayer for their conversion.

There was no general agreement among the revivalist preachers concerning which physical responses were appropriate and which were not. However, some people experienced the "barks," the "jerks," and other bizarre physical expressions. Most camp meeting leaders agreed that, in order to move people spiritually, it was also necessary to move them physically and emotionally.[12]

Revivalism developed an order of worship that was designed to gain converts. Usually a Sunday service had three parts. First was the song service. This was often viewed as preliminary and as an emotional warm-up for the sermon. Second was the sermon. It was charged with

---

[11]Webber, *Worship, Old and New*, p. 83.
[12]White, *Protestant Worship: Traditions in Transition*, pp. 172-74.

emotion, was hard driving, and designed to call people to conversion. Third was the harvest of new converts. After the sermon, people were urged to come forward for baptism.

This three-part order of service has become basic in many churches today. With such an arrangement, it is not surprising that preaching became the center of worship and that the meeting house was called the auditorium (a place to hear). Church buildings were constructed with an elevated platform on which a desk or podium was placed. Three chairs also appeared on the platform — one for the person presiding, one for the song leader, and one for the preacher. In time, these chairs often became quite large and ornate, looking like seats designed for royalty, not common people. Preaching was the chief item in Sunday services, usually taking up half or more of the time.[13]

The Rise of Rationalism and its Affect on Worship

In modern Protestantism there has also been an emphasis in worship on rational understanding. Many Protestant groups during the 1700s developed a commentary approach to reading Scripture. A minister, or someone trained, would read the Bible and comment on it, giving an interpretation. The speaker encouraged questions or comments from the assembly. Then the minister delivered a sermon which never lasted less than an hour and might last for two or three hours (with a break for people to stretch). Presbyterians emphasized lectures on Scripture and expository preaching. They rejected the use of all ceremonial practices in worship unless they were prescribed in the New Testament. Worship remained simple and appealed to the mind alone, not to the senses of touch, sight, smell, or taste. It

---

[13]*Ibid.*, pp. 177-83.

appealed to the sense of hearing only if it meant hearing the Word of God as it was read or preached.[14]

The American Restoration Movement

This stress on rational understanding influenced Thomas and Alexander Campbell who were Presbyterian ministers in Scotland before moving to America. It is impossible to separate what has been called the Restoration Movement, with which men like Barton W. Stone, Walter Scott, and the Campbells are so intimately tied, from the developments of the Revivalists and the leaders of the Frontier tradition. Stone, the Campbells, and other leaders in the Restoration Movement inherited much from the movements that preceded them. Indeed, they helped shape the movement throughout the 1800s. These men, who were appalled at the lack of unity among believers in Christ, appealed to all believers to abolish their human creeds and come together by practicing simple New Testament Christianity. There was a spirit of hope and optimism on the American frontier. The United States had recently adopted a remarkable Constitution. Why could believers not let the Bible be the Christian Constitution that would put an end to sectarianism?[15]

A Constitution for Christian Worship?

This understanding of the New Testament as a Constitution led to important views concerning worship. Thomas Campbell stated in his *Declaration and Address* that the New Testament was as perfect a constitution for the worship, discipline, and government of the New

---

[14]Webber, *Worship, Old and New*, pp. 80-81.
[15]Colbert S. Cartwright, "Disciples Worship: A Rich and Relevant Heritage," *Mid-Stream* 28 no. 3 (1989): pp. 264-265.

Testament church as the Old Testament was for the worship, discipline, and government of the Old Testament church. Alexander Campbell basically agreed with his father, but saw the New Testament as a "constitution for worship" only in that it set forth the essential aspects of worship, not a liturgy or a prescribed order of worship.[16] In 1828 Alexander Campbell commented:

> The New Testament contains no liturgy, no congregational service, as did the Old Testament. In the writings of the great Jewish apostle, Moses, there is a ritual, a liturgy, a tabernacle or temple service laid down; but no such thing is found in the apostolic epistles.[17]

This seems to reflect Alexander Campbell's lifelong attitude toward the use of liturgy in worship. He believed that the local congregation must be free to express its own wishes, needs, and interests in corporate worship. While there was no prescribed liturgy, it was imperative that all be done "decently and in order" (1 Cor. 14:40). Campbell left decisions concerning the order of worship to the discretion of each congregation.[18]

Contained in the 1827 edition of the *Christian Baptist*, edited by Alexander Campbell, is a 33-page description of the worship services of seven different congregations, including congregations in England, Ireland, Scotland, and America. A New York congregation described its worship activities as practiced in March, 1818:

> The elders presided during the worship period. Worship opened by the congregation kneeling in prayer, which was led by an elder or one appointed by them. A portion of the Bible is read by one of the elders relative to the Lord's supper, this is followed by another hymn. A passage of scripture is read for

---

[16]Hieronymus, p. 4.
[17]*Ibid.*, p. 2.
[18]*Ibid.*

the collection of poor saints, and a prayer for proper use of the funds, and then the collection. Next, one chapter is read from the Old Testament and one in the New Testament, and time is allowed for comments by any of the brethren. Exhortations from the Bible follow by the elders or brethren. There is a song, prayer and separation.

In the evening elders or those approved by them preach the gospel to the lost, second a love feast is observed. There is a meeting conducted one week day evening. The holy kiss and the washing of feet is observed on Sunday evenings. Elders are frequently paid for the labors. Presently we have two elders and three deacons.[19]

In 1835, Campbell wrote about a congregation that he had visited. He did not claim that their particular order of worship was the only correct one. However, he complimented it highly as an example of how a congregation could order its worship. It was as follows: a call to worship, a hymn, a reading from one of the Gospels, a prayer, a reading from one of the Epistles, a communion hymn, a statement about the Lord's Supper, a prayer for the bread, the breaking and distribution of the bread, a prayer for the cup, distribution of the cup, a prayer, the offering, the sharing by various members toward the "edification of the body" (referring to the sermon), several songs, and a benediction.[20]

Alexander Campbell's Unique Influence on Worship

Two of Campbell's teachings made him somewhat distinctive in his day. One was that the Lord's Supper was central to Christian worship. There could be no legitimate worship after the New Testament model, he taught, without the observance of the Lord's Supper.

---

[19]Dabney Phillips, "Worship in the Early Restoration Churches," in *Harding College Lectures* (Austin, TX: Firm Foundation Publishing House, 1978), p. 147.

[20]Hieronymus, p. 5.

The other had to do with his view of preaching. Campbell insisted that he did not "preach" during worship. He viewed his messages as teaching for the purpose of edification. He believed that the evangelist had his proper role in winning converts, but not in the Christian worship assembly. His understanding of preaching was that it was evangelistic in nature. This certainly reflects the revivalistic mood of preaching in Campbell's day. He did not believe the worship service was the place to try to sway people to become Christians. Rather, he saw the assembly as a time for teaching and edification of the saved.[21] This view clashed with the more common view in the first half of the 1800s when many worship services had become weekly revival services.

This was the period when audiences were swayed and moved by powerful preachers. Ralph Martin writes:

> The persuasive powers of human speech enhanced the authority of those leaders who could command a hearing. And the same was true of church leaders who excelled as platform orators and, so the phrase ran, "pulpiteers." The preacher's rostrum became the church's sounding board and the minister's throne. This led to a style of worship that was heavily intellectualized. . . .[22]

Campbell, indeed, was a powerful orator and a persuasive speaker. However, he was unlike many other preachers of his day. He employed a conversational style of presentation. Generally he was quite unemotional, rarely making a gesture. Campbell relied on the power of truth and rationality as the means of informing and persuading people. It was common for one of his sermons to last two or three hours. That kind of length was characteristic of other preachers in the Restoration

---

[21]*Ibid.*, pp. 4-5.
[22]Martin, *The Worship of God*, p. 8.

period as well. Although Campbell never regarded himself a pulpiteer in the worship service, his highly rational, intellectual style of teaching and debating mightily influenced other preachers in the Movement. His style helped to lead to a long period of preaching in Restoration churches in which rationalism was admired and emotion was disparaged.

The Restoration Movement motto became: "Where the Scriptures speak, we speak; where they are silent, we are silent." Thomas Campbell applied that motto to every aspect of the Christian life, including worship. He wrote, "Nothing ought to be received into the faith or worship of the Church, or to be made a term of communion among Christians, that is not as old as the New Testament." Thomas Campbell considered the developments which had occurred in worship tradition since the first century as invalid. In doing so, Campbell and his Restoration descendents, perhaps unwittingly, formed a new tradition of their own. James F. White reflects: "In a sense, it is a tradition of no tradition, but that attitude soon became a tradition in its own right."[23] Later, Thomas Campbell's son Alexander wrote:

> I have endeavored to read the Scriptures as if no one had read them before me, and I am as much on my guard against reading them today through the medium of my views of yesterday, as I am against being influenced by any foreign name, authority, or system, whatever.[24]

Campbell investigated Scripture afresh and changed many of his views because of his honest and open-minded study. However, Campbell was chasing an elusive dream. No one is totally free from his culture and the thinking of his time. Regardless of his rhetoric,

---

[23]White, *Protestant Worship: Traditions in Transition*, pp. 172-74.
[24]Cartwright, p. 264.

Campbell could not help being profoundly influenced by those who came before him as well as by his contemporaries. Their views and the circumstances of his day provided "glasses" though which he filtered his own study. That is the way it always works — it is impossible any other way. Intelligent and honest as we might be, no man is an island, Campbell included. Likewise, we in the Restoration heritage are profoundly influenced by Campbell and others even as we endeavor to study Scripture afresh.

What Does Church History Teach Us About Worship Today?

Perhaps at this point, if not long before, you are asking yourself, "Why spend so much time on church history when the book is supposed to be about worship?" Good question. Here's my answer. This survey of Christian worship throughout the centuries is intended to help us see that we are indeed debtors to our past. It helps us understand the origin of many of our beliefs and practices in worship.

As we consider worship renewal, it is helpful to know that many of our current worship practices are not actually a biblical prescription but rather an outgrowth of culture and tradition. That means that it is not unbiblical to make changes in many of these practices. People become upset when changes are made because they falsely believe that we are tampering with the "blueprint" of Scripture when in fact that is not the case at all. By examining worship practices down through history, we can see that we have inherited a lot of tradition.

The fact is that we have been changing all along through the years. Much of that change has occurred so slowly that we have not been aware of it, and it has not alarmed us to any great extent. As changes were coming slowly we had time to adapt and adjust to them.

However, with the rapid changes being forced on us in the world in which we live now, we don't have as much time to adapt and adjust as before. Therefore, we have to work harder to understand the process of change and what is necessary to reach people in our fast-paced world.

Change is not in itself a bad thing. Change is inevitable; it's a natural part of being finite and earth-bound. Obviously, some change is not beneficial. However, some change is both necessary and good. Growth itself requires change. If one is incapable of changing or unwilling to change, he cannot grow. Consider the physical growth of plants and people: those who do not change are abnormal. They are either ill, deformed, or stunted in some way. It is only as they change that they grow. Not only does the body change, but the mind also changes, expanding its concepts and understanding. It questions, explores, learns, adjusts, and progresses in the process. Indeed, the essence of Christian living is changing constantly from the "old man" to the "new creation."

Rather than trying to throw tradition away, I am encouraging us to get back to the earliest traditions of Christian worship. Cultural considerations are important. We must be culturally relevant and maintain biblical principles at the same time. Some things are negotiable; others are not. Let us be willing to make changes in those areas that are negotiable — this is the reason for worship renewal. If there are changes which we can make that are in keeping with Scripture and will also better connect with people today and help lead them into the presence of God, then let us make those changes as effectively and as quickly as possible. "Quick" is dangerous. We must understand the dynamics of change and how to be effective change agents. The emphasis is on as quickly *as possible* — which almost always takes a while.

It also helps us to know that none of us has arrived at a perfect understanding of the Bible and of worship. None of us can claim that we have the perfect, infallible interpretation on every point of Scripture. Our thinking has been deeply affected by the thinking and teaching of people and things that are influential in our lives: parents, college professors, books we have read, mentors, preachers, friends, associates, mates, etc. One's rhetoric may insist that it is possible simply to read the Bible and all understand it the same and understand it perfectly, but that obviously is not the case.

Too many preachers in the past have unfairly and inaccurately accused other religious groups of being insincere and dishonest. If others were sincere and honest, we claim, they would have to reach the same conclusions we have reached. That simply is not the case. It never has been, nor will it ever be. That is not even the case within a family where everyone deeply loves one another and is committed to each other — if it is a healthy family. There are some families where a parent is so demanding of conformity that no deviation from his or her views is tolerated, but those families are sick. They are so dysfunctional that individuals in the family will inevitably demonstrate signs of emotional instability and/or illness and even physical illness.

All of this means that we have to give others the same courtesy that we want them to extend to us: to believe that they are honest, sincere, and zealous in their attempts to understand the Bible and to fulfill its call upon their lives — even if they disagree with us. None of us comes into this world in a vacuum. None of us has a pure, undefiled line of access to the mind of Christ, for it is impossible for fallible, sinful human beings not to see Scripture through our own filters of history, culture, and experience.

John Robinson (1572-1625) was an English Separatist preacher who encouraged many of his fellow believers to emigrate from Holland to the new world in America. He had chosen to remain in Holland with that portion of the group who either could not or thought it unwise to leave. His parting words to the pilgrims who were emigrating convey the attitude of openness and willingness to continue studying that I am encouraging in this book. He said:

> I charge you before God and his blessed angels, to follow me no further than I have followed Christ; and if God should reveal anything to you by any other instrument of him, to be as ready to receive it as ever you were to receive any truth by my ministry; for I am confident the Lord hath more truth and light yet to break forth out of his Word. I bewail the condition of the reformed churches, who are come to a period in religion, and will go no further than the instruments of their reformation. The Lutherans cannot be drawn to go beyond what Luther says; for whatever part of God's will has been imparted and revealed to Calvin they will rather die than embrace it. And the Calvinists, as you see, stick where Calvin left them. This is a misery much to be lamented; for though Luther and Calvin were precious shining lights in their times, yet God did not reveal his whole will to them; and were they living now they would be as ready and willing to embrace further light as that which they had received. I beseech you to remember your church covenant, at least that part of it whereby you promise and covenant with God and with one another, to receive whatsoever light or truth shall be made known to you from the written Word of God.[25]

Excellent counsel to be three and a half centuries old!

---

[25]Ilion T. Jones, p. 264.

DISCUSSION QUESTIONS
ON CHAPTER SIX

1. What leads to and characterizes spiritual revival?

2. How would you describe the worship services where you assemble? Are they stagnant or are they in a state of revival?

3. How much emphasis should be placed on the invitation and baptism in the worship service? Are they the primary reason for assembling?

4. What innovative methods did the revivalist preachers use to reach people on the American frontier?

5. Is it possible to be innovative in the style of worship and still be true to Scripture? Support your answer.

6. The dominant shapers of the Restoration Movement emphasized rational thinking almost to the exclusion of emotional involvement in worship. What is the result of that emphasis?

7. Does the New Testament give us a Constitution or blueprint for Christian worship? If not, what does it provide?

8. What was Campbell's view of preaching in the worship assembly? Is that the view of the preacher and elders where you worship?

9. What kind of change is bad? What kind of change is good?

10. Is your congregation continuing to grow in its understanding of the Lord's will as it relates to worship?

7

Come Before His Presence with Singing

Singing in Old Testament Worship

God's people are a people of song. The first place the Bible mentions God's people singing is in Exodus 15 after the Lord safely led the Israelites through the Red Sea and drowned their Egyptian pursuers in a rousing defeat. The people recounted in song how God had saved them by His majestic hand and how He had led them with unfailing love.

In early Jewish life, songs of praise seem to have been spontaneous expressions of adoration for God. It was common for the Hebrews to attribute praise coming from parts of God's creation. Job stated that the stars sang and David said that the mountains sang praises to God. King David, the sweet singer of Israel, was a musician and composer of psalms, many of which were written to be sung. With David, there seems to have been a change in the way music was used among the gathered assembly. It became a part of the professional responsibility of the worship leaders, the Levites (1 Chr. 15:16), and therefore became more formalized. As priest-musicians, these performers gave full time to their musical service.[1]

When we think of worship in the Old Testament we cannot help but think of the Psalms. In Hebrew the book of Psalms is called *Tehillim*, or "Hymns of Praise."[2]

---

[1]Donald Hustad, *Jubilate!* (Carol Stream, IL: Hope Publishing Company, 1981), pp. 79-81.

[2]Millgram, p. 60.

The Psalms convey an intense and sure conviction that God is near and concerned about His people. These psalms express the heart of the pious people who wrote them. Concerning the Psalms, Abraham Millgram wrote:

> They are rooted in a deep and unquestioning love for God, the King, the Creator, and above all the merciful Father. The psalms speak to the heart of man in words of sublime tenderness and utter simplicity; they therefore reach into the heart of the suppliant and arouse his noblest sentiments. They express vividly and powerfully the psalmists' firm faith, hope, and trust in the God of Israel, the God of redemption and salvation. At times despondency bordering on despair overcomes the psalmist, but only to throw into greater relief his overflowing faith in the living God, whose salvation never fails.[3]

In ancient Hebrew worship, Scripture was never spoken without melody. Donald Hustad says, "They were always sung in a lusty cantillation."[4] The Psalmist exclaimed, "Shout to God with loud songs of joy!" (Ps. 47:1).

Singing at the temple possibly was antiphonal since some of the psalms are obviously couched in a responsory pattern. Antiphonal singing predates the exile (Exod. 15:1-21). After the Babylonian exile we read of responsive singing between two choirs of musicians (Neh. 12:24, 31). The Levites served as the professional leaders of these songs. Jewish laymen primarily watched and listened and probably frequently joined in the traditional response "Amen" and "Alleluia," and possibly in an antiphonal refrain like "for his steadfast love endures for ever" (Ps. 136).[5]

There is no conclusive evidence that there was

---

[3]Millgram, p. 60.
[4]Hustad, p. 81.
[5]Hustad, pp. 82-83.

singing in the early synagogue. Ralph Martin, however, believes that singing developed in synagogues in the Greek-speaking world. Philo attests to singing among members of the Qumran community when they assembled to worship.[6] Many other scholars believe that synagogue worship did include singing. Millgram believes that the Jewish people increasingly took the Psalms to their heart and never tired of them. When the synagogue became the spiritual home of the Jewish people, many of the psalms were incorporated into every service. Millgram writes, "The psalms thus became the spiritual girders of the synagogue worship."[7]

Traditional animal sacrifices could only be offered in the temple. Therefore when Israel was deported to Babylon in the years following 597 B.C., the people substituted sacrifices of praise and prayer for those of animals and grain. Singing may have entered synagogue worship through the Levitical singers who continued to practice their art after being taken into Babylonian exile.

Singing in New Testament Worship

In the opening pages of the New Testament we are greeted with an outburst of singing as Mary rejoices at the announcement that she will give birth to God's Son (Luke 1:46-55). Then Zechariah breaks out in what scholars believe is a song at the birth of his son John, the forerunner of the Christ (Luke 1:68-79). Next, the angels glorify God, singing praise at the birth of Jesus (Luke 2:14). Then Simeon sings praise when Jesus is presented at the temple to be circumcised (Luke 2:29-32). Many scholars believe that the early church knew these hymns

---

[6]Ralph Martin, "New Testament Hymns: Background and Development," *The Expository Times* 94 no. 3 (1983): p. 132.

[7]Millgram, pp. 62-63.

even before they were written down in the gospel accounts.[8]

One thing seems clear concerning singing in the early church. First century Christians completely abandoned the professionalism of both the temple and the synagogue. Ephesians 5:19-20 and Colossians 3:16 command all believers to sing. The early church used the psalms as a foundation for much of their own singing in worship.

Franklin Segler believes that the Psalms constituted the core of personal prayer and corporate worship for all forms of Judaism and for all the churches of Christendom. They were the liturgical food of the inner life of Jesus and provided support for Paul and Silas in prison (Acts 16:25).[9]

Everett Ferguson says that hymns were often addressed to Christ, and even the Old Testament Psalms were understood in the church as about Christ.[10] Not only were the Psalms used by the early church, but they were also used by churches for centuries afterward as musical expressions of praise. For years, many churches have forfeited a beautiful part of the heritage of worship by reducing the public use of Psalms to a non-musical status.[11] In recent years it has been refreshing to hear contemporary Christian songs which are refocusing on the Psalms as a powerful musical resource.

The early church wrote new songs which they sang in addition to ones they adopted from the Psalms. Paul's letter to the Corinthian Church indicates this. First Corinthians 14:26 says, "When you come together, everyone has a hymn. . . ." Some of those hymns quite possibly are found in Scripture. Many scholars believe that passages such as John 1:1-18, Philippians 2:6-11,

---

[8]Webber, *Worship, Old and New*, p. 36.
[9]Segler, p. 23.
[10]Ferguson, *Early Christians Speak*, p. 156.
[11]Hieronymus, p. 134.

Colossians 1:15-20, Revelation 4:8 and 11, 7:12, 11:17-18, and 15:3-4 were set to music and sung in early Christian worship.[12] It is interesting that for almost 300 years after the sixteenth century Protestant Reformation, Christian groups influenced by John Calvin used only metrical psalms for congregational worship. Calvin held the conviction that "only God's Word is worthy to be sung in God's praise." But even in New Testament times, Christians were writing and singing new hymns.

Paul wrote of "psalms, hymns, and spiritual songs" (Eph. 5:19; Col. 3:16). Scholars are divided on the question of whether these were three different terms for the same thing or if they reflect three different types of music. It seems that the second interpretation is more correct. The "psalms" of Ephesians 5:19 and Colossians 3:16 probably refer to the Old Testament psalms.[13] "Hymns" *per se* would be tributes of worship directed to God (Rev. 4:8, 11; 15:3-4; Luke 1 and 2).

The hymn is the most common and most popular medium of praise among Christians today. The oldest hymns date to the early days of the church.[14] Augustine defined a hymn as "a song with praise to God." Three things stand out in Augustine's definition: A hymn is praise; it is intended to be sung; it is directed to God.[15] Paul Schilling expands on Augustine's definition: "A hymn is a lyric poem that is suitable for singing in corporate worship and that voices the worshipers' feelings and attitudes toward God and God's intentions for their lives."[16] Scholars such as Ralph Martin believe that the

---

[12]Webber, *Worship, Old and New*, p. 36.

[13]Martin, *The Worship of God*, pp. 51-52.

[14]Horton Davies, *Christian Worship: Its History and Meaning* (New York: Abingdon Press, 1957), p. 95.

[15]Martin, *The Worship of God*, pp. 42-43.

[16]S. Paul Schilling, *The Faith We Sing* (Philadelphia: The Westminster Press, 1983), pp. 29-30.

hymns sung in the churches established by Paul were centered around Jesus and the events of salvation which Jesus came to fulfill. Ferguson affirms Martin's position and adds, "The praise of Christ continued to be a central element in songs produced in the centuries after the New Testament."[17]

"Spiritual songs" can mean at least two things. One, the adjective may mean "sacred" as opposed to "secular" songs. Two, the adjective can mean "songs inspired by the Spirit." Martin prefers the second interpretation. He believes that these songs were the result of immediate inspiration, as in 1 Corinthians 14:26, where improvised composition is implied.[18]

We really know very little about how Christians actually rendered their hymns in the earliest centuries. We can draw conclusions from Jewish singing, Greek music, and medieval church music. These sources indicate that their singing probably was more of a chant than a melody. There is no evidence of songs with melodies until the fourth century. Even after melodies came to be written there were not harmonies. Songs were sung in unison.

Until the latter part of the fourth century the Psalms were sung as a response to the direction of a leader called a cantor. This is referred to as "responsoral singing" in which the cantor sang the main content as a solo, then the congregation repeated the last words or responded with a refrain of acclamation. In the late fourth century, in addition to responsoral singing, the congregation learned to sing antiphonally. The congregation was divided into two choirs who chanted alternately to one another. The parallelism of the Psalms suggests antiphonal chanting. When the Psalms were recited in the synagogue, the congregation took part in responsive singing.[19]

---

[17]Ferguson, *Early Christians Speak*, p. 156.
[18]Martin, *The Worship of God*, p. 53.
[19]Ferguson, *Early Christians Speak*, pp. 160-61.

Which Style of Music?

One's preference in music generally is a matter of taste. Preference is affected by education, musical training, and exposure to different types and styles of music. Since these matters differ with each Christian, it is difficult, if not impossible, to select and sing songs that will please everyone.

Music is often a source of conflict in the church. Some people want to sing newer, contemporary songs, while others want only the old familiar ones. Some like stately, dignified anthems of European origin like Luther's "A Mighty Fortress Is Our God," while others prefer Southern gospel favorites such as "I'll Fly Away." Often we become obsessive about music because our first response to it is emotional, not rational. By nature, music unlocks our feelings at their deepest levels. The conflict of old songs versus contemporary songs is not new. New songs became a necessity as the gospel moved out into the Gentile culture of the early centuries. New songs were needed to express sensitivity to the Greek culture and at the same time not to reject the best of their Jewish heritage.

For a time during the Protestant Reformation the churches influenced by Calvin, such as the Baptists, Presbyterians, and Congregationalists, sang only the Psalms in their worship, and then only in unison. Calvin was skeptical of "hymns of human composure." He allowed only the 150 Psalms to be sung, with the exception of the Ten Commandments and the *Nunc Dimittis* (the first two words of Simeon's song in Luke 2:29-32 in the Latin Version of Scripture).

Isaac Watts (1674-1748), among others, was dissatisfied with the narrow limits of singing only the Psalms. He created hymns of free expression as well as updating the way the Psalms were sung, "making David speak like a

147

Christian." Watts, who has been called the father of English hymnody, greatly influenced Charles Wesley (1707-1788) who composed more than 7,200 hymns.[20] By 1790 many of these same churches were singing contemporary religious poetry in choral settings in multiple part harmony. This period was not unlike our own regarding the strong feelings about what kind of music should be used in worship. Stephen A. Marini argues that the new forms of music that developed in the eighteenth century marked the most significant liturgical change in colonial American religion. It started a fundamental debate, not only about what ought to be sung and how it ought to be sung, but also about the nature of worship itself, the interpretation of Scripture, the constitution of the church and the powers of regeneration.[21]

The conflict between old and new songs is evident in the preface to a song book published several years ago:

> For some years we have noticed a tendency among many people to drift away from the good old songs that were loved and cherished by our fathers and mothers and to adopt the modern "jig" and operatic tunes. As a result of this there has been a great decline, and, in our humble judgment, the progress has been downward or backward. The singing is not as sweet and soul stirring as it was in our younger days. We have lately observed that in many places there is a desire to return to the old tunes, but a suitable book for all occasions containing only the old music could not be had. We believe that in the following pages you will find the cream of the old music. The book contains none of the "modern sort," but we have endeavored to give a variety.[22]

---

[20]Morgan Simmons, "Hymnody: Reflections on Our Faith," *Reformed Liturgy and Music* 21 (Summer 1987): p. 141.

[21]Stephen A. Marini, "Rehearsal for Revival: Sacred Singing in the Great Awakening in America," in *Sacred Sound: Music in Religious Thought and Practice* (Chico, CA: Scholars Press, 1983), p. 71.

[22]Alton Howard, "The Contributions of Modern Church Music to Worship," in *Harding College Lectures* (Austin, TX: Firm Foundation Publishing House, 1978), pp. 165-66.

Those words were written by C.H. Cayce in Martin, Tennessee on March 30, 1912. It is important to see that the "old tunes" and "the old music" that Cayce wanted in 1912 were once new songs themselves. In other words, every song at one time was a new song. It is highly probable that when those "old songs" that Cayce loved were first written, there were people who disliked them because they were new. I am not advocating dispensing with the old hymns. Rather, I am arguing that positive contributions can be made to worship by learning new songs which tell the same old story in new and fresh ways. God's people have been writing and singing new songs for thousands of years. Israel sang a new song after her release from Egypt (Exod. 20). David wrote, "He put a new song in my mouth, a hymn of praise to our God" (Ps. 40:3). The birth of Christ was welcomed with a new song (Luke 2:14).

We should keep the best songs of the past, and add to them the best new songs we can find. Some among us are talented enough to write new songs. Those who have tried to canonize music have hindered the growth of the church, both numerically and spiritually. New music has usually accompanied periods of spiritual revival. During some periods of revival the emphasis has been on purifying doctrine. Often the emphasis has been on personal spirituality, with an accompanying growth in evangelism and ministry.

Perhaps the most notable of the developments in the revival movements has been the flowering of new hymns, which quickly became very popular. Typically, these new songs abandoned traditional sacred symbols and borrowed poetic styles and images from popular, non-sacred music styles of the day.

No song could be more sacred and loved than "Amazing Grace," but the first listeners to that melody would not have agreed. It was a plantation love song.

Not until the moving lyrics of a converted slave trader, John Newton (1725-1807), were wedded to this tune did it become spiritual. In early America, the tune to the hymn "Revive Us Again" (or "Hallelujah, Thine the Glory") was a drinking song. Its original title was "Hallelujah, I'm a Bum." Needless to say, the last line — "revive us again" — was not a prayer for spiritual renewal! When evangelist Billy Sunday introduced the innovative "Brighten the Corner Where You Are," much of the Christian community rose up in arms because of the syncopated beat to the song. Its long-short-long beat was the hallmark of the ragtime era. That meter is also the distinctive characteristic of the old favorite "Since Jesus Came Into My Heart." When this song was introduced, many believers were shocked at singing the name of Jesus to a syncopated beat.[23]

Jack Boyd, professor of music at Abilene Christian University, and editor of *Great Songs of the Church*, says that musical traditions in churches within the Restoration heritage come from the frontier music/shaped note tradition of the 1880s and 1890s.[24] Much of that supposed religious music was originally designed for recreational use. Most of us today do not realize that this music came out of what Boyd calls "the Great Sentimental Age of American Music," roughly 1860 to 1915 (Civil War to World War I). Many of the

---

[23]Personal correspondence from Dr. Jack Boyd, professor of music at Abilene Christian University in Abilene, Texas.

[24]It is interesting to note that Alexander Campbell despised placing musical notation in hymnbooks. His own hymnbook included only the words to the songs without the music. In the *Millennial Harbinger*, 1847, pp. 178-179, he wrote, "I would prefer to have an organ, or a fashionable choir as a means of my worship than the words of a hymn set to the notes of a tune upon which to fix my eyes while engaging in the worship of God." Isn't it strange that today there are so many people who fuss about the very thing that would have made Campbell so happy — having only the words to songs without musical notes?

most popular musical tunes used in the hymns of that day were carefully disguised dance music. "Standing on the Promises" is a march, written in the time of John Philip Sousa when marches were one of the most common ballroom dances. "Jesus is All the World to Me" is an Irish jig, the same style and speed as "When Johnny Comes Marching Home Again." Songs such as these allowed toe-tappable dance music into assemblies of worship when such tunes with secular words or no words at all would have been resoundingly denounced from the pulpit.[25]

With the passage of time, these new "secular" forms and sounds became so much a part of the new "sacred" worship language that it no longer seemed new. Gradually, it took its place along with the best loved of the old music. Later revivals arose with new songs, gradually replacing the songs which were new and seemed so strange in the former revival.[26]

So it continues today. New songs continue to be written, many of them borrowing from the forms and styles of contemporary secular music. The new songs appeal to many people in the younger generation — they "connect" with the segment of the population that has grown up with contemporary forms of music.

It is essential that we distinguish between *form* and *content*. The content is the message — the words of the song. The form is the method used to communicate the message — the musical style. Content is what we say. Form is how we say it. What some find objectionable in the new contemporary songs is the form, not the content. That is where preferences for certain musical styles come into play. The truly important issue is the message of the song — the content. If the content is

---

[25]Personal correspondence from Dr. Jack Boyd.
[26]Hustad, pp. 120-21.

biblical, the form essentially becomes a matter of taste.

An increasingly smaller percentage of America's city and suburban dwellers have any connection with farming. For the most part, we are no longer a seafaring people. Yet many of the old songs we sing in worship rely heavily on farming and seafaring metaphors which many people do not understand. Although "Bringing in the Sheaves" is a precious song to many older Christians, my three teenagers have no concept of what that means. "Let the Lower Lights Be Burning" talks about trimming a "feeble lamp" for "some poor sailor, tempest tossed." How many younger people and unchurched people know what "lower lights" means? Probably not many.

Many of the songs in our books use language that no one speaks in daily conversations anymore. "Hark, the gentle voice of Jesus calleth" is the first line to one of our best loved songs. I make no effort to discontinue singing it. However, when is the last time you called a friend on the telephone and said with old English flair, "Hark, my brother, wilt thou come to a dinner prepared for thee?" It is not wrong to do so, but the point is made: we simply do not talk that way anymore. We will probably continue to sing songs such as these, but let's add to them songs which speak of current concerns and have a newer sound which connects with my children and millions of other people who do not have the historical or Christian background to understand the old songs.

Music and songs need to change to keep relevant. What does it say about us when we do not continue to create new church music, when we feel like the only songs that are good songs are ones that are at least one hundred years old? There is a difference in taste and style of church music, and no one has the right to bind his or her tastes on anyone else. Therefore, we need to be open enough to allow hymns to be set to contemporary images and music.

Some of the music styles that appeal to younger people today seem both unpleasant and inappropriate to the older generation. It would be helpful for all Christians to know that this tension is not new. Leaders who are sensitive to others need to help educate them about the nature of the problem and plead for understanding, tolerance, and sensitivity from all concerned. Those who yearn for more contemporary praise and worship songs must show genuine love, respect, kindness, thoughtfulness, and acceptance of their brothers and sisters whose musical preferences are for the old standards. The opposite is true as well.

It can well be argued that the most powerful influence in the lives of young people is their music — more powerful than parents, school, or even peers. In his book, *The Closing of the American Mind*, Allan Bloom indicates that if, in our culture, we do not communicate with the young through music, we simply do not communicate.[27] It's sad that brilliant musicians whose hearts are ruled by greed, sensuality, and wickedness know how to move people emotionally but so often have nothing worthwhile to say. It's sadder still how many times Christians bore many people with the otherwise unsearchable riches of Jesus because of the lack of creative skill in our means of communicating the message.

No question about it, to enhance the beauty of truth with the right emotional feel, in a way that pleases the majority of worshipers, is a delicate matter. The more diverse the congregation, the more difficult it becomes. However, those who lead singing must strive to understand what is appropriate for the members of their congregation. In the kind of diverse memberships which make up most of today's suburban churches, that means

---

[27]Allan David Bloom, *The Closing of the American Mind* (New York: Simon and Schuster, 1987).

a sensitivity to both those who prefer the old songs and those who want the new songs. Worship leaders whose hearts are set on ministry will not try to shock or alienate any segment of the congregation. Sensitive leaders are more interested in building bridges than walls.

The Power of Music

Someone has said that music is the language of the emotions. Music stimulates the emotions like nothing else. Therefore, music is incredibly powerful as a means of communication. Ronald Allen and Gordon Borror write: "Words alone can be and often are very strong, but couple them with the 'right' music and they can be burned into the mind and consciousness indelibly."[28] Most of us who are adults remember popular songs from our childhood. All we need to hear is a few notes or bars of a song and we not only can hum the entire tune, but we usually can remember many of the words. Just a few notes of a song can bring back memories and feelings that may be 20, 40, or 60 years old.

If you lived through the depression, something probably happens inside you emotionally when you hear a band strike up "Happy Days Are Here Again." It brings back all the memories, pleasant and difficult, you experienced during those bleak years in American history. I grew up during the 1950s and '60s. When I hear songs like "Yesterday" by the Beatles or "Little Deuce Coupe" by the Beach Boys, I am transported back in time to my own teenage years. Many of the emotions of those bygone days become as fresh in my mind as this morning's newspaper. So it is with many of the spiritual songs I learned as a youngster, then as a teenager and college student. Many of those songs are still as meaningful to

---

[28]Allen and Borror, p. 160.

me today (some are even more meaningful) as they were when I first learned them.

Singing may be the most popular element of Christian worship because it unites the whole assembly in active participation to a degree which is hardly true of any other component in worship. For more than a century in the Middle Ages, congregational singing was forbidden in worship. Luther protested, "Let God speak directly to His people through the Scriptures, and let His people respond with grateful songs of praise."[29] Music induces an attitude of worship. Webber writes, "It elicits from deep within a person the sense of awe and mystery that accompanies a meeting with God. In this way [it] releases an inner nonrational part of our being that words with their more rational and discursive meanings cannot unearth and set free to utter praise."[30]

Webber's words make sense in light of the Bicameral brain theory which says that the right side of the brain is not analytical. The right side of the brain does not count or sort or dissect data like the left side of the brain does. Rather, the right half of the brain is the emotive and creative side where we process feelings and things like the arts. According to this theory, music is "heard" primarily through the right side of the brain. Preaching and teaching appeal primarily to the left side of the brain which is analytical in nature. When both are put together in one worship service the whole person, both the rational and the emotional being, is addressed.[31] When powerful words and moving music are combined into a song, the entire person is touched in ways that are impossible with words alone or music alone.

---

[29]Coleman and Lindquist, pp. 25-26.

[30]Webber, *Worship, Old and New*, p. 176.

[31]Thomas Oden, *Pastoral Theology: Essentials of Ministry* (San Francisco: Harper and Row, Publishers, 1983), p. 96.

Most worship services in Restoration Churches have stressed aspects of worship that appeal more to the left side, the analytical side of the brain. That meets the needs of "left brained" people very well, but it does not minister as well to those who are primarily "right brained" people. In the future, worship leaders will be wise to provide a balance that meets the wide spectrum of personality types that make up the worshiping family of God in their congregations.

A Theology of Singing

In churches of Christ a great deal of attention has been given to the non-use of instrumental music and to practical ways we can improve congregational singing. Little attention, however, has been given to the theological meaning of singing. What are we doing when we sing? What is accomplished? Theology is present in all hymns. Sometimes it is good theology, and sometimes it is bad theology, but all hymns make some kind of theological statement. Hymns say something about God, the divine character and purpose, the nature and destiny of human life, the way of salvation, human responsibility before God, and related matters. When matters as vital as these are the subjects of our songs, it becomes important that we pay close attention to the content of the words we sing.[32]

Alexander Campbell understood the importance of the theology which is expressed in music. In the introduction to his 1853 hymnbook, *Psalms, Hymns, and Spiritual Songs*, he wrote:

The Christian Hymn Book, next to the Bible, moreover, wields the largest and mightiest formative influence upon the young and old, upon saint and sinner, and of any other book in the

---

[32]Schilling, p. 25.

world. Poetry. . .partakes so much of the spirit of its author, that it insinuates itself into the soul with more subtlety and power than any other language of mortals. . . .Permit me, I also say, to dispense the psalmody of a community, and I care not who dictates its creed or writes it catechism. If the hymn book is daily sung in the family, and in the social meetings of the brethren, it must imbue their souls with its sentiments more than all the other labors of the pulpit or of the press.[33]

Campbell staunchly opposed written creeds of faith. However, he declared that the hymnal of any people is "the best substitute in the world for what is usually called a confession of faith." It was "the doctrinal embodiment and exponent" of a community's faith, hope, and love. In the October, 1851 issue of the *Millennial Harbinger*, he wrote:

Were I, indeed, obliged or Providentially called upon, to publish what is usually called a confession of my faith — a full exhibit of my attainments in Christian knowledge — I would rather present to the world a copy of my Christian Psalmody — the psalms, hymns and spiritual songs which I adopt and use, than any other documentary evidence which I could offer; not only of my faith and hope in God through the Lord Jesus, but also of my measure of knowledge in the mystery of God, and of Christ, and of man's redemption.[34]

S.D. Schilling agrees with Campbell's sentiments. He writes, "The editors of our major hymn books understand well the importance of the theological affirmations of the hymns they offer for the use in worship, even if worshipers cannot."[35] Pierre Jean de Beranger (1780-1857) was correct when he said, "Let me make the songs of the people, and I care not who makes their laws."[36]

---

[33]Hieronymus, pp. 195-96.

[34]*Ibid.*, p. 196.

[35]S.D. Schilling, "Theology in Hymnnody," *Reformed Liturgy in Music* 21 no.3 (1987): p. 145.

[36]Hieronymus, p. 196.

This is why the person who chooses the songs for worship is potentially the most important "teacher" in the congregation. His musical preferences will be a powerful shaping force in the belief patterns of the church.[37]

Purposes of Singing

Singing fulfills a number of different purposes.

1) *Singing acts as an aid to worship by putting us into the right frame of mind and heart.* Music sets the tone for most of human activity. From elevators, to supermarkets, to movies, music sets the stage. Can we be any less attentive to the role music plays in preparing us for an encounter with the living God?

2) *Singing allows us to express our deepest thoughts and emotions to God, and it does so in a way that no other medium provides.*

Music can take us where the intellect alone cannot go. It has the capacity to convey love and devotion, praise and joy, concern and sorrow in ways that are too difficult in the merely spoken word. Every act of worship can find meaningful expression through song. In meaningful worship, people experience an emotional release. Congregational singing is the perfect vehicle to carry unleashed feelings into the presence of God as gifts of worship.

3) *Singing can help us gain a stronger conviction of the truths expressed in the songs.*

Hebrews 13:15 instructs us to offer to God a sacrifice of praise, "the fruit of lips that confess his name." Singing is a way of acknowledging God, of praising Him and confessing our faith in Him.

---

[37]Robert Dale, *To Dream Again* (Nashville: The Broadman Press, 1981), p. 54.

4) *Singing allows everyone to participate actively.*

Singing is one of the few elements of corporate worship in which all can be so actively involved. It is even a unique delight to witness deaf worshipers signing with vigor as the whole body sings together.

5) *Singing is also one of the best mediums through which to offer praise to the Lord.*

Some people have the mistaken idea that singing is only for good singers. Singing is for believers — all believers. The relevant question is not "Do you have a voice?" but "Do you have a song?" If you have a desire to praise God, perhaps no other avenue is more suited to express it as singing.

6) *Singing teaches, admonishes, encourages and edifies.*

First Corinthians 14:26, Ephesians 5:19, and Colossians 3:16 support this claim. Songs are effective teaching tools because of the power of repetition. As songs are sung repeatedly through the years, they have a strong impact on our beliefs. They are also effective teaching tools because they link ideas with emotion.

7) *Singing helps us remember the great acts of God.*

Because singing teaches, it helps us remember. As worshipers, a primary task is to recall the great things God has done.

8) *Singing provides a marvelous medium through which to express thanks, love and devotion to God* (Jonah 2:9; Eph. 5:20).

9) *Singing expresses joy* (James 5:13).

As marvelous as the songs of the Hebrews were, a great many of them express a sense of unfulfilled longing. There was great joy in the early church (Acts 2:1-13,47; 3:8; 5:41-42; 8:39; 13:52). "The kingdom of God is . . . righteousness, peace and joy in the Holy Spirit" (Rom. 14:17). It should not be surprising that there is great joy associated with the songs of Christianity. As we sing, let us do so with great enthusiasm. John

Wesley was concerned that people's praise should be enthusiastic:

> Sing lustily, and with a good courage . . . Beware of singing as if you were half dead or half asleep; but lift up your voice with strength . . . Be no more afraid of your voice now, nor more ashamed of its being heard, than when you sang the songs of Satan.[38]

10) *Singing helps to evangelize the lost.*

Unbelievers who attend the assembly are often touched by the music and words of the hymns. Many of the songs we sing invite others to come to the Lord in obedient faith.

11) *Singing gives expression to the indwelling Holy Spirit and the Word of Christ.*

Ephesians 5:18 associates singing with being filled with the Spirit, and Colossians 3:16 associates singing with the indwelling word of Christ. Everett Ferguson says there is no need to interpret one passage in terms of the other, as if the one is what the other means. He writes:

> Both statements are true and belong together; singing is the result of the presence of the Spirit and of the Word of Christ. Praise is a consequence of being filled with the Spirit and possessing the word of Christ. When the Spirit and the Word of Christ dwell in a person, it finds expression in song. The knowledge of salvation in Christ, the acceptance of God's grace, the receiving of the Holy Spirit as the first route to redemption — this leads to song.[39]

Standards of Good Worship Music

On what basis do we judge songs for Christian worship? Some of the guidelines which follow rest solidly on

---

[38]Instructions reproduced in many Methodist hymnals.

[39]Everett Ferguson, "The Theology of Singing," in *Harding College Lectures* (Austin, TX: Firm Foundation Publishing House, 1978), p. 79.

scriptural principles, while others fall into the realm of opinion. With that disclaimer, let me suggest several "standards" that can guide our selection of music.

1) *Songs should be doctrinally sound and faithful to Scripture.*

Songs that teach erroneous theology have no place in worship. Careful song selection insures accurate teaching.

2) *Songs should point us to God.*

There is an important place in worship for songs with a horizontal focus — songs which are directed to one another and which encourage fellow Christians as we sing "to one another in psalms, hymns, and spiritual songs" (Eph. 5:19). Many of the songs in our hymnbooks focus on one another as we sing about our hopes, joys, fears, etc. However, in our efforts to edify one another, our primary goal is to praise God.

Wendell Willis writes: "Singing, like all worship, should point to the one worshiped, not to individual worshipers." That means that many of our songs need to be directed to God and to Jesus Christ. Songs such as "We Praise Thee, O God" have that vertical focus. Many songs in our hymnals do not even mention God, Christ, or the Holy Spirit. Worship ought to reflect our awareness of God's majesty and goodness. All worship is a response to what God has done. The content of hymns should emphasize the unique aspects of Christianity.[40] The hymns preserved in the first century focus on Jesus Christ and recite the events of salvation which He accomplished (John 1:1-18, Phil. 2:6-11, Col. 1:15-20, and 1 Tim. 3:16). The first century Christians placed Jesus on a par with God, and they praised both God and Jesus in their worship.

Many times we sing songs simply because we like

---

[40]Willis, pp. 54, 58-59.

them or because we do not see anything wrong with them. Sometimes we sing certain songs because they make us feel good. We may do all this without regard to whether those songs genuinely are pleasing to God. The primary requirement for singing in worship is that our songs please God. Music that is enjoyed simply as an end in itself is out of place in worship. In his pocket hymnal, *Sacred Melody*, Charles Wesley had these directions: "Let not weakness or weariness hinder you. Sing lustily and with good courage. Above all sing spiritually. Have an eye to God in every word you sing. *Aim at pleasing Him more than yourself*" (italics mine).

Some people worship their praise and praise their worship. The act of praise itself must not be the object of our worship. Only God and Jesus deserve that position. Worship is the vehicle in which we express our adoration to the Heavenly Father and our encouragement to one another. It is possible for individuals to adore the music itself more than the One about Whom the song is written. It is possible to praise the style of worship or the emotional feelings it produces rather than the Lord Himself. When the act of worship becomes the object of worship it becomes idolatry.

Music used in public worship must lead us into the presence of God. Ralph Martin writes, "Nothing is so worthy of our singing as the glory and majesty of God, His creative power and redeeming grace. The greatest hymns are never far from the sublime scenery of our redemption."[41] These songs should celebrate God's activity in history and in the present — the culminating act being the salvation He provided through Jesus.[42]

Before moving on to point three, let's spend a little more time on the idea of focusing praise solely upon

---

[41]Martin, *The Worship of God*, p. 47.
[42]*Ibid.*, p. 59.

God. In their book *Come and Worship*, Michael Coleman and Ed Lindquist emphasize what they call "praise and worship music," by which they mean primarily songs directed to God and not to fellow Christians. They insist that "praise and worship music" is distinguished from other forms of music in the following ways: First, it expresses praise, which the Bible says is the doorway to God's presence. (See Ps. 100:4). When we praise, we share in a heavenly activity like the angels who sing to God around His throne (Rev. 4; 5; 14:2-3; 15:2-3). Although our singing is imperfect compared to that of the angels, it is thrilling to know that we share their praise to God and to Jesus.

Second, praise music is vertical. Horizontal music talks *about* God, while vertical music talks *to* God. Some songs address God in the second person (you), while others address God in the third person (He). Both horizontal and vertical music are valid ministries and have a place in the church. However, vertical songs address God more directly in the second person.

Third, praise music can be sacrificial. Praise and worship songs have nothing to do with our emotions or how we feel. Hebrews 13:15 speaks of "a sacrifice of praise." We are to offer praise no matter what our circumstances (1 Thess. 5:16-18). The songs we lift up to God should be our best effort, offered in love, humility, and gratitude. Instead of the sacrificial system of the old covenant where God's people were required to offer animals, Christians are to offer a sacrifice of praise. Even under the old covenant, God wanted His people to "offer the fruit of [their] lips" (Hos. 14:2). The idea of vocal praise as a sacrifice was developed extensively in Judaism and can be seen in intertestamental literature, the Dead Sea Scrolls, and rabbinic literature. The New Testament connects singing with the spirit, making it a spiritual activity (1 Cor. 14:15; Eph. 5:19; Col. 3:16).

Fourth, praise music is a "delivery system" for Scripture. Many of the praise and worship songs which have been written in recent years are taken directly from Scripture. Setting biblical passages to music is a powerful way to help people proclaim Scripture, memorize it and use it. Once songs are in your mind, the music and lyrics tend to remain there. Coleman and Lindquist reported a survey in *U.S.A. Today* which asked people if they could recall the lyrics to 18 songs which the Beatles made popular during the 1960s and 1970s. Even after 20 years, most people could remember more than 92 percent of the words.[43] This fact gives us insight into why Satan has tried so hard to keep God's people from developing and singing good songs and why he has tried so hard to flood our culture with music that is godless.

3) *Some of our songs need a horizontal focus, but with a vertical perspective.*

Having declared that God must be the primary focus of our worship, there must also be songs that are horizontal in focus. Songs should carry a message that edifies, instructs, and admonishes fellow Christians (Eph. 5:19; Col. 3:16). First Corinthians 14:26 says that our singing and whatever we do in the assembly is to be done for edification. Worship should include a balance of objective and subjective songs. Objective songs focus entirely on God, Christ, the Holy Spirit and what they have done for us. Subjective songs deal with things like confession, petition, moral reflection, intercession, evangelism, and our own personal faith experience. Objective songs look upward, while subjective songs look inward.[44]

4) *Songs should be clear and understandable.*

The Apostle Paul wrote, "I will sing with the spirit,

---

[43]Coleman and Lindquist, 24-26.
[44]Martin, *The Worship of God*, pp. 44-45.

and I will sing with the understanding also" (1 Cor. 14:15). It is important that people comprehend the meaning of the words they sing. A few years ago Terry Bell wrote a bulletin article that drives this point home with both humor and power:

Another Great American Hymn...
"Found A Peanut"

It was in the summer of 1972 that I learned a great spiritual lesson. I was the guest of honor one Sunday at a village church service in South India. The villagers had just the year before, learned an English hymn which they wished to sing for me as their worship began. It seems that an American missionary had taught them this song one night while sitting around the campfire. The Tamil song leader lifted his hand, and in fine American style began the song, as this village congregation struggled with the English lyrics to "Found a peanut, found a peanut, found a peanut one day." Every face looked so spiritual.

But in some ways, what's the difference? Thousands of their American counterparts sing words they don't understand every Sunday. Now, mind you there's nothing wrong with 18th century hymns, but there is something wrong with singing words we don't understand, and there is something wrong with sanctifying all the old and condemning all the new. In many of our congregations, the unwritten policy is . . . "if the guy who wrote it ain't dead, we ain't gonna sing it." We need a revolution in the area of Christian music.

My conclusion is simple . . . alas the area of our singing has become a trysting place for me. I've spent many a direful night, rent asunder, with ebon pinion brooding o'er the vale. What e'er betide, the bowers will not fail, even from ether-plains. It's time to raise our Ebenezers and fain become gladsome. In mirth we have moaned, our suits disdained. Now is the time to have our spiritual thirst assuaged as we fain the supernal among the zephyrs wafting in the dale from days of yore.

I've often wondered why this kind of language is any more spiritual than . . . "Found a Peanut."[45]

---

[45]Church bulletin of the Broadway Church of Christ, Lubbock, TX, for July 29, 1990.

If the language is so old or the words so unfamiliar that they block understanding, they may be out of place in worship. Leaders must either explain the meaning or stop using songs that hinder comprehension. Leaders also need to select songs that will connect meaningfully to the people they lead. Unless worship leaders are keenly aware of the wide diversity of people who make up many of our churches, the entire congregation is likely to be subjected to the likes and dislikes of the minority who happen to be in charge. When this is the case, Lynn Anderson says, "This leaves the rest scrambling to 'translate' or else feeling emotionally left out!"

5) *Songs should be easy to sing* (as a general rule).

Songs with elaborate arrangements and special parts may detract from the purpose of worship. They may also discourage less musically inclined members from singing for fear their own voices will detract. Difficult songs may also tempt others to sit and listen as to a performance. It is important to ask: does the music support or distract from the congregation's efforts to praise God?

One of the advantages of many of the modern praise songs is that the tunes usually are simple and have choruses which are repeated often, making them easy to learn and to sing. This does not mean that a congregation must never try to learn songs that are musically challenging. Several years ago I was a member of a congregation which learned to sing "The Hallelujah Chorus." It took them a while to learn it, but now they sing it well. It is one of the congregation's favorite hymns. Churches can learn challenging musical pieces, but leaders must be careful not to try to sing too many difficult or new songs.

6) *Songs should speak to the whole person.*

Human beings are physical, intellectual, spiritual, social, and emotional beings, and we need to keep a proper balance in all parts. Everett Ferguson writes:

Singing engages mind, heart, and the organs of speech: the intellect, the emotions, and the physical self are involved. . . . hence, the tongue — the physical body — is the instrument on which God is praised. The mind understands; the heart responds in thankfulness; the tongue expresses it. All are involved in song.[46]

7) *Good songs involve everyone in the assembly* (generally).

Congregational singing (with everyone participating together) should be the general practice. However, before building that case, let me address a matter that is controversial in many congregations. It is what some have called *special music*. The question is, "Is it scriptural for singing to take place in worship when that singing is being done by anything less than full congregational participation?" Is it permissible to have a solo or a duet or a quartet or a chorus sing as part of the worship service?

This issue deserves more extensive treatment than I have time or space to give it here. But I will answer the question this way. There is abundant evidence of antiphonal singing and responsory singing in both the Old Testament and in the early church. Ephesians 5:19 says, "Speak to *one another* in psalms, hymns and spiritual songs." It is possible to obey that command by having everyone in the congregation speaking to one another in song at the same time. It is also possible to obey that command by having an individual speak via a song to others in the assembly. The same thing can be said of Colossians 3:16 which instructs us to "teach and admonish *one another* with all wisdom, and as you sing psalms, hymns and spiritual songs with gratitude in your hearts to God."

---

[46]Ferguson, "The Theology of Singing," pp. 80-81.

It is almost certain that at least some first century churches had solo singing. First Corinthians 14:26 reads, "When you come together, everyone has a hymn, or a word of instruction, a revelation, a tongue or an interpretation . . ." In the Gospel Advocate commentary series, J. W. Shepherd commented on v. 26: "A graphic picture is given of the assembled church, eager to contribute, each his part, to the services." Jimmy Allen of Harding University says in his survey of First Corinthians on v. 26, "Apparently, there was solo singing by gifted people in the assembly at Corinth." Tertullian (A. D. 160-220) says that solo singing was practiced in Christian gatherings. Speaking of the Christian love and worship at the love feast, he says, "then each, from what he knows of the Holy Scriptures, or from his own heart, is called before the rest to sing to God" (*Apology* 39:18, Loeb Classical Library).

G.C. Brewer was one of the most respected preachers in the Restoration Movement in this century. In 1957 he wrote *The Model Church* in which he said:

> It is no violation of anything in the New Testament — rather, it is sanctioned by it — for one man to sing to the audience. Nor is it wrong for two persons, four persons, or six persons together to stand before the assembly and admonish them with a song or speak to them through a hymn — provided always, of course that the singers are themselves worshipers and that they do not do all the singing and thereby take away the right and privilege that belongs to every Christian — to praise God in song.[47]

It is my conviction that if a message can be spoken in worship, it can be sung in worship. As we have already indicated, there are occasions when a sung message communicates more effectively than a spoken message.

---

[47]G.C. Brewer, *The Model Church* (Nashville: Gospel Advocate Company, 1957), p. 150.

Suppose a man presiding at the Lord's Table knows a new and moving song based on the Lord's death, burial, and resurrection — a song which no one else had learned. He could recite the words without music, and it could be quite meaningful. But allow him to sing those words to a soul-stirring melody, and it would make a more profound spiritual impact than word alone could accomplish.

Howard Norton published these editorial comments in *The Christian Chronicle*:

> This writer grew up in a church of Christ that had a children's chorus at every single Sunday service. We also had quartets, trios, and duets; but there are people in our fellowship today who are ready to fight rather than allow an occasional special song to be a part of the worship service. Why? Because their Bible says it is wrong? No, because we have not done it traditionally. Some object to special singing because they fear the entertainment syndrome. We also fear the entertainment syndrome, but even congregational singing can degenerate into entertainment instead of worship.[48]

Why is it that when a man stands up to preach, prances all around a stage, waves his arms, inflects his voice, gets dramatic when he tells an emotional story, and tries to get us to laugh at an occasional joke we call him a good preacher? Many of the same folks who would call a singing group or a drama group "entertainment" would never think of referring to the preacher's actions as "entertainment." The fact is that "good preachers" (the kind that most congregations desperately try to employ and keep) are men whose presentations have some entertaining qualities. You may not like the word "entertaining," but that's what you mean when you say, "I really enjoy his sermons." There's a word which describes preachers who are so dull and uninteresting that they

---

[48]Howard Norton, "Church Needs Doctrinal Balance," *Christian Chronicle* 47 (January 1990), p. 22.

continually bore the congregation — unemployed.

The same thing can be said of song leaders, some of whom are famous because of the way they lead singing. If song leaders' or preachers' purpose is to entertain, then each one has some serious problems. Sure, there is always the possibility that special music (even congregational singing) can degenerate into entertainment, just as preaching can. We need to understand what music is for. Music is for communication, for emphasis, for emotion, for mood. In a sense, these things have some entertainment value, but they transcend mere entertainment. Some people will "hear" a sermon more quickly, and it will penetrate more deeply if couched in a song than any other way the message could be presented.

Now, having argued for the use of special music, I still want to affirm that singing in the assembly usually is a corporate activity.[49] Congregational singing exemplifies the unity of the church. Singing together symbolizes the one body of Christ. The Apostle Paul prayed that the Roman Christians would have a spirit of unity "so that with one heart and mouth you may glorify the God and Father of our Lord Jesus Christ" (Rom. 15:5-6).

8) *The selection of songs should be appropriate for each segment of worship.*

Although this is a subjective matter, "O Worship the King," is an appropriate lead in to the service and might seem strange at the end. "The Old Rugged Cross" is generally used around the Lord's Supper because it focuses on what the Lord's Supper commemorates. If the song selection is badly out of kilter with what is supposed to be happening, it is confusing and distracting to worshipers, but if used rightly, even non-traditional placement of songs could lead the worshiper's thoughts into new directions.

---

[49]Willis, pp. 59-60.

What a marvelous privilege to sing praises to God. With the Psalmist let us exclaim:

> Come, let us sing for joy to the Lord;
>   let us shout aloud to the Rock of our salvation.
> Let us come before him with thanksgiving
>   and extol him with music and song.
> For the Lord is the great God,
>   the great King above all gods.
>
> Psalm 95:1-3

DISCUSSION QUESTIONS
ON CHAPTER SEVEN

1. Why do you think the Psalms were so treasured by the Jews and early Christians?

2. What is antiphonal singing? Responsory singing? Is there biblical basis for this?

3. Why is music a controversial issue in churches today? Is this controversy new?

4. Why would people want to write and sing new songs today? Why does it seem to take so long for new songs to be accepted?

5. What are the characteristics of a good song for worship?

6. What is the difference between psalms, hymns, and spiritual songs?

7. Did early Christians ever have someone sing a solo or one group sing to another? Support your answer.

8. When people like different styles of music, how can a congregation meet the needs of all its members?

9. What does "left-brain," "right-brain" theory say about the types of music we sing in worship?

10. Why is music such a powerful tool for worship?

11. Respond to the statement: "Let me make the songs of the people, and I care not who makes their laws."

12. How do Coleman and Lindquist define "praise music?"

8
Worship Requires a Sacrifice

In many congregations, the act of giving does not seem as important an element of worship as singing, praying, preaching, reading the Word, and the Lord's Supper. Sometimes it is treated as a necessary distraction and not as a vital part of our worship to God. However, giving is as vital to worship as anything else we can do.

Giving As Part of Old Testament Worship

Almost from the opening pages of Scripture we read of individuals who brought gifts to God. Cain and Abel each offered to God a gift. No one knows for sure exactly why God rejected Cain's gift and accepted Abel's offering. In all likelihood, it had to do with obedience to God's undisclosed directions, and it probably also had something to do with the state of each man's heart when he gave. Note how the passage reads, and pay special attention to the two italicized words of Genesis 4:3-4: "In the course of time Cain brought *some* of the fruits of the soil as an offering to the LORD. But Abel brought fat portions from some of the *firstborn* of his flock."

It seems that Abel gave God the newest and the best of his flock — some of the *first*born. These were the precious little lambs with great value and potential. From a human perspective, it does not make sense to sacrifice the youngest and best. It makes more sense to sacrifice something that is less valuable, and more easily replaceable, like potatoes and onions. Besides, there would have been a lot of potatoes and onions. Giving a whole bunch of produce was not going to be much of a sacrifice for Cain. But giving some of the firstborn of Abel's little lambs — now that is a sacrifice!

This explanation seems to fit what Hebrews 11:4 says, "By faith Abel offered God a better sacrifice than Cain did." Although it may not have made logical sense, Abel was willing to do what God said on the basis of his faith in God. The clear implication is that Cain was not willing to make his offering on that basis. The same choice faces us today. Will we give God a gift that is a genuine sacrifice, or will we give in to the temptation to offer God merely some of what we have in abundance? That is a penetrating question which is at the heart of worship. God does not want the trinkets we pitch His direction. He wants all we are and all we have. After all, it all belongs to Him anyway. The issue is not ownership, but stewardship. The spirit of worship is that we want to give everything back to God.

In Genesis 22:5 we learn something of Abraham's understanding of worship. In obedience to God's command, Abraham prepared to offer his son Isaac as a sacrifice. He left his servants behind and told them that he and his son were going up the mount to worship the Lord. Worship the Lord? How do you call sacrificing your only son worship? God never intended to have Abraham kill Isaac. God was testing Abraham's *willingness* to sacrifice. All worship involves sacrifice, whether it is our time, our egos, our dreams, or our possessions. God desires for us to let go that we might receive from Him.

A friend of mine, who says, "Giving is a gut check," is right. God does not want from us a piece of paper with George Washington's picture on it. He wants us to give in order that we might trust Him more. He wants us to give in response to His love. Sometimes the prayers we offer before the collection betray our lack of biblical understanding of giving. We pray, "Bless this gift to the furtherance of the Lord's work. Help the elders use it wisely." This seems like little more than a spiritualized method of meeting the weekly budget and little else. What really is at stake is whether or not we are responding to God's gift to us.

A more appropriate prayer might be, "Loving Father, as we give to You today, we do so out of love for You and out of gratitude for the indescribable gift You gave us in Christ Jesus. As we place our contribution in the plate may we also give ourselves fully to You." Rather than rush through the collection with breakneck speed, we would honor the Lord more to reflect on His gifts to us. Well worded prayers can assist us. Well chosen songs before, during, and after the collection can help. Let us make our time of financial contribution in worship more than a perfunctory matter.

In the truest sense of worship, all of life must be laid before God as an offering. Sacrificial giving is not some effort to meet an expectation or even to satisfy a need. Rather, giving in worship is one way of expressing our faith in God and our love for Him.

In Old Testament times, people did not go to worship God without taking a sacrifice. God told the Israelites, "No one is to appear before me empty-handed" (Exod. 34:20). Exodus 35 and 36 tell the marvelous story of the offerings of both materials and time the Israelites made to construct the tabernacle. Those who had willing hearts were to give various supplies needed to construct the tent of meeting. Their generosity was their response of faith to the God who delivered them and promised to dwell among them. The response of the people was so overwhelming that Moses had to tell the people not to bring any more offerings, because they had more than enough (Exod. 36: 4-7).

Animal sacrifices were offered to God as an acknowl-edgment that all life comes from Him. Those animal sacrifices also atoned for the sins of the people. In most of the sacrifices at the temple, some of the meat went to the priests to provide for their needs. In every case, the offerings, whether animal or grain, were to be the best, not the leftovers or the rejects. God expressed anger through the prophet Malachi at His people because they were offering blind, crippled, and diseased animals as sacrifices. It was an insult to God, and He refused to accept them (Mal. 1:6-14). The Jews of Malachi's day prove that it is possible to give without worshiping, but it is not possible to worship without giving the best. God wanted their first-fruits, the firstborn given to Him.

In the first century, sacrifices were still being offered at the temple. In addition to those, a new practice had been added. Sometime after the exile, every male Jew in the empire was assessed a half-shekel "temple tax." Jews living outside Palestine took up their collection and sent it to the temple in Jerusalem by special representatives. Their collection helped sustain the temple worship and also provided a sense of unity among Jews around the world. The synagogue also took a collection which was primarily used to help the poor and destitute. These Jewish practices of giving and sacrificing are important background to the act of giving in Christian worship.

Giving as a Part of New Testament Worship

Jesus had much to say about money. Someone has estimated that one out of seven words recorded by Jesus deals with our relationship to our possessions. Seventeen of Jesus' 36 parables deal with stewardship. Our Lord taught that it was more blessed to give than to receive (Acts 20:35). The book of Acts bears witness to the concern and generosity of the early Christians for those in need (Acts 2:44-45; 4:32-37; 6:1-7).

The most detailed passages in the New Testament concerning the collection as a part of worship come from Paul's letters to the church in Corinth. Paul wrote: "Now about the collection for God's people: Do what I told the Galatian churches to do. On the first day of every week, each one of you should set aside a sum of money in keeping with his income, saving it up, so that when I come no collections will have to be made" (1 Cor. 16:1-2). These words may seem a bit out of place after such an exalted discussion of the resurrection in chapter 15. However, Paul wrote in 1 Corinthians 15:58, "Always give yourselves fully to the work of the Lord . . . ." It is in that context that Paul said in the very next verse, "Now concerning the collection . . . ." (1 Cor. 16:1). This collection was for the poor saints in the Jerusalem church. We do not know why there was such poverty in that church. We only know that Paul urged them to give to help their brothers and sisters.

This passage is a gold mine of principles. In it there are at least five characteristics of Christian giving.

1) *Giving is a universal practice in the church.*

"Do what I told the Galatian churches to do," Paul wrote (1 Cor. 16:1). Everywhere Paul went, he instructed churches that giving is essential for Christians. It is not optional. Every Christian is to give of his or her means. Jesus had taught his followers, "Freely you have received, freely give." They had received food, shelter, clothing, and life itself from God. We have received those things too, and much more. If we are Christians, we have received forgiveness, salvation, and eternal hope. As we have received freely of God's grace, let us freely give so that others may receive the same.

2) *Giving is a weekly activity.*

Paul commanded them to give "on the first day of every week" (1 Cor. 16:2). Although we have other clear

177

indications in Scripture, this is the clearest passage that assures us they met each first day of the week. It was the Lord's Day, the day of resurrection. Just as important as it was to break bread when they assembled for worship (Acts 20:7), it was also important that they set aside an amount to be offered as a gift.

3) *Giving must be a personal act.*

Who was to give? ". . .each one of you," Paul said in verse 2. No one is left out. Each individual has the opportunity and the command to give. The amount does not matter to God, not as long as the heart is right. The person Jesus chose to hold up as an illustration of a generous heart was the widow who gave her last pennies (Mark 12:42-43). The amount mattered little to Jesus. What touched Him was that in faith and trust she gave all she had — little though it was. Even children should be taught to give. If nothing more than a few coins, children need to learn early the privilege, the responsibility, and the joy of giving. It is not enough simply for them to watch Daddy and Mommy put their money in the collection. It needs to be a personal act for them as well. Habits, both good and bad, often start early.

4) *Giving is to be a predetermined amount.*

Paul taught, "Set aside a sum of money. . . ." (1 Cor. 16:2). What we give the Lord ought to be planned in advance. This is not meant to discourage spontaneous giving. Needs arise often that require an immediate response of generosity. However, when we gather in assembly on the Lord's day, we should have given thought to the amount we intend to offer. God does not want our leftovers. He is not pleased with our last minute, spur-of-the-moment decisions. Some Christians give more thought and planning to what they will buy and how much they will spend on birthday and Christmas presents than what they will give for God's work.

There are three reasons why we should predetermine

our gifts. One, obedience to God requires it. Paul said to set aside a sum of money. Two, response to Christ demands it. Jesus came to earth with a plan. His birth, His teaching, His death, His ascension did not come about by accident. It all happened according to the fore-thought and planning of the heavenly Father. If Jesus did that for us out of a predetermined plan, should we not do likewise? "For you know the grace of our Lord Jesus Christ, that though he was rich, yet for your sakes he became poor, so that you through his poverty might become rich" (2 Cor. 8:9).

Madam Chiang Kai-shek tells the story of a hero of the Chinese rice fields during an earthquake. From his hilltop farm he felt the quake and saw the distant ocean swiftly withdraw from the shore line, like some hungry animal crouching back for a leap. He knew that the leap would be a tidal wave. In the valleys below, he saw his neighbors working low fields that would be flooded. They must be gathered quickly to his hilltop. His rice barns were dry as tinder. So with a torch he set fire to them and rang the fire gong that hung beneath the eaves. His neighbors saw the smoke and rushed to help him. Then from their safe perch on the hill, they saw the waters cover over the fields they had just left. Imme-diately they knew their friend had saved their lives, and they knew the cost to their friend. In gratitude, they erected a monument in his honor. It read: "He gave us all he had, and gave it gladly." Jesus gave all He had, and gave it gladly and with predetermination. In gratitude, let us give back to Him with the same kind of joy and predetermination.

The third reason we should give a predetermined amount is because godly priorities demand it. Predetermined giving puts God first. When the bills start piling in we may be tempted to put our contributions off until the creditors are happy. God expects us to pay our debts; that is not the point. Without a predetermined plan, we probably will be able to give God only the left-overs. We must give to God first, and then learn to live on what is left. "Honor the Lord with your wealth, with the firstfruits of all your crops; then your barns will be filled to overflowing, and your vats will brim over with new wine" (Prov. 3:9).

5) *Giving should be a proportional amount.*

Paul commanded each one to give ". . .in keeping with his income" (1 Cor. 16:2). The New Testament does not prescribe a percentage of income to give. We know that God loves a cheerful giver (2 Cor. 9:7). We also know that Paul commended the Macedonian brethren for being generous and for "giving as much as they were able and even beyond their ability." He also praised them for their "eager willingness" to share (2 Cor. 8 and 9).

That still does not provide us a specific amount or percentage of our income to give. Perhaps the Old Testament can provide some helpful guidelines. The minimum amount the Jew was commanded to give was ten percent, a tithe (Lev. 27:30-33). In addition to that, many Jews gave other free will offerings. Abraham gave a tithe of all he had to Melchizedek (Gen. 14:20). Jacob offered to God a tithe of all he had (Gen. 28:20-22).

The prophet Malachi charged God's people with robbery because they were giving God less than their tithe (Mal. 3:8-9). Someone may object, "Yes, but that was the Old Covenant. We're under the new covenant and not obligated to the regulations of the Old." That is true, but does God expect less from us than from the Jews? Jesus announced, "For I tell you that unless your righteousness surpasses that of the Pharisees and the teachers of the law, you will certainly not enter the king-dom of heaven" (Matt. 5:20). Is our inheritance with Jesus Christ richer than the inheritance the Hebrews had under the Old covenant? Jewish Christians of the first century probably could not have contemplated giving less than ten percent.

Although it is not proper to legislate a tithe in the Christian era, it is my judgment that a tithe is a good starting place for Christians. Those who criticize this guideline are usually people who feel that a tithe calls for too much. I have never heard anyone say, "I don't believe in the tithe because it keeps me from giving as much as I would like to give." The January, 1989 issue of *Moody Monthly* reported the findings of a Gallup Poll which indicated that the greater a household's income, the smaller percentage it gave to charity. The statistics across the board are sad: those making $10,000 to $30,000 a year gave 2.5 percent; $30,000 to $50,000 gave 2.0 percent; $75,000 to $100,000 gave 1.7 percent.

Those statistics represent a broad sweep of Americans, believers and non-believers together. As you might expect, Christians give at a higher percentage than non-Christians. But do not take too much consolation. If the polls are correct, less than five percent of Christians give a tithe. Using the Jewish standard, 95 percent of Christians are robbing God. If our hearts really are where our treasures are, these figures indicate that the majority of Christian hearts are not with the Lord's work.

Joe Barnett tells the story about a treasurer of a congregation who resigned and the church asked another man to take his position. The man ran the large grain elevator in this farming community. He agreed to take the job on two conditions: one, that no report from the treasurer would have to be given for one whole year, and two, that no one would ask him any questions during that year. Members gulped, but they finally agreed because he was a trusted man in the community, he was well known, and most of them did business with him at his grain elevator. At the end of the year he gave his report:

— the indebtedness of $250,000 on our church building has been paid.

— the missions quota has been paid and oversubscribed by 200 percent.

— there are no outstanding bills.

— there's a cash balance of $12,000.

Immediately the shocked congregation began asking how such a thing could happen. He said, "Most of you bring your grain to my elevator, and as you did business with me during this past year, I simply withheld ten percent on your behalf and contributed it to the church in your name. You never missed it." What wonderful things could be accomplished if every believer would give ten percent to God's work.

Some time after Paul's first letter to the Corinthian church, he felt it necessary to send them another letter in which he reminded them of their commitment to give to the poor saints in Jerusalem (2 Cor. 8 and 9). Perhaps they needed some encouragement, even a little prodding, to keep their commitment. Perhaps they needed some inspiration or even a model of generosity to spur them on. If that was what they needed, Paul provided the Corinthian Christians an excellent example in the Macedonian churches. As Paul held up the Macedonian Christians, he held up Jesus as the supreme example of giving. Paul directly tied Jesus' sacrificial gift of Himself to the grace of God (2 Cor. 8:1, 9).

Stop! I want you to read 2 Corinthians chapters 8 and 9 before you go any farther. As you read, be looking for characteristics of giving. Have you read those two chapters? What did you discover about giving? I see at least six principles concerning giving from this important passage:

1) *Giving is a privilege.*

The text says, "Entirely on their own, they urgently pleaded with us for the privilege of sharing in this service to the saints" (2 Cor. 8:4). Is that not amazing? Here were a group of Christians who were in extreme poverty themselves, suffering severe trial, but giving "as much as they were able, and even beyond their ability (2 Cor. 8:2-3). Their rich generosity welled up out of a sense of overflowing joy in the Lord. Imagine that! They displayed an almost reckless happiness at being able to share with others in need. No doubt, they were motivated by the gift of Jesus on their own behalf.

Do you feel happy when you give? Is there an "over-flowing joy"? There needs to be because "God loves a cheerful giver" (2 Cor. 9:7). I love the story about a father who wanted to teach his young son a good lesson. He gave the boy a quarter and a dollar for the contribution for worship. "Put whichever one you want in the collection plate and keep the other for yourself," he told the boy. After the services were over, the father asked his son which amount he had given. "Well," said the boy, "I was going to give the dollar, but just before the collection the preacher reminded everyone that the Lord loves a cheerful giver. I knew I'd be a lot more cheerful if I gave the quarter, so I did." Sound like any experiences you have ever had?

The word *cheerful* in 2 Corinthians 9:7 is the Greek word from which we get our word *hilarious*. That is great! God loves hilarious givers! It would be wonderful to see smiles on faces when brothers and sisters drop contributions in the offering plate. Imagine a husband smiling as he says to his wife, "Put it all in, Honey. Just put all the money in." And she responds, "Isn't it wonderful that we can share like this with others?" And as they pass the plate down the row they look at each other and laugh for joy!

Ben Rogers tells the following story. Suppose you go for your annual checkup and the doctor begins to poke, prod, and press various places, all the while asking,

"Does this hurt? How about this?" If you cry out in pain, one of two things has happened. Either the doctor has pushed too hard, without the right sensitivity. Or more likely, there is something wrong, and the doctor will say, "We'd better do some more tests. It's not supposed to hurt there!" So it is when preachers start talking about giving, and certain members cry out in discomfort, criticizing the message and the messenger. Either the preacher has pushed too hard. Or more likely there is something wrong. In that case, the preacher needs to say, "My friend, we're in need of the Great Physician because it's not supposed to hurt there."

If we understand giving as God intended it, giving is not an obligation — it is a privilege.

2) *We must give ourselves first.*

"They gave themselves first to the Lord and then to us" (2 Cor. 8:5). That explains the source of their willing sacrifice. They gave themselves because Jesus had given Himself first. They knew that Jesus had made Himself poor in order to make them spiritually rich (2 Cor. 8:9). Once they were guilty, undeserving aliens and enemies, but now they had become adopted children and joint-heirs with Christ. They simply wanted to give themselves back to the Lord. They gave not just their money and possessions, they surrendered their very lives to Him.

When Fiji was still a cannibal island, James Calvert and a group of determined missionaries decided to go there with the gospel. The captain of the ship in which they traveled tried to talk them out of going. "You'll risk your life and all those with you if you go among those savages," he reasoned. Calvert's magnificent reply was, "We died before we came here." That is the spirit of giving oneself. When God's grace takes root in us, we cannot help but give ourselves. The gift of God's grace teaches us the grace of giving.

3) *We are to excel in the grace of giving.*

Paul commended the Corinthian Christians for the way they had excelled in faith, knowledge, earnestness, and love, but he also challenged them: "see that you also excel in this grace of giving" (2 Cor. 8:7). Excelling in the grace of giving has more to do with how we give and why we give than with the amount we give. God wants us to give cheerfully, generously, gratefully, as we have prospered.

4) *We reap what we sow.*

Every farmer knows the truthfulness of Paul's words, "Whoever sows sparingly will also reap sparingly, and whoever sows generously will also reap generously" (9:6). A farmer looking for a large harvest will not skimp on the seed he puts in the ground. Neither should Christians who contribute to the Lord's work. Solomon wrote:

> One man gives freely, yet gains even more;
> another withholds unduly, but comes to poverty.
> A generous man will prosper;
> he who refreshes others will himself be refreshed.
> (Prov. 11:24-25)

> He who is kind to the poor lends to the Lord,
> and he will reward him for what he has done.
> (Prov. 19:17)

> He who gives to the poor will lack nothing,
> but he who closes his eyes to them receives many curses.
> (Prov. 28:27).

To the Galatian church, Paul wrote:

> A man reaps what he sows. . . Let us not become weary in doing good, for at the proper time we will reap a harvest if we do not give up. Therefore, as we have opportunity, let us do good to all people, especially to those who belong to the family of believers.
> (Gal. 6:7,9-10)

185

I do not believe that God wants us to give with the immature motivation that we will get something in return. There are better reasons to give. But the truth remains as sure as God's promises stand. If we sow generously, we will reap generously. The disciple of Christ cannot lose: when he gives all, he gains all; when he loses his life, he finds it. Jim Elliot, martyred as a missionary to the Auca Indians in South America in 1956, summed it up like this: "He is no fool who gives what he cannot keep to gain what he cannot lose."

5) *God will replenish what we sow.*

We can never outgive God's ability to refill the store-house. Note the *italicized* words in 2 Corinthians 9:8: "And God is able to make all grace abound to you, so that in *all* things at *all* times, having *all* that you need, you will abound in every good work." Did you notice that little three-letter word "all"? It is significant. God is the great, inexhaustible source of all life and blessings. Everything belongs to Him. "The earth is the LORD's, and the fullness thereof" (Ps. 24:1, KJV). There is the song I learned at camp several years ago that goes like this:

> He owns the cattle on a thousand hills,
> The wealth in every mine.
> He owns the rivers and the rocks and rills,
> The stars and moon that shine.
> Wonderful blessings, more than tongue can tell.
> They are my Savior's, so they're mine as well.
> He owns the cattle on a thousand hills,
> I know the Lord will care for me.

As stewards of God's grace and goodness, we become agents of His grace and goodness to others. There is a tremendous circular promise God makes. As long as God gives to us, we are to give to others. As long as we give to others, God keeps giving to us. And the cycle never stops. God's inventory never runs low. God's gifts know no recession as long as we give the way He teaches us to give. Nowhere are we taught that God will bless us abundantly for selfish purposes. On the contrary, God sternly warns against greed. The parable of the rich fool is a warning to anyone who would hoard this world's goods for himself. God gives and replenishes our supply so that we can pass His blessings on to others. God wants us to "abound in every good work" (2 Cor. 9:8).

Wayne Horton tells about the time when Abraham Lincoln's business was failing. His partner asked how much longer he thought they could keep going. Lincoln said, "It looks like our business is about winked out." He further said, "If there was a way, I'd sell this business and buy one book, a copy of *Blackstone's Commentary on English Law,* but there's no way to sell the business, so I guess I'll never be a lawyer." A little later a family in a wagon came by. They were moving west and they were about out of money. Lincoln was offered a barrel for 50 cents to help them along. He took his last 50 cents from his pocket and gave it to the man in exchange for a barrel he did not need. Later that evening, Lincoln was looking in the barrel. At the bottom he found some old papers and to his surprise, a copy of *Blackstone's Commentary on English Law.*

Jesus promised, "Give, and it will be given to you. A good measure, pressed down, shaken together and running over, will be poured into your lap. For with the measure you use, it will be measured to you" (Luke 6:38). God's promise to replenish does not get any more plain: "Now he who supplies seed to the sower and bread for food will also supply and increase your store of seed and will enlarge the harvest of your righteousness. You will be made rich in every way *so that you can be generous on every occasion*" (2 Cor. 9:10-11). Paul was not suggesting that Christianity be viewed as a sound business investment bringing certain material rewards. He was not guaranteeing us a $150 return on a $100 gift/investment. God is not in competition with Merrill Lynch. God may not give back to us more of the same thing we have given. He may choose to bless us in some other way than money for money. One thing is for certain. When we give to help the Lord's work, God will always give back blessings enough to enable us to continue giving. Jesus promised, "Seek first his kingdom and his righteousness, and all these things will be given to you as well" (Matt. 6:33).

6) *Generous giving results in thanksgiving and praise to God.*

The natural response to God's grace and goodness is a heart of thankfulness, gratitude, and praise. Look at what Paul says will result from generous giving:

> . . .your generosity will result in thanksgiving to God. This service that you perform is not only supplying the needs of God's people but is also overflowing in many expressions of thanks to God. Because of the service by which you have proved yourselves, men will praise God for the obedience that accompanies your confession of the gospel of Christ, and for your generosity in sharing with them and with everyone else. And in their prayers for you their hearts will go out to you, because of the surpassing grace God has given you. Thanks be to God for his indescribable gift! (2 Cor. 9:11-15).

Seldom was Paul at a loss for words, but God's gracious gift of Jesus was so marvelous, so valuable, that he could not find words adequate to describe it.

So often we come to worship with misplaced emphasis. We come seeking a blessing when we should come seeking to make an offering. Our offerings in worship are an expression of our gratitude and appreciation to God for all He does for us. Our gifts are a symbol of the sacrifice we make — a sacrifice of ourselves and all that we possess. Paul wrote, "I urge you, brothers, in view of God's mercy, to offer your bodies as living sacrifices, holy and pleasing to God — this is your spiritual act of worship" (Rom. 12:1). The writer of Hebrews commands, "Through Jesus, therefore, let us continually offer to God a sacrifice of praise — the fruit of lips that confess his name. And do not forget to do good and to share with others, for with such sacrifices God is pleased" (Heb. 13:15-16).

Ours is not a choice of either giving ourselves or our possessions to Him who gave them. If we comprehend the salvation we graciously have been given, we will return both life and possessions. We will give both the praise of our lips to God and the material means at our disposal to help those in need. When our hearts are right, no one will have to beg us to give. Generosity will overflow from a grateful heart. Isaac Watts captured the thought extremely well:

> When I survey the wondrous cross
> on which the Prince of Glory died,
> My richest gain I count but loss,
> And pour contempt on all my pride.
>
> Were the whole realm of nature mine,
> That were a present far too small;
> Love so amazing, so divine,
> Demands my soul, my life my all.

DISCUSSION QUESTIONS
ON CHAPTER EIGHT

1. Read John 3:16. What did God's love motivate Him to do?

2. In 2 Corinthians 8:1-9, Paul ties giving with the grace of God. How are they connected?

3. How is giving an act of worship?

4. Is it possible to worship God acceptably through giving if one has not first given themselves to God? Support your answer.

5. Read 2 Corinthians 9:7. What is a cheerful giver? How cheerful may we be when we give? Why does God love a cheerful giver? How does cheerful giving influence worship?

6. The Old Testament commanded a tithe. Should Christians give a tithe today? Support your answer.

7. Is it possible to worship and not give?

8. In 2 Corinthians 9:11-15, Paul ties giving and thanksgiving together. How does a thankful heart relate to worship?

9
Listen Up — God is Speaking

If you spend much time reading the history of Christian worship, you'll find that the two primary elements observed by the church throughout the ages have been the ministry of the Word (including both the reading of Scripture and preaching) and the ministry of the Lord's Supper. Hearing the Word of God and sharing in the Lord's Supper are foundations of Christian worship. In the earliest days of the church there was equal emphasis on both the Word and the Supper. However, during the Middle Ages, the Catholic Church gradually magnified the place of the Supper (or Eucharist, as they called it) above the Word.

Leaders of the Protestant Reformation sought to restore the unity of the Word and the Supper, but were not wholly successful. John Calvin wanted the church to observe the Lord's Supper weekly, but his view failed to win broad approval. Ulrich Zwingli's view that the Lord's Supper should be taken quarterly held sway throughout most of the Protestant world. Protestants, in contrast to Roman Catholics, have tended to magnify the place of the Word over the Lord's Supper.[1] Churches tied to the Restoration Movement have maintained the view that there must be an emphasis on both the Word and the Supper.

---

[1]Hunter Beckelhymer, "The Place of Preaching in Worship: A Theological Rationale," *Encounter* 44, no. 3 (1983): p. 280.

Reading the Word of God

The Importance of Scripture to the Jews

The Israelites always had Scripture at the center of their worship. After the Hebrew nation left Egyptian bondage, the Lord called Moses to the top of Mt. Sinai to receive His laws and commands. Exodus 24:1-7 describes a setting of worship in which Moses read the Book of the Covenant to the people. They responded by pledging their obedience to the words of God. God had warned Israel against idolatry or making any graven images which the people might worship (Exod. 20:4-5). This injunction probably explains why the ancient Jews showed little development of the visual arts. However, they had few equals in the arts of the Word. Over the centuries they displayed a deep respect for poetry, history, law, narrative, and preaching. They lovingly nurtured Scripture. They were a people of the Book.

The Old Testament book of Nehemiah tells the story of Ezra the scribe who made the reading of Scripture central to Jewish worship. Ezra played an important role at a critical time in the nation's history. Nebuchadnezzar and the mighty Babylonian army had destroyed Jerusalem, along with Solomon's temple, in 597 B.C. For the next 70 years the Israelites lived in Babylonian exile, far removed from their beloved homeland. Under Persian rule, the Hebrews were finally allowed to go back to Jerusalem. Led by Nehemiah, the people rebuilt the walls of the city, and under the direction of Ezra, the people began to rebuild their spiritual lives.

Before going any farther, stop and read Nehemiah 8:1-8. Did you notice any principles in that passage concerning the use of the Word? I see at least five.

1) *It is important to read Scripture aloud in the public assembly.*

Did you notice how long Ezra read from the Law?

From daybreak until noon! What is more, Ezra read from the Book of the Law for several days (v. 18), and the people listened attentively! (v. 3). It was not Ezra's charisma that made the deep impression; the people were focused on the book.

2) *They showed respect for the Word of God.*

When Ezra opened the book, the people stood out of reverence. Nothing is said about them sitting down, so possibly they stood for half a day listening to the Lord's Word. They knew they were not hearing the *Jerusalem Daily Times* — they were listening to God speak.

3) *The people were actively involved in the reading.*

Good listening itself is hard work, but they did even more than listen attentively. They lifted their hands and responded, "Amen! Amen!" They even bowed down with their faces to the ground as they worshiped the Lord (v. 6). As the Word of God was being read, no one was passing notes, snoozing, or making out their grocery shopping list. They engaged in focused participation.

4) *Qualified teachers instructed the people.*

The people needed help understanding the meaning of the Law which they had just heard (vv. 7-8). The Law of Moses was in the Hebrew language. However, the Israelites had been away from their native land and language for 70 years. No doubt, many of them could no longer speak, read, or understand the language. Even if some could understand the language, many of them were unable to apply it. Therefore, they needed instruction. This is still the place of preaching and teaching in the church today — making the meaning of God's Word clear and applicable.

5) *The reading of the Word of God ought to lead to obedience.*

It certainly did among the people who listened to the Word of God as Ezra read it. Finish reading Nehemiah 8 and then read the ninth chapter. The people confessed their sins, repented of their wickedness, worshiped God, and committed themselves to following God's ways. If we read the Bible in our worship assemblies in check-list fashion just to say we have done it, we are insulting God. If we read it merely to gain facts and intellectual stimulation, we are probably only fueling our prideful egos. But if we read Scripture with the intent to hear and follow God's voice, the effort will lead us to genuine obedience to God's will.

Scripture Reading – The Primary Element in Synagogue Worship

It was during that long Babylonian exile that many scholars believe the synagogue was born. It was the synagogue and not the temple which fostered the study of Scripture and elevated it to the position it has continued to hold in Judaism. The primary element in synagogue worship was the reading and exposition of Scripture. The Law was read, first in Hebrew and then in Aramaic paraphrases, known as Targums.[2] Actually there were two readings. The first reading came from the Law. Not only was it a longer reading, but it was also predetermined for each Sabbath. The shorter reading came from the prophets and could be selected at random by the person chosen to read. After the reading, there would be an exhortation based on the day's text.

An important reference to this pattern is Luke 4:16-27 where Jesus went to the synagogue in his hometown of Nazareth. When He was handed the scroll of Isaiah He stood to read the passage which He selected for the occasion. When He had finished reading, He sat down and interpreted and applied the passage. The early church quickly adopted this Jewish custom of public reading from the Law and Prophets. As evangelists like

---

[2]Martin, *Worship in the Early Church*, pp. 66-67.

Paul and Barnabas entered new cities on their missionary journeys they visited the synagogues where there
were readings from the Law and the Prophets, followed
by exposition and application of the texts (Acts 13:14-
44). While teaching in the synagogue, New Testament
evangelists showed how Jesus Christ fulfilled the Law
and the Prophets (Acts 17:2-3).

Scripture Reading in Early Christian Worship

The first Christians were Jews. It should not be
surprising that they would bring to their newly found
faith and worship the custom of reading from Scripture.
The Scriptures pointed them to Jesus as the Christ. The
Apostle Paul clearly expected even his Gentile readers to
be acquainted with the Old Testament. Paul often made
references to subtle details and undertones of the Old
Testament (Rom. 4:1-23; 9:7-9; Gal. 3:6-9; 4:21-31; 1 Cor.
6:16; 10:1-10; 2 Cor. 3:7-18). This leads us to believe that
readings from the Old Testament were common among
the Gentile churches. Many scholars believe that the
church replaced readings from the Law with recitations
from the Psalms. The Psalms were long used by the Jews
as acclamations of praise to God. The early Christians
easily incorporated the Psalms into their own worship.[3]

Paul wrote to the young preacher, Timothy, "Until I
come, devote yourself to the public reading of Scripture,
to preaching and to teaching" (1 Tim. 4:13). Timothy
understood "Scripture" to be the Old Testament. The
canon of the New Testament had not yet been
completed when Paul wrote those instructions.
However, Paul regarded his own letters as inspired by
the Holy Spirit and expected that they would be read
in Christian assemblies. "After this letter has been read
to you, see that it is also read in the church of the

---

[3]Hieronymus, p. 38.

Laodiceans and that you in turn read the letter from Laodicea" (Col. 4:16). "I charge you before the Lord to have this letter read to all the brothers" (1 Thess. 5:27). From these passages it is evident that reading the Word of God was considered an act of worship in biblical times.

Justin Martyr, a second century teacher and apologist, gives us a detailed description of one congregation's worship. He wrote, "the memoirs of the Apostles or the writings of the prophets are read as long as time permits" (*1st Apology* 67). Over the last several centuries, Protestant churches have elevated the place of preaching in worship. Preaching is an important part of worship and one key way to minister the Word to people. However, the sermon must not take the place of simply reading God's Word in the assembly. These words of Martin Luther have the ring of truth: "When I declare the Word of God I offer sacrifice. When thou hearest the Word of God with all thy heart, thou dost offer sacrifice."[4] The real question that churches must face is whether or not they want Scripture to be at the center of Christian worship. Revivalism needed only a verse or two to launch into a sermon, but the church needs a steady, strong diet of God's Word, both read and preached.[5]

The Value of Bible Reading in Worship

The Scriptures reveal what no other book discloses. The Bible is the record of God's covenant with humanity. It tells of His love and mercy. It is a witness of His saving acts on behalf of all people. It tells of Jesus and the salvation He brings. It records human experiences

---

[4]Wiersbe, p. 121.

[5]James F. White, "The Missing Jewel of the Evangelical Church," *The Reformed Journal* 26, no. 6 (1986): p. 14.

and how people have worshiped God, both acceptably and unacceptably. The Bible tells of God's expectations and His grace, of His goodness and faithfulness, of His righteousness and justice. It is the sword of the Holy Spirit (Eph. 6:17). I love the words of the Scottish preacher and writer, Thomas Cuthrie:

> The Bible is an armory of heavenly weapons, a laboratory of infallible medicines, a mine of exhaustless wealth. It is a guidebook for every road, a chart for every sea, a medicine for every malady, and a balm for every wound. Rob us of our Bible and our sky has lost its sun.

Books of science, literature and history may enlighten us, but no book gives life except the Bible. Indeed, it is a living Word. People will never be transformed into Christ's likeness unless they encounter Him in the Word of God. God's Word is truth (John 17:17). The world's perspective of reality is a false one. Only Scripture paints a true picture of reality. Satan has blinded many people to the truth, leading them to believe that Scripture is irrelevant to their modern lives. George Barna writes, "Until people see the Bible as a practical guidebook for their everyday existence, it will probably continue to remain on the shelf next to *The Complete Works of Shakespeare* or *War and Peace*."[6]

Christians must be drawn back into the inspired pages of Scripture. Reading Scripture is necessary both individually and collectively when we assemble to worship, for it is in Scripture that we encounter the Lord and begin to grow up in Him. Franklin Segler writes, "The Bible is the life book of the church. It provides objective content for worship. It points man to God, the source of truth and life."[7] We cannot appreci-

---

[6]George Barna, *Moody Monthly* July/August (1989): p. 72.
[7]Segler, pp. 65-66.

ate the God of the Word until we appreciate the Word of God.

Although it records events of the past, the Bible is much more than stories of ancient times and people and places far away. Its message is relevant to life here and now. Paul wrote, "All Scripture is God-breathed and is useful for teaching, rebuking, correcting and training in righteousness, so that the man of God may be thoroughly equipped for every good work" (2 Tim. 3:16-17).

A Dozen Suggestions Concerning the Reading of God's Word

Here are twelve suggestions that will help restore the Word to its rightful place in worship.

1) *Read Scripture aloud in worship – and read more of it.*

We must read it more frequently than many of our churches are accustomed to doing. For a people who are proud of our Restoration heritage and claim to be "a people of the Book," most of our congregations read the Bible surprisingly little in our assemblies.

In many congregations there is a reading of Scripture before the sermon, but it is usually very brief — perhaps only a few verses. If we truly are going to be a people who "speak where the Bible speaks and are silent where the Bible is silent," we must become more intimately acquainted with the Word. Preachers may need to shorten sermons or congregations may need to lengthen worship services to allow more time for the reading of Scripture. No preacher's wit or wisdom takes the place of reading the Word. Charles Schulz, the creator of the cartoon strip "Peanuts," drew a high school boy telling his girlfriend, "I think I've finally begun to unravel the mystery of the Old Testament." She responded, "Yea? How's that?" "I've started to read it," he quipped. Let us start reading Scripture in our assemblies, and more of it.

We cannot appreciate the God of the Word until we appreciate the Word of God.

2) *Follow biblical commands and examples for the public reading of God's Word.*

Reading the Word in worship was extremely important to the Jews in the synagogue and to the early Christians in their assemblies. We are creatures of habit and tradition, seldom questioning why we do what we do or fail to do. Such is the case regarding the reading of Scripture in worship. Many Christians have been members of churches which for years, and perhaps all their lives, have never given much attention to the reading of Scripture in worship. When we ignore the public reading of Scripture we are out of step with biblical and historical examples.

3) *Show reverence for God's Word when it is read in worship.*

People demonstrate their lack of reverence in a number of ways. When the Bible is being read in worship it is not unusual to see people fidgeting and fumbling with things, shuffling in and out of the assembly, talking and passing notes. Most people would not do those things during a prayer. Even at secular events such as a football game, a hush blankets the stadium when someone offers a prayer. Why would we show respect when we are talking to God and not show the same reverence when God is talking to us? That is, after all, what Scripture is — God speaking to us!

We also demonstrate an irreverent attitude if we complain when asked to stand at the reading of God's Word. Those of us who are healthy will stand on our feet for hours at a sporting event or in the shopping mall. Given that fact, is it not sinful that a Christian would grumble at being asked to rise at the reading of God's Word? Is there anyone who is physically capable of standing who would not rise if the President of the

United States were to walk into the room? Should we not be more anxious to stand out of respect for God when He speaks to us?

There is no verse in the New Testament which *commands* us to stand when Scripture is read. Therefore, it would be wrong to insinuate that one is sinning if he or she sits during a Scripture reading. I certainly am not advocating that we stand up every time the preacher reads a verse of Scripture in his sermon. If he referred to several, we would all be see-sawing up and down throughout the entire lesson. That would be most distracting, not to mention exhausting. What I am suggesting is that we plan for longer readings of Scripture which are not a part of the sermon — readings which stand alone in our services just like prayers and the Lord's Supper stand alone to receive our undivided attention. Let us read an entire chapter or chapters of the Bible, and like the Israelites in Ezra's day, let us listen attentively and reverently.

4) *Encourage Christians to bring their own Bibles to worship.*

Most of the time, Christians should read along with the worship leader and follow the preacher as he studies various passages with the assembled group. At times it may be more meaningful simply to listen to the reading. However, for the most part, we should be like those noble Bereans (Acts 17) who examined the Scriptures daily to see if what they were being taught was true to the Word. That Berean-type examination takes place not only at home after the assembly is dismissed, but also during the sermon itself.

5) *Select good readers for public reading of Scripture.*

If the Bible is read poorly in the assembly, it becomes a hindrance to worshipers trying to listen to the voice of God. Consider starting a readers' group to train readers. Encourage the reading of Scripture in Bible classes to give boys and men the opportunity to gain experience in reading publicly. Most congregations would not think of calling on people to lead singing who do not sing well, who stammer and stutter and mispronounce the words of the songs. Neither should we call on men to read Scripture who read poorly. God's Word deserves to be read publicly as well as it possibly can be read.[8]

6) *Place Bibles in the pews.*

This is not to discourage people from bringing their own Bibles. However, supplying the pews with Bibles provides copies for those who come without one, and it also allows everyone to read from the same translation of Scripture.

7) *Devote entire services to reading the Word of God.*

Why not? If the Bible is as important as we claim it is, we need to schedule more opportunities to read it in assembly. This would be easy to schedule, especially on Sunday evening and mid-week assemblies. Devoting the entire service to Scripture reading does not mean that the assembled group cannot sing and pray as well. Just make Scripture reading the heart of the service. With a little forethought and creativity, this can be one of the most meaningful times for a congregation.

One congregation devoted a Sunday night to reading the Old Testament story of Job. During the week, prior to the worship service, the preacher selected key verses representing the thoughts of each of the book's characters. Different men, dressed in authentic garb, stood on the platform and read the lines of the major characters in the story: Job, Bildad, Eliphaz, Zophar, and Elihu. There was even a strong, low voice off stage who spoke the words of God, and an evil-sounding voice off stage speaking the words of Satan. On another Sunday evening the congregation focused on the readings from

---

[8]Webber, *Worship is a Verb*, p. 77.

the book of Revelation which depicted John's visions of the scenes of worship around God's throne in heaven. Those sections of Scripture were interposed with songs and prayers that highlighted the thoughts of the readings.

Not every reading requires this type of elaborate planning. The point is to make time to read longer sections of the Bible in public worship assemblies.

8) *Encourage families to read the Bible together at home.*

Deuteronomy 6:4-9 establishes the biblical foundation for keeping the Word of God in the forefront of the home. Church leaders should strive to help parents learn how to share the Bible effectively in their homes. Although it is vitally important that the assembled people of God hear His Word, nothing can take the place of families reading Scripture in their own homes. It is in the home that children best learn a deep love and respect for the Word. The truth is that if we are not reading the Bible at home, reading it in assembly will not be as meaningful as it could and should be.

9) *Read and study the Bible personally and individually.*

Most of us take the Bible for granted. Not long ago I counted the Bibles which I and my family own. You probably would expect a preacher to have a few more copies than the average person, but even I was shocked when I counted more than 30 copies of Scripture in my office and home. Yet, I confess that there are days when I do not read and study even one of those copies. It wounds my wicked pride to make that confession, but it's true, and I am ashamed. However, I wonder how much more I would hunger and thirst for the Word if it were not so readily available.

Many Americans followed the story of Terry Anderson, the Associated Press chief Middle East correspondent, who was kidnapped by Shiite fundamentalists and held as a hostage in Lebanon for seven years. At times he was beaten. Most of the time he was blind-folded and chained. He was physically abused more often than he can recount. The news of his release made headlines worldwide. What did not make as much news were these words which he penned shortly after his release:

> Constantly over the years, I found consolation and counsel in the Bible I was given in the first few weeks. The comfort was from the real, immediate voices of people who had suffered greatly, and in ways that seemed so close to what I was going through. I read the Bible more than 50 times, cover to cover, in those first few years.[9]

Do you not suppose Terry Anderson listens more attentively to Scripture when it is read aloud now than he did before his capture? Without question, his heart has been made more sensitive by the suffering he endured. Whether or not it will take suffering in our lives to make us more sensitive to God's word, I do not know. But I do know that the public reading of Scripture is sweeter to those who make a habit of reading and studying it privately. Many Christians find it helpful to pick a quiet time and place for Bible reading. It might also be helpful to find a private place and time to read the Bible aloud. Involving both the senses of sight and sound will aid you in retaining what you read.

One other thing that is helpful during personal Bible study is to memorize Scripture. The Restoration preacher, Walter Scott, urged church leaders to memorize a chapter of Scripture a day.[10] Few of us have time to memorize a chapter a day. Even if we memorized a verse a week, having just that much Scripture written on our hearts would be a tremendous blessing and strength.

---

[9]Terry Anderson, "Ex-Hostage Anderson Slips Gently Back Into Chaos of 'Real World,'" *The Tennessean*, March 15, 1992, Section A, p. 26.

[10]Hieronymus, p. 120.

Charles Swindoll tells a story about being in Canada for eight days with two more days to go. He was lonely and with nothing he really wanted to do. As he was walking toward the elevator he heard two young women talking and laughing as they used the hotel phone. He smiled and passed on by and punched the "up" button on the elevator. He got on. So did these two young women. He punched "6," but they didn't punch any button, so he asked them what floor. One looked at him rather sensuously and said, "How about floor six — you got any plans?"

> There he was, all alone with two girls in Canada. And frankly, he was flattered, but he had a decision to make. The things that popped into his mind immediately were not his wife and kids, nor his position or reputation. It was not even the possibility of being seen or set up. None of those things hit him at that instant. The thing that popped into his mind were memorized verses of God's word. "Do not be deceived: God is not mocked. A man reaps what he sows" (Gal. 6:7). "Put on the full armor of God that you may be able to stand firm against the schemes of the devil" (Eph. 6:11). "Even so, consider yourselves to be dead to sin, but alive to God in Christ Jesus. Therefore do not let sin reign in your mortal body that you should obey its lust" (Rom. 6:11-12). Looking back at the two girls, Swindoll replied, "I've got a full evening planned. I'm really not interested." Swindoll wrote, "How grateful I was for the memorized Word."[11]

10) *Engage the congregation in unison and responsive readings from Scripture.*

Psalm 136 is a good example of a passage that can be read responsively. Each of the twenty-six verses of that psalm is followed by the refrain "His love endures forever." The worship leader reads the verse and the congregation responds by reading the refrain in unison.

---

[11]Charles Swindoll, *Three Steps Forward, Two Steps Back* (Nashville: Thomas Nelson, 1980), pp. 100-101.

These practices are centuries old in the church, even going back to antiphonal recitation of Scripture among Jews in the Old Testament.[12] It is a marvelous way of involving the entire assembly in the reading of God's Word.

11) *Invoke God's blessings on the reading of His Word.*

Concerning His Word God said, "It will not return to me empty, but will accomplish what I desire and achieve the purpose for which I sent it" (Isa. 55:11). Both in our times of public worship and in our personal study, let us pray that God will bless the reading of His Word, that it will accomplish its purpose in every heart that hears it.

12) *Consider a regular cycle of Scripture readings.*

Synagogue worship was careful to insure that in due time every section of the Scriptures would be read. Everett Ferguson writes, "The synagogue employed regular cycles of reading, and later lectionary texts of the New Testament suggests that Christians from an early day did the same."[13] It seems almost certain that the early church read from the Prophets (that they might establish the Messiahship of Jesus) and from the Epistles as they received them. As time went on, the Church read from the Gospels and the Epistles on a regular cycle.[14]

Many Christian bookstores carry what is called a lectionary. It is a three-year cycle of suggested Scripture readings for worship. Your congregation might benefit from using a lectionary as a guide for selecting Scripture readings. No doubt, there are some who would object to its use, but that fear is unfounded. It is not a *creed* book. It is merely a tool, nothing more than a suggested sequence of Scripture readings that provide a balance of Scripture from every portion of the Bible. If followed, it will take a congregation through the Bible every three years.

---

[12]Hieronymus, p. 130.
[13]Ferguson, *Early Christians Speak*, p. 87.
[14]Hieronymus, p. 122.

Someone might object that the reason the early church had a cycle of readings was because they did not have printed copies of Scripture available to them as we do. The only access they had to the Scriptures was through a lectionary system of readings. Since we have copies of Scripture, the objection goes, we do not need a cycle of readings like they did. Besides, the argument continues, the New Testament does not command us to use a lectionary — therefore we should not use one. It is correct that early Christians did not have copies of Scripture as we do. However, many Christians who have multiple copies of Scripture have never yet read through the Bible from beginning to end. When they do read they tend to read from the same sections over and over, thus remaining ignorant of entire portions of God's Word. One advantage of using a cycle of readings in the assembly is that people get a balance of Scripture.

One year my congregation was encouraged to purchase copies of *The One Year Bible*, which is divided into 365 portions that gives the reader a section of Scripture each day from the Old Testament, the Psalms, the Proverbs, and the New Testament. As the title indicates, it will take the reader through the Bible in one year. In conjunction with the daily readings, the preachers and the adult Bible class teachers delivered lessons each Sunday from one of the passages in the previous week's schedule. There are other excellent tools such as *The Narrated Bible*, edited by F. LaGard Smith, which also take the reader through the Bible in a year. Obviously, the two resources I have mentioned are designed for personal daily reading and are different from a published lectionary. However, with some creativity, any number of resources can be used to provide a balance of Scripture readings in public worship.

Whether the church uses a published lectionary or devises its own scheme of reading through the Bible over a given period of time, such a plan is no more unscriptural than many other things that aid us in worship such as song books and individual communion cups. If it helps the congregation encounter God, give it a try.

Preaching the Word

The ministry of the Word also involves preaching. Preaching has always held a vital place in the life of God's people. Moses often spoke for God. When the people listened and obeyed, they were blessed, but when they turned deaf ears and ignored the word of God preached through Moses, they suffered the consequences. The prototype of the preacher was the Hebrew prophet who knew his message was from God and who delivered it to people whether or not they were receptive. Just as the synagogue elevated the reading of the Word in services of worship, it also gave rise to exegesis and exposition of Scripture. It is not surprising, then, that preaching played a key role in the birth of the church (Acts 2) and in its continued expansion and maturity.

The book of Acts records the contents of several sermons. Common themes run through the preaching of the young church. The preaching emphasized that Jesus had fulfilled the prophecies of Scripture and that the hope of Israel was a present reality (Acts 2:16; 3:18,24; 10:43). This fulfillment was proven by the life, death, and resurrection of Jesus the Messiah (Acts 2:30; 10:37-39; 5:30; 2:24,32; 3:15; 2:33). Having raised Jesus from the dead, God exalted Him as Lord of all (Acts 2:33-36; 3:13; 4:11).

Their preaching also emphasized the Holy Spirit's presence in the church as the guarantee of God's favor toward His people (Acts 2:17-21,44; 5:32). They preached that Christ will come again as Judge and Savior

(Acts 3:20; 10:42; 17:31). Sermons also appealed for repentance and baptism which resulted in forgiveness, an assurance of salvation, and the gift of the Holy Spirit (Acts 2:38; 3:19; 10:43). Those early sermons recorded much more than the mere facts of God's activity in Christ. Their sermons also declared that God was in Christ reconciling the world to Himself (2 Cor. 5:19). Their preaching not only informed, it also called for a decision. It demanded a response to the God who had provided atonement through Jesus the Christ (1 Cor. 1:18; 2 Cor. 2:15-16).

The preaching of the Apostle Paul echoes the themes found in the sermons in Acts. His sermons were based primarily on three truths. First was the resurrection of Jesus through which God inaugurated a new stage of world history (1 Thess. 1:9-10; 1 Cor. 15:11-19; Rom. 8:34). Second was his reliance upon the Holy Spirit. Paul taught that human wisdom was inadequate for living the Christian life (2 Cor. 3:17-18; 2:3-14; 1 Cor. 2:4,13). Third was the message of reconciliation (2 Cor. 5:18-21). This seems to be Paul's theological rationale for preaching: "We are therefore Christ's ambassadors, as though God were making his appeal through us. We implore you on Christ's behalf: Be reconciled to God" (2 Cor. 5:20).

The book of Acts provides several examples of evangelistic sermons directed to unbelievers. Strangely, the New Testament does not provide the contents of a sermon delivered to believers. Paul preached to a gathering of Christians in Troas (Acts 20:7-12), but we do not know the contents of the lesson. However, as Ilion Jones writes, "Preaching occupied such a prominent place in the New Testament church that it can be said with assurance that their worship would not have been complete without it."[15] In John R. W. Stott's excellent book on

---

[15]Ilion T. Jones, p. 76.

preaching, *Between Two Worlds*, he insists that preaching and worship belong indissolubly to each other:

> All worship is an intelligent and loving response to the revelation of God, because it is the adoration of his Name. Therefore acceptable worship is impossible without preaching. For preaching is making known the Name of the Lord, and worship is praising the Name of the Lord made known. Far from being an alien intrusion into worship, the reading and preaching of the word are actually indispensable to it. The two cannot be divorced. Indeed, it is their unnatural divorce which accounts for the low level of so much contemporary worship. Our worship is poor because our knowledge of God is poor, and our knowledge of God is poor because our preaching is poor. But when the Word of God is expounded in its fullness, and the congregation begins to glimpse the glory of the living God, they bow down in solemn awe and joyful wonder before His throne. It is preaching which accomplishes this, the proclamation of the Word of God in the power of the Spirit of God. That is why preaching is unique and irreplaceable.[16]

Preaching in Second Century Worship and Beyond

The Church in the second century continued to preach the message of God. Justin's *Apology* states that after a reading of the memoirs of the apostles or the writings of the prophets, one who was called the president would get up and give a discourse urging and inviting them to imitate what they had heard. This is evidence that preaching was alive and well in the second century church. Preaching declined during the period from Augustine to Martin Luther, and sermons ceased to be a vital part of worship services. We must credit Luther with restoring preaching to a central place in worship. John Calvin was also a great believer in expository preaching, and he helped put preaching back into the worship services of Protestant churches.

---

[16]John R. W. Stott, *Between Two Worlds* (Grand Rapids: Eerdmans, 1982), pp. 82-83.

The Power of Preaching

There is great power in preaching. Although the gospel seems like foolishness to unbelievers, Paul proclaimed it in Corinth as the power of God (1 Cor. 1:17-25). To the Romans he declared, ". . .I am eager to preach the gospel also to you who are at Rome. I am not ashamed of the gospel, because it is the power of God for the salvation of everyone who believes. . ." (Rom. 1:15-16). The power of preaching is evident in Peter's sermon recorded in Acts 2 and in the cities where Paul and others preached and established churches. Preaching has the power to change lives. In reality, it is the gospel that changes lives, but it takes preaching to communicate that good news. Romans 10:14-15, 17 reads:

> How, then, can they call on the one they have not believed in? And how can they believe in the one of whom they have not heard? And how can they hear without someone preaching to them? And how can they preach unless they are sent? As it is written, "How beautiful are the feet of those who bring good news!" . . . .Consequently, faith comes from hearing the message, and the message is heard through the word of Christ.

The preaching of the gospel has led to changes in the lives of thieves, idolaters, liars, slanderers, gossips, drunks, drug addicts, cheats, and crooks. It has changed people whose lives were sexually immoral, greedy, selfish, proud (1 Cor. 6:9-11).

Preaching also has the power to change those who are already Christians. It helps us face up to our sin and calls on us to repent. It confronts us with the bad news of our guilt so that we can accept the good news of God's grace and forgiveness through the blood of Christ. It turns our eyes inward to see the weakness there and then lifts our eyes up to see God's holiness. Preaching reminds us of God's great deeds in the past so that we have faith to trust Him to work in our lives in the present and the future. It teaches us the truth so that we are not blown by every wind of doctrine (Eph. 4:14). It inspires us and strengthens us when we are weak. It challenges our selfish comforts and prompts us to Christ-like service and obedience. Nothing else has such power.

Although preaching is done by feeble men, God's powerful gospel shines through humble human channels and gives life to hearers. Somewhere I came across a letter written to the editor of the *British Weekly*. It reads:

> Dear Sir:
>   It seems ministers feel their sermons are very important and spend a great deal of time preparing them. I have been attending a church service quite regularly for the past 30 years and I have probably heard 3,000 of them. To my consternation, I discovered that I cannot remember a single sermon. I wonder if a minister's time might be more profitably spent on something else?
>   Sincerely . . .

That letter produced a real storm of editorial responses as readers of the *British Weekly* expressed their feelings on the subject. The uproar finally ended when this letter was published:

> Dear Sir:
>   I have been married for 30 years. During that time I have eaten 32,850 meals — mostly of my wife's cooking. Suddenly, I have discovered that I cannot remember the menu of a single meal. And yet, I received nourishment from every single one of them. I have the distinct impression that without them, I would have starved to death long ago.

A Word of Caution About Preaching and Preachers

No doubt about it — preaching is exceedingly important to the worshiping church (Rom. 10:14-17; 1 Cor. 1:17-31). However, a word of caution is appropriate here. Preaching is not the only element in worship. It is one of several elements, each of which is exceedingly important. Those who view preaching as less important see it as something to be endured and gotten out of the way so the congregation can get on to other things. Those who view preaching as *the* most important thing look at the other elements of worship as preliminaries to be gotten out of the way so that the congregation can enjoy "the main event." Both concepts are tragically incorrect. There needs to be a balance of all the elements in worship so that each complements the others. Ronald Allen and Gordon Borror write:

> Viewing the preacher's singular act of proclamation as significantly more important than the entire congregation's acts of adoration, praise, confession, thanksgiving, and dedication, is espousing an expensive heresy which may well be robbing many a church of its spiritual assets.[17]

For those of you who think your preacher is the greatest in the world — be careful — very careful. You do not worship the preacher — you must not. Honor him? Yes. Love him? Definitely. Encourage him? By all means. Adore him? Only God deserves your adoration. A guest preacher had been scheduled to fill the pulpit of Plymouth Church in Brooklyn one Sunday morning. Henry Ward Beecher usually delivered the sermon there. When the visiting preacher stepped to the pulpit, numerous people in the congregation rushed to the exits disappointed that their hero preacher was absent. Witnessing this rapid flight from the sanctuary, the guest preacher raised his hand and said, "All those who came here to worship Henry Ward Beecher may now withdraw — all who came to worship God may remain."

We must be careful that we do not become idolatrous in our love of preaching or preachers, especially if your

---

[17]Allen and Borror, p. 9.

preacher happens to be especially dynamic. C. Welton Gaddy writes:

> Far too easily the magnetism of a particular preacher can be confused with the power of the Word of God. Personal charisma can be identified as spiritual power. Church members may even gather to hear the preacher rather than to worship God.[18]

Preachers are men with feet of clay, and as we are all aware, sometimes those clay feet crumble miserably. Indeed, God works through clay vessels (Isa. 64:8; Jer. 18:1-6; Rom. 9:21; 2 Cor. 4:7), but let us be certain our faith is in the Potter and not the clay.

The Word of God Must Be Central in Preaching

Those who preach must be sure that God's Word is central to their message. It really doesn't matter a whole lot what the preacher's opinions are on world events. What matters is that he communicate the Word of God to those who hear him. C. Welton Gaddy writes:

> A disciplined faithfulness to the Bible in proclamation spares worship from the ignoble trivia of nice little talks, editorial opinions, and locker-room type appeals of spiritualized "Go get 'ums." Confessions of "in my estimation" and "I think" give way to the declaration "Thus says the Lord."[19]

Haddon W. Robinson makes the same point powerfully in his book, *Biblical Preaching*:

> A preacher can proclaim anything in a stained-glass voice at 11:30 on Sunday morning, following the singing of hymns. Yet when a preacher fails to preach the Scriptures, he abandons his authority. He confronts his hearers no longer with a word

---

[18]C. Welton Gaddy, *The Gift of Worship* (Nashville: Broadman Press, 1992), p. 71.
[19]*Ibid.*, p. 208.

from God but only with another word from men. Therefore most modern preaching evokes little more than a wide yawn. God is not in it.[20]

The primary purpose of preaching is to present the gospel to those who hear. In his book, *Fundamentals of Preaching*, John Killinger writes:

Years ago, when ships were the only way communications could be carried from the old countries to America, people in America anxious for news from relatives and loved ones would assemble at the dock as soon as a mast was sighted. The moment a gangplank was thrown up and sailors began to disembark, hands would stretch out and cries would go up from the crowd beseeching, "Is there any word? Is there any word?" And I can testify, as one who has often gone to church with the masses of modern men and women who feel isolated, cut off from community, lost in this wasteland of electronics and gadgetry, that we enter the sanctuary with the same plea: "Is there any word?"[21]

No matter how relevant a preacher's message, if it is not devoted to passing on the gospel, it is out of place in the Sunday service.[22] William Willimon's words are strong:

Whenever [preaching] is used to motivate the congregation to respond to the denomination's latest programs, or the pastor's own crusade, or social action, or personal commitment — or to educate, titillate, soothe, excite, coerce — or any other often worthwhile purpose, then it is safe to say that the worship of God has been perverted into a means of achieving our own human purposes rather than an occasion to respond to God's purposes.[23]

---

[20]Haddon W. Robinson, *Biblical Preaching* (Grand Rapids: Baker, 1980), p. 18.
[21]John Killinger, *Fundamentals of Preaching* (Philadelphia: Fortress Press, 1985), p. 13.
[22]White, *Christian Worship in Transition*, p. 16.
[23]Willimon, *Word, Water, Wine and Bread*, p. 123.

Preaching is also much more than passing along correct information about God. Preaching needs to help people know much more than the facts. It needs to help people come face to face with the personal God who loves them and demands their grateful response of faith, love and obedience. G. Campbell Morgan wrote:

> It is possible for a man to analyze the Bible and lose it in the process, to prepare a synthesis of the Bible and lose his soul at the work; to make himself perfectly familiar with the letter, and to find out that the letter killeth because he has lost touch with the spirit.[24]

A preacher who prepares his lesson, but fails to meet God Himself in the preparation, will never transform the lives of those who hear his sermon.[25]

These words from the pen of Warren Wiersbe are a fitting conclusion to this chapter:

> The purpose of preaching is not to inform the congregation of the minister's homiletical gifts; it is to bring the congregation face to face with the living God. . . .The purpose of the Word of God is to reveal the God of the Word; and when you meet the God of the Word, you must do something about His will.[26]

---

[24]Wiersbe, p. 124.
[25]*Ibid.*, p. 128.
[26]*Ibid.*

DISCUSSION QUESTIONS
ON CHAPTER NINE

1. How much Scripture does your congregation read in the assembly? Do you think enough Scripture is being read?

2. How do you feel about being asked to stand when the Bible is being read to the congregation?

3. The Jews had a system of readings that assured that they would read through the Scriptures in a certain period of time. Do you think such a method would be helpful to your congregation?

4. What could your congregation do to make Bible reading more effective in worship?

5. Describe unison and responsive readings. How might they help your assembly?

6. How important is preaching to worship?

7. How much of the assembly time should preaching comprise?

8. How would you help a congregation that seems to hold its preacher and his preaching in such high regard that they are in danger of idolizing him?

9. What must be at the center of preaching if it is truly to be biblical preaching?

10
Prayer is More
Than a Shopping List

Prayer has been called the soul of worship. Although prayer should be an intensely personal and individual matter in a Christian's private relationship with God, it is also an indispensable part of the Christian worship assembly. In corporate worship, prayer is an expression of unity, community, fellowship, and oneness as the entire congregation calls upon the name of the Lord.

Prayer as a Part of Old Testament Worship

Throughout history people have sought God through prayer. In the days of Adam and Eve, "men began to call on the name of the Lord" (Gen. 4:26). From the beginning of Abraham's relationship with God, he "called on the name of the Lord" (Gen. 12:8; 21:23). Beginning with the earliest biblical examples, prayer was a response to what God had done in the past, was doing in the present, or had promised to do in the future. Many of the prayers in the Bible are similar to conversations one friend has with another. Although there was no disrespect, many of the prayers show a directness and a familiarity in prayer that may surprise us. In Genesis 15:1-5 Abram had a conversation with God concerning his heir. In Genesis 18:16-33, Abraham negotiated with God concerning God's decision to destroy the wicked city of Sodom. Moses had a similar conversation with God in an attempt to convince the Lord to spare the Israelites from God's anger after they persuaded Aaron to build the golden calf (Exod. 32:7-14).

In the Old Testament, prayer was also closely connected with sacrifice. Abram, Isaac, Jacob, and their descendants often prayed where they had built altars to the Lord (Gen. 13:3-4; 26:25; 28:20-22). Prayers accompanied the sacrifices both in the tabernacle and later in the temple. After the Babylonians destroyed the temple in 597 B.C. and carried Israel into Babylonian captivity, animal sacrifices ceased. During those seven decades of exile, prayer became a substitute for sacrifices. In the synagogue, members were invited to pray by the use of the phrase "come and offer" a prayer rather than "come and pray." Prayer in the form of praise, adoration, and thanksgiving was an offering, equivalent to the offering of material sacrifices.[1]

Prayer was a central item in Israel's worship. The faithful Jew prayed three times a day (Ps. 55:17; Dan. 6:10). The Old Testament contains many examples of prayer. One Old Testament scholar, Ludwig Kohler, finds about 85 original prayers in the Old Testament. In addition there are 66 psalms and 14 parts of psalms which may be called prayers.[2] Although time does not permit the study of these passages, some of the most notable examples of prayer in the Old Testament are: Hannah's prayer for a son (1 Sam. 2:1-10), Solomon's prayer at the dedication of the temple (1 Kgs. 8:22-54; 2 Chr. 6:12-7:15), Elijah's prayer for fire on Mt. Carmel (1 Kgs. 18:30-39), Hezekiah's prayer for deliverance from Sennacherib and his Assyrian army (2 Kings 19:14-19; Isa. 37:14-20), Daniel's prayer of confession after the Persians overthrew the Babylonians (Dan. 9:1-19), Ezra's prayer of confession for the returned exiles (Ezra 9:5-15), and the Israelites' prayer of confession after returning from Babylonian captivity (Neh. 9:5-37). Many of the

---

[1]Ilion T. Jones, p. 33.
[2]Ludwig Kohler, *Old Testament Theology* (Philadephia: Westminster, 1957), p. 251.

Psalms are moving examples of prayer. There are prayers of confession (Ps. 51), prayers seeking communion with God (Ps. 63), prayers for protection (Ps. 57), prayers for healing and mercy and deliverance (Ps. 6), and prayers of praise too many to mention (Ps. 90).

Prayer as a Part of New Testament Worship

As the New Testament story opens, it does so with prayer. A priest named Zechariah was serving in the temple. As he was burning incense inside, "all the assembled worshipers were praying outside" (Luke 1:8-10). An angel of the Lord appeared to Zechariah and assured him that God had heard his prayer. The heavenly messenger promised the old priest that he and his barren wife, Elizabeth, would have a son whose name was to be John. John would prepare the way for the Messiah (Luke 1:11-18). Later, after Jesus was born and Joseph and Mary presented Him for circumcision at the temple, Simeon praised God and addressed the Lord:

> Sovereign Lord, as you have promised,
> you now dismiss your servant in peace.
> For my eyes have seen your salvation,
> which you have prepared in the sight of all people,
> a light for revelation to the Gentiles
> and for glory to your people Israel (Luke 2:29-32).

Jesus and Prayer

We know practically nothing of Jesus' childhood, although we may assume that Jesus was taught to pray by both His parents' instruction and example. No doubt, Jesus also learned the habits of prayer from His experiences in the synagogue. One thing is certain concerning the biblical record — during Jesus' ministry He was a man of intense prayer. Why did Jesus pray? Why would the very Son of God need to pray? We must not forget that Jesus took on human flesh during His life on earth. Although He was in His very nature God, He humbled Himself when He became a man (Phil. 2:6-8). As a human being, He was subject to the same physical and emotional needs as any other man. He prayed because He needed communication with His father. He prayed because He needed God's care and guidance and provision. Jesus prayed, not merely as an example for us, but out of a genuine sense of His own dependence on His Father. If Jesus needed to pray, how much more do we, both individually and in our assemblies!

Jesus clearly expressed His mind on prayer by His teachings. Among other things, He taught His disciples to pray with persistence (Luke 11:5-8), with humility and penitent hearts (Luke 18:10-14), with sincerity and simplicity (Matt. 6:5-8; Mark 12:38-40), with intensity and determination (Mark 14:38), with expectancy (Matt. 7:7-11; Mark 11:24), and with a forgiving spirit (Mark 11:25-26).

Jesus' best known teaching on prayer is found in the Sermon on the Mount (Matt. 6:9-15). Although this has often been called the Lord's prayer, it might be more appropriate to call it Jesus' model prayer. In only ten lines, Jesus teaches us how to pray. Although individuals should pattern their private prayers after Jesus' model, the prayer is a corporate prayer. Jesus said, "*Our* Father." Although God is *your* Father and *my* Father, He is not yours or mine alone — He is the Father of us all. What a privilege to address God with the intimate name "Father." For most of us, "father" means parentage, protection, discipline, affection, love, provision, compassion, instruction, and reward, just to name a few. After addressing our Father, the prayer begins with praise to God: "Hallowed be your name." This is where prayer ought always begin — not with our long shopping list of requests, but with acknowledgment of God's majesty, power, goodness and holiness. Before we start asking God to meet our needs, Jesus would have us declare to God that He is worthy of all praise, glory, and adoration. The prayer then moves to a concern for God's kingdom and His will in the world and also in our own lives.

Only after addressing God and His concerns first does Jesus teach us to pray for ourselves. The prayer helps us express our total dependence on God by asking for provisions for life itself, for the forgiveness of our sins, and for protection and deliverance from evil and the evil one. If we carefully consider each line (and sometimes individual words of those lines), there are enough things to pray about that we would never exhaust it. Apparently, this was the way the model prayer was used in the early church. Everett Ferguson says, "The Lord's prayer was not received verbatim as a fixed form but was an outline or sketch of a prayer which one either filled in or supplemented with his own petitions."[3]

Even more commanding than His words, was Jesus' example of prayer. His followers witnessed the strength that prayer gave Jesus, so much so that they asked Him to teach them to pray (Luke 11:1). Periods of prayer preceded the critical moments of His work: at His baptism immediately before He began His public ministry (Luke 3:21), before choosing the twelve disciples (Matt. 10:2-4), before His transfiguration that prepared His disciples for a fuller revelation of who He was (Mark 9:2-8), and before Gethsemane (Luke 22:40-46).

Occasionally, Jesus spent all night in prayer (Luke 6:12). At other times He got up before daybreak to pray (Luke 4:42). Although He prayed in crowds and with His disciples, Jesus also spent time alone in prayer (Mark

---

[3]Ferguson, *Early Christians Speak*, p. 140.

6:46; Luke 5:15-16). Jesus' prayers were primarily times of deep communion with God (Luke 9:28-36), joyful thanksgiving (Luke 10:21-22), and intercession for others (John 17).

Jesus considered prayer essential to ministry. On one occasion, Jesus rebuked the twelve after they attempted, unsuccessfully, to cast out an evil spirit that had tormented a boy since his childhood. When the disciples asked why they could not drive it out, Jesus replied, "This kind can come out only by prayer" (Mark 9:29). J.S. Stewart said that prayer "was not only an important part of His life: it *was* His life, the very breath of His being."[4] Indeed, Jesus died as He lived — praying to God, "Father, into your hands I commit my spirit" (Luke 23:46).

Prayer In The Early Church

The book of Acts opens with the disciples "joined together constantly in prayer" (Acts 1:14). They prayed for God's guidance in choosing a man to fill the role left vacant by Judas' suicide (Acts 1:24). From the start, the first Christians "devoted themselves to the apostles' teaching and to the fellowship, to the breaking of bread and to prayer" (Acts 2:42). Although Jesus' disciples were no longer under the old covenant, many of those in Jerusalem continued to go to the temple at the prescribed hours of prayer (three times daily — morning, noon, and afternoon) to pray. This is what Peter and John were doing when they healed a crippled man at the Beautiful Gate of the temple (Acts 3:1). For that act of kindness, the Jewish Sanhedrin hauled Peter and John in for questioning. They threatened the two and warned them not to speak or teach any more in the name of Jesus. After releasing Peter and John, the two disciples

---

[4]Quoted in Martin, *Worship in the Early Church*, p. 29.

went back and reported all that the chief priests and elders had said to them (Acts 4:1-23). The response of the group was just what you would hope — "they raised their voices together in prayer to God" (Acts 4:24). After praying for boldness to preach and power to do great works in Jesus' name, the place where they were meeting was shaken, literally, and they were all filled with the Holy Spirit (Acts 4:24-31).

Early Christians considered prayer so important that the Apostles appointed helpers in their work so they could devote more of their time to praying. When those special servants had been selected, they were presented before the Apostles who prayed and laid their hands on them (Acts 6:1-6). When Peter was in prison, the church gathered to pray for his release (Acts 12:5).

The local church in Antioch assembled for prayer before they sent Paul and Barnabas out on their missionary journey (Acts 13:2-3). Prior to appointing elders in Asia Minor, Paul prayed and fasted (Acts 14:23). At midnight in a Philippian jail, Paul and Silas were praying and singing hymns to God (Acts 16:25). Part of the church in Ephesus met with Paul for prayer before he set off for Jerusalem (Acts 20:36). In route, Paul's journey took him through Tyre, where all the disciples and their wives and children accompanied Paul and his companions out of the city and knelt with them on the beach to pray (Acts 21:5).

There is no way to understand the dynamic life of the early church apart from its practice of prayer. Neither is it possible to observe their worship without seeing the importance prayer played in it. C. Welton Gaddy writes, "Worship without prayer is as inconceivable as a meal without food."

Paul's prayers for the churches are evident in many of his letters to them (Rom. 1:8-12; 1 Cor. 1:4; Eph. 1:15-19; 3:14-21; Phil. 1:3-11; Col. 1:3-14; 1 Thess. 1:2-3;

2 Thess. 1:11-12). Not only did Paul pray for his brothers and sisters in the churches, but he requested that those churches also pray for him and for all the saints (Rom. 15:30-31; 2 Cor. 1:11; Eph. 6:18; Col. 4:3-4; 1 Thess. 5:25). Paul urged his fellow Christians to be "faithful in prayer" (Rom. 12:12), to "pray in the Spirit on all occasions with all kinds of prayers and requests" (Eph. 6:18), to "devote" themselves to prayer (Col. 4:2), and to "pray continually" (1 Thess. 5:17). Paul's answer to anxiety was prayer offered to God with an attitude of trust and thanksgiving (Phil. 4:6).

Prayer is Communion With God

Too often we become concerned with the mechanics of prayer. Should we use "Thee," "Thou," and "Thine," or is it proper to use conversational idioms, addressing God as "You" and "Yours"? Should we kneel? Is a prayer heard without the words "in Jesus name," and is it acceptable to say those words at some place in the prayer other than immediately before the "Amen"? Questions of mechanics are important. However, in our desire to *do it right*, we may forget that prayer is fundamentally communion with God.

Sometimes we may wonder why we need to pray to God when He already knows everything about us. I think it's because God knows that what we need most is *Him*. Communion with God is the thing that surpasses every other need we have. Yes, God grants requests in prayer, but blessed is the person who longs for God Himself more than for what God gives.

Prayer is more a matter of the heart than art. Even if we get the forms and the mechanics right, we have not prayed unless we have entered into God's presence and communed with Him. Paul taught that we are to pray with both the mind and the spirit (1 Cor. 14:15). Our intellect is present when we pray, but prayer is more an expression of our hearts, feelings, fears, longings and frustrations. Prayer expresses our heart-felt praise and concerns and joys and dependence on God, our Creator. Prayer is the vehicle that allows us to tell God our shame and guilt from sin, our relief for His forgiveness, and our thankfulness for His goodness and grace. Those issues are matters of the heart. The power of this communion with God is intensified when we pray with other Christians. Jesus promised, "I tell you that if two of you on earth agree about anything you ask for, it will be done for you by my Father in heaven. For where two or three come together in my name, there am I with them" (Matt. 18:19-20).

Communion with God in prayer is more powerful than we can imagine (Eph. 1:19). God is "able to do immeasurably more than all we ask or imagine, according to his power that is at work within us" (Eph. 3:20). It was Paul's prayer that God strengthen us with power through His Spirit in our inner being (Eph. 3:16). Much of that power is unleashed through the prayers of righteous people (Jas. 5:16).

Conditions for Effective Prayer

A number of conditions are necessary for prayer to be fully effective. These are not meant to be merely mechanics. Mechanics alone do not make words into a prayer. The following conditions are more matters of the heart than mechanics.

Condition One: Faith

The determining factor in prayer is the character of God. What makes prayer meaningful and powerful is not faith in prayer. We do not trust in the act of prayer itself as if prayer were some magic words we recite together. Prayer is powerful and effective because of our faith *in God* to Whom we address our prayers. God hears and answers the prayers of His people. Jesus promised:

> Ask and it will be given to you; seek and you will find; knock and the door will be opened to you. For everyone who asks receives; he who seeks finds; and to him who knocks, the door will be opened. Which of you, if his son asks for bread, will give him a stone? Or if he asks for a fish, will give him a snake? If you, then, though you are evil, know how to give good gifts to your children, how much more will your Father in heaven give good gifts to those who ask him! (Matt. 7:7-11).

Jesus also declared, "If you believe, you will receive whatever you ask in prayer" (Matt. 21:22; Mark 11:24). John wrote, ". . .if we know that he hears us — whatever we ask — we know that we have what we asked of him" (1 John 5:15). Those words are as true for the prayers of an assembled congregation at worship as they are for an individual seeker in the privacy of his own home. Through the prophet Jeremiah, God promised to hear and answer the prayers of His people:

> Then you will call upon me and come and pray to me, and I will listen to you. You will seek me and find me when you seek me with all your heart. I will be found by you, declares the LORD (Jer. 29:12-14).

How faith strengthening are the words of Peter, "For the eyes of the Lord are on the righteous and his ears are attentive to their prayer" (1 Pet. 3:12). The penetrating question is: Do we really believe God means what He says in His Word about these matters? Could it be our lack of faith that keeps us from taking advantage of prayer's power?

A lack of faith will devastate the effectiveness of our prayers, whether we are talking about individual and private prayer or the corporate prayers of the congregation. When we ask God for something we "must believe and not doubt, because he who doubts is like a wave of the sea, blown and tossed by the wind. That man should not think he will receive anything from the Lord; he is a double-minded man, unstable in all he does" (Jas. 1:6-8). It is the prayer of faith that reaps results (Jas. 5:13-18).

Condition Two: Pure Motives

James says that sometimes we do not get what we desire because we do not ask God. But even when we ask, we sometimes do not receive because we ask with wrong motives. We are driven by the desire to use what God would give us to spend selfishly on ourselves (Jas. 4:1-3). Given our human nature, we don't always know whether our motives are pure. It makes sense, then, that one of the things we ask God to grant us is a pure heart so that we will ask with pure motives.

Condition Three: Submission to God's Will

Everyone agrees that Jesus' prayers were effective. That was due, in part, to His submission to God's will. Jesus came to do His Father's will (John 4:34; 6:38). That does not mean that Jesus had no human will of His own. Nor does it mean that there never was an occasion when Jesus struggled to accept His Father's will.

When Jesus was in Gethsemane contemplating His impending crucifixion, He did not want to go through it. Luke alone related something that caught his attention as a physician. The anguish and stress which Jesus was experiencing in that garden was so intense that in His deeply earnest prayer "his sweat was like drops of blood falling to the ground" (Luke 22:44). However, in the teeth of that ordeal, Jesus said, "Yet not as I will, but as you will" (Matt. 26:39), and in the end He said, "may your will be done" (Matt. 26:42). It must have been this most difficult of Jesus' hours to which the writer of

227

Hebrews wrote: "During the days of Jesus' life on earth, he offered up prayers and petitions *with loud cries and tears* to the one who could save him from death, and he was heard because of *his reverent submission.* Although he was a son, he learned obedience from what he suffered. . . ." (Heb. 5:7-8).

Had Jesus not been submissive to God's will, His life and ministry would have been a failure. His ministry fulfilled God's plan, and Jesus was able to fulfill it precisely because He did pray. Effective prayer and the will of God are inseparable. Jesus taught us to pray, "thy will be done" (Matt. 6:10). John writes, "This is the confidence we have in approaching God: that if we ask anything *according to his will*, he hears us" (1 John 5:14, emphasis added). E. Stanley Jones wrote:

> [Prayer is] surrender to the will of God and cooperation with that will. If I throw out a boathook from the boat and catch hold of the shore and pull, do I pull the shore to me, or do I pull myself to the shore? Prayer is not pulling God to my will, but the aligning of my will to the will of God.[5]

Condition Four: Obedience

One of the most sobering passages concerning God turning a deaf ear to prayer comes in Isaiah 1:10-17. God rejected the Jews' sacrifices, although they were extravagant. God was sick of their meaningless offerings. Their incense was detestable to Him. The Lord hated their special holy days, feast days, and festivals. God said, "When you spread out your hands in prayer, I will hide my eyes from you; even if you offer many prayers, I will not listen" (Isa. 1:15). Why had God rejected their offerings and refused to listen to their prayers? The next several verses in the chapter tell us: their lives were full of wickedness, injustice, and disobedience to God. Some

---

[5]E. Stanley Jones, *A Song of Ascents*, p. 383.

time later, the prophet Jeremiah warned the people of Judah that God was sick of their words of praise that did not square with the disobedience of their lives (Jer. 7:1-11).

The Scriptures give us great assurance that God will hear and answer us when we pray to Him (Jer. 29:12; 1 John 5:14-15). But that is true only if we obey Him. That does not mean that we never make a mistake, but it does mean that we must commit ourselves to a life of obedience to His commands. John writes, "Dear friends, if our hearts do not condemn us, we have confidence before God and receive from him anything we ask, *because we obey his commands and do what pleases him*" (1 John 3:21-22, emphasis added).

Condition Five: Humility

Pride and arrogance guarantee a relationship out of step with God. The Bible says, "God opposes the proud, but gives grace to the humble" (Prov. 3:34; Jas. 4:6). This works in every area of life, including prayer. Jesus illustrated this lesson in His parable of the self-righteous Pharisee and the humble tax collector in Luke 18:9-14. Both men went up to the temple to pray. The Pharisee stood up arrogantly and "prayed *about* himself." He was so proud of his spiritual achievements. What a contrast to the tax collector who would not even look up to heaven, but beat his breast and pleaded for God's mercy on him, a sinner. Jesus declared that God justified the humble tax collector and not the proud Pharisee. King David wrote:

> The righteous cry out, and the LORD hears them;
> he delivers them from all their troubles.
> The LORD is close to the brokenhearted
> and saves those who are crushed in spirit (Ps. 34:17-18).

Jesus said, "For everyone who exalts himself will be

humbled, and he who humbles himself will be exalted" (Luke 18:14).

Condition Six: In Jesus' Name

To pray in the name of Jesus means to come to God through and by the authority of Jesus. Prayer is a privilege made possible by Jesus who is our mediator with the Father (1 Tim. 2:5) and our "living way" to Him (Heb. 10:20). We come before God as those who belong to Jesus, having been baptized in His name (Acts 2:38). We now have spiritual life in His name (John 20:31). Everything we do is to be done in the name of Jesus (Col. 3:17). Jesus has authorized us to make our prayer requests to God (John 14:13-15; 15:7; 16:23-26). Using the name of Jesus is a privilege, and we must never use it carelessly or casually. The sons of Sceva used it in a cavalier fashion. They wanted the power which Jesus had, but they were unwilling to submit to Jesus' Lordship. As a result, an evil spirit overpowered them and gave them such a beating they ran out of the house naked and bleeding (Acts 19:15-16).

Closing a prayer "in Jesus name" is not just a formula tacked onto the end of the prayer to make sure it is effective. Prayer in the name of Jesus reflects our awareness that we are dependent upon God's faithfulness.[6] There is no specific command or even an example requiring us to verbalize "in Jesus' name" with every prayer. It is not a liturgical formula. Therefore we must not recite it as compulsory ritual but use it as a wonderful, regular reminder of how it is we come before God — because of Jesus Christ, in union with Jesus Christ, and enabled by the authority of Jesus Christ.

The Postures of Prayer

The Bible makes no issue of the physical postures of

prayer. These are often mentioned in passing as matters of ordinary behavior. However, in a culture which feels various degrees of discomfort with certain physical expressions of worship and postures for prayer, it is important to see what the Scriptures say about this matter. Prayers were offered from the sitting position (Matt. 5:1; 6:9-13). In times of great intensity, prayers were sometimes offered in a prostrate position (Mark 14:35). Heads and bodies were often bowed in prayer. Frequently, people knelt in prayer (1 Kgs. 8:54; Ezra 9:5; Luke 22:41). The kneeling and prostrate postures are signs of submission, and they acknowledge God's greatness (Matt. 4:9; Phil. 2:9-11).

The most common posture for prayer in the first century was standing with hands and face uplifted toward heaven (Mark 11:25; Luke 18:11, 13) This was also the practice in the Old Testament (1 Sam. 1:26; 1 Kgs. 8:22). David writes, "Hear my cry for mercy as I call to you for help, as I lift up my hands toward your Most Holy Place" (Ps. 28:2). Again, David writes, "I will praise you as long as I live, and in your name I will lift up my hands" (Ps. 63:4). The Psalmist writes, "Lift up your hands in the sanctuary and praise the LORD" (Ps. 134:2). That was also the practice of the synagogue. This practice was undoubtedly carried over by Jewish Christians into their worship. Paul wrote, "I want men everywhere to lift up holy hands in prayer, without anger or disputing" (1 Tim. 2:8).

Everett Ferguson explains this posture for prayer as it most likely was practiced in the church during and just after the close of the first century. He says that the characteristic posture for Christian prayer was standing with arms outstretched and slightly raised and the palms turned up to heaven. People knelt as a sign of humility,

---

[6]Willis, pp. 68-69.

but they stood as a sign of joy and boldness. Ferguson says that the dominant note of the early Christian prayers was praise, expressed most clearly in the recorded doxologies of the day. Standing was the practice on the Lord's day in honor of the resurrection. Stretching out the arms became a symbol of the cross for Christians.[7]

The posture one takes in prayer depends on the needs, the concerns, the emotions, and the circumstances of the situation. However, one thing ought to be perfectly clear from this quick survey — there are more ways to posture oneself than the ones which we traditionally use. We have no trouble bowing our heads or praying from a standing or sitting position. But very few of us have experienced worship assemblies where people regularly lift their hands and faces to heaven. However, it is not only permissible by biblical standards, it is also urged on us.

There are those who long to lift their hands in praise and in prayer to the Lord, but they are afraid of the repercussions if they do. In the name of all that is right and biblical, and in the name of Christian freedom, we must give people both the freedom and the permission to posture themselves in whatever ways are biblical. Someone always raises the issue of "decently and in order" (1 Cor. 14:40), insinuating that to lift one's hands in public assembly is indecent and/or disorderly. It was not indecent or disorderly in biblical days; why should it be so today? Is it not more a matter of preference and custom and culture? Is it not more a matter of that with which we feel comfortable? Culture and traditional standards are to be taken seriously, but I maintain that we need to set our standards by Scripture and not by cultural norms or personal comfort zones.

---

[7]Ferguson, *Early Christians Speak*, pp. 141,143,147.

We have not always been as restrained and reserved in our physical postures. Many older Christians, especially those who grew up in small, rural congregations, remember when kneeling for prayer was the rule rather than the exception. Some of them remember people raising a hand in prayer. We may have become so sophisticated and fearful of what others might think, that we have rejected biblical postures in worship that would aid us in praising God as He wants and deserves to be praised.

Worship will not be constantly reserved and restrained in heaven. It will be reverent. It will be awesome. If the book of Revelation is any indication, there will even be times of absolute silence in heaven. But the primary picture I get of heaven from the Scriptures is a place of joyful praise, a place where every knee will bow and every tongue confess that Jesus Christ is Lord to the praise of God's glory (Phil. 2:9-11).

Elders and ministers and other church leaders are going to have to teach biblical truth concerning these matters. But teaching alone will not get the job done. They are going to have to give people permission and even encourage Christians to practice biblical postures of praise. Even more than either teaching and permission, leaders are going to have to model these things before the congregation before people will feel a genuine freedom and courage to try to worship God in the way His saints have worshiped Him throughout the centuries.

The Holy Spirit's Role in Prayer

Shortly before Jesus was taken for a mock trial and crucifixion He promised that He would send the Comforter, the Holy Spirit, to be with His disciples forever. Although Jesus was going back to the Father,

He was not going to leave them as orphans. The Holy Spirit, Jesus assured them, would be with them and would live in them (John 14:16-17). Just before His ascension into heaven, Jesus reminded them again of His promise that God would send the Holy Spirit to them (Acts 1:3-5). "You will receive power when the Holy Spirit comes on you," Jesus said (Acts 1:8). On the day of Pentecost, seven weeks after Jesus' crucifixion, God fulfilled the promise. "All of them were filled with the Holy Spirit . . ." (Acts 2:4). Peter told the people that when they repented of the their sins and were baptized in the name of Jesus Christ, their sins would be forgiven and they would "receive the gift of the Holy Spirit," a gift for them and for their "children and for all who are far off — for all whom the Lord our God will call" (Acts 2:38-39).

From the beginning of the church the Holy Spirit has played a key role in the lives of God's people. It should not be surprising that the Holy Spirit is also active in Christians' prayers. After Peter and John were released from questioning by the Sanhedrin, they went back to their Christian family and prayed about the events which had just occurred. They also asked God for boldness to speak the gospel in face of opposition. "After they prayed, the place where they were meeting was shaken. And they were all filled with the Holy Spirit and spoke the word of God boldly" (Acts 4:31).

When Paul was admonishing the Ephesians to put on the full armor of God, he told them to take "the sword of the Spirit, which is the word of God. And pray in the Spirit on all occasions with all kinds of prayers and requests" (Eph. 6:17-18). Jude also instructed believers to "pray in the Holy Spirit" (Jude 20).

What do we do when we feel weak and do not know what to pray or how we ought to pray? Paul wrote, "the Spirit helps us in our weakness. We do not know what we ought to pray for, but the Spirit himself intercedes for us with groans that words cannot express. And he who searches our hearts knows the mind of the Spirit, because the Spirit intercedes for the saints in accordance with God's will" (Rom. 8:26-27). Those words ought to bring us great assurance and comfort. Jesus has not left us orphans either. The Holy Spirit helps us as we pray.

Special Words of Prayer

Amen

No word of prayer is more recognized around the world than the word "Amen." It is found 57 times in Scripture, 30 of which are in the New Testament. Although it is spoken often, many people do not understand its meaning and usage. "Amen" at the end of the prayer does not mean "the prayer is finally over," or "now we can go home," or "now, let's eat." "Amen" was used in Israel to affirm prayers, oaths, blessings and curses (Deut. 27:15-26; 1 Chr. 16:36; Neh. 5:13; 8:6; Ps. 106:48). "Amen" has two primary meanings in our prayers. Most commonly it means affirmation. It is like saying, "Yes, this is true. I believe and support it" (Eph. 3:21; Rev. 5:14). "Amen" is used occasionally as a petition, such as in Revelation 22:20, "He who testifies to these things says, 'Yes, I am coming soon.' Amen. Come, Lord Jesus." Used in this way it is asking, "Let this be so, according to your will."

It was a common practice in the Old Testament for all the people to say "Amen" (1 Chr. 16:36; Neh. 5:13; 8:6; Ps. 106:48). It was also a common practice in the early church. The Apostle Paul instructed those who led prayers in the Corinthian church to pray words that everyone could understand. Otherwise, "how can one who finds himself among those who do not understand say 'Amen' to your thanksgiving, since he does not know what you are saying?" (1 Cor. 14:16). Even though the prayer was led by one person, everyone in the congregation voiced their "Amen" at the conclusion of their prayer.

During the Restoration Movement there have been rare outbursts of emotional expression during preaching. However, Alexander Campbell insisted that "at the close of all social prayer . . . the whole congregation that unites in the petitions should, like the primitive Christians say with an audible and clear voice, *Amen*" (1 Cor. 14:16-17).[8] Not as many Christians do that today as used to, at least in most white congregations. That is not the case with most of the black churches who continue to be much more actively involved in worship, both physically and vocally. We need to restore the "Amen" to the congregation. We need to get used to saying it anyway, since the inhabitants of heaven exclaim it frequently (Rev. 5:14; 7:12; 19:4). Christians today need to voice their approval just as much as the Israelites and early Christians did centuries ago.

Abba

The most precious word of prayer is "Abba." It was one of the first words a young Hebrew child learned to utter. It was a child's personal term for his or her father, equivalent to our term "Daddy." It conveys all the tender love and affection typical between a good father and his child. It was an endearing name one would use to address only the one who filled the male parenting role. This is the word Jesus used in Gethsemane when He prayed to His father: "Abba, Father, everything is possible for you. Take this cup from me. Yet not what I will, but what you will" (Mark 14:36). "Abba" is found two

---

[8]Colbert S. Cartwright, "Disciples Worship: A Rich and Relevant Heritage," *Mid-Stream* 28, no. 3 (July 1989), pp. 273-274.

other times in Scripture. One of those is in Romans 8:14-17,

> Those who are led by the Spirit of God are sons of God. For you did not receive a spirit that makes you a slave again to fear, but you received the Spirit of sonship. And by him we cry, "Abba, Father." The Spirit Himself testifies with our spirit that we are God's children. Now if we are children, then we are heirs — heirs of God and co-heirs with Christ.

Paul reaffirms this same message in Galatians 4:6-7. Through the blood of Jesus, we have confidence to enter the throne room of God (Heb. 4:14-16; 6:19-20; 10:19-22). And by the Holy Spirit we are able to cry "Abba, Father." May we never treat the holy name of God with irreverent familiarity. It does not seem appropriate to think of God as our "good buddy," our "chum," or our "pal." Those words are too flippant, even jesting, to describe the relationship Jesus has granted us with the Father. When the Bible says to come "boldly" to the throne of grace, it doesn't mean brashly. The very thought that the all-holy God would even allow the likes of us, as unholy as we are, to come into His presence ought to fill us with an incredible sense of awe, gratitude, and reverence. Yes, He is our Father, but there should be something more than a casual "Hey, there!" when we approach Him. We must not go barging in thoughtlessly before our Father. Prayer can become too formal and ceremonial to be real, but it can also become too casual to be real. It is possible to be God's friend (Jas. 2:23), but not God's running mate. However, with reverence and love we do have the marvelously wonderful blessing of being able to address God, "Abba, Father." Let's take advantage of it!

Maranatha

Another word of prayer is "Maranatha." The Apostle

Paul closed his first letter to the Corinthians by writing, "Come, O Lord!" (1 Cor. 16:22). This expression in the Aramaic language is "Maranatha." Ralph Martin says that it was a common devotional exclamation. It can mean either, "The Lord has come" (is coming), or if the letters are divided, as "Marana Tha," it means "Our Lord, come!" Martin writes:

> It looks backward to all that the coming of Christ into the world has meant, and is an acknowledgment of praise. It looks forward to His appearing, and is a cry of expectation. It has also a present significance, as it bids the assembled Church to recognize that the Lord is in their midst and has come to greet His people.[9]

"Marana Tha" is a prayer of invocation addressed to Jesus. The next to the last verse in the Bible reads, "He who testifies to these things says, 'Yes, I am coming soon.' Amen. Come, Lord Jesus" (Rev. 22:20)

Enhancing Prayers in Public Worship

As with every element of worship, we should seek to make our public prayers as meaningful and effective as possible. Following are several suggestions to help prayer leaders improve prayer in our worship assemblies.

1. *Be prepared.*

Those who lead in prayer shoulder great responsibility. It is difficult to lead the thoughts for an entire body, to be aware of their needs and struggles, their joys and challenges. Therefore, he should give a lot of consideration to what will represent the thoughts of the majority of his fellow worshipers. There are times when extemporaneous prayers are appropriate. However, as a general

---

[9]Ralph Martin, *Worship in the Early Church*, p. 131.

rule, leaders should make advance preparation just as we expect the preacher to prepare his sermon. In some places there seems to be some resistance to such planning. The argument is that a spontaneous prayer comes more from the heart. Where did anyone ever get the idea that unplanned, thoughtless prayers were more heart-felt and more spiritual than those prepared in advance?

J.H. Jowett said:

> We frequently fix upon the sermon when we seek to account for the comparative impotency of a service, when perhaps the real cause of paralysis is to be found in our dead and deadening prayers. There is nothing mightier than the utterance of spontaneous prayer, when it is born in the depths of the soul. But there is nothing more dreadfully unimpressive than extemporary prayer which leaps about on the surface of things, a disorderly dance of empty words, going we know not whither, a mob of words carrying no blood, bearing no secret of the soul, a whirl of insignificant expressions, behind which is no vital pulse, no silent cry from lone and desolate depths.[10]

Most leaders would be helped by outlining and writing out their prayers. This does not mean the leader has to read the prayer publicly. However, writing a prayer will keep prayers from wandering.

2. *Open the worship service with an invocation.*

Many congregations do not know what an invocation (or a benediction) is or how to use one. We simply haven't used the word. An invocation is not merely a prayer at the beginning of a graduation ceremony or banquet. To invoke means "to call upon for aid, for protection, and for blessing." An invocation is brief and comes at the very first of the service. It is not a prayer for people or about issues, but a humble acknowledg-

---

[10]Andrew Blackwood, *The Fine Art of Public Worship* (New York: Abingdon-Cokesbury Press, 1939), pp. 166-67.

ment that those gathered look heavenward with thanks-giving, asking God's presence in what is about to be said and done. Prominent in the invocation is adoration and praise to God. The purpose is to express the desires of the people to become conscious of God's presence and to receive His blessing. Morgan Phelps Noyes gives us an example of a good invocation:

> Almighty God, unto whom all hearts be open, all desires known, and to whom no secrets are hid; cleanse the thoughts of our hearts by the inspiration of your Holy Spirit, that we may perfectly love you, and worthily magnify your holy name; through Jesus Christ our Lord, Amen.[11]

3. *At times a call to prayer is helpful.*

We do this frequently, anyway, although we probably don't realize it, when the leader says, "Let us pray," or "Would you pray with me?" A better way might be to read a brief passage before the prayer such as: "Ask, and it will be given you; seek and you will find, knock and the door will be opened to you" (Matt. 7:7). "Whatever you ask in my name, that will I do, that the Father may be glorified in the Son" (John 14:13, NASB). "In everything by prayer and supplication with thanksgiving let your requests be made known to God" (Phil. 4:6, NASB). "Continue stead-fastly in prayer" (Col. 4:2, RSV). "I urge that supplica-tions, prayers, intercessions, and thanksgivings be made for all" (1 Tim. 2:1, RSV). "Let us then with confidence draw near to the throne of grace" (Heb. 4:16, RSV).

4. *Address prayer to God.*

That may seem too elementary to mention, yet it is surprising how many leaders address the congregation. A prayer is not the time for the leader to preach a sermon. Nor is it the time to make announcements. I

---

[11]Morgan Phelps Noyes, *Prayers for Services* (New York: Charles Scribner's Sons, 1934), p. 36.

once heard a preacher cleverly disguise an announcement he had forgotten to make earlier. In his closing
prayer he said something like, "And Lord, help us in our
very important deacons meeting tonight in room 100
right after we are dismissed. In Jesus' Name. Amen."

5. *Be brief.*

This is not to say that there is not an appropriate
place for long prayer or for extended services of prayer.
However, some prayers are so long that people eventually "tune out." From my childhood I still remember
certain men who were always long-winded with their
prayers. A buddy and I would play a game where each of
us would guess how long the prayer would last. As soon
as the first word was spoken we were marking the
second hand on our watches. Admittedly, that was
immature behavior, but I am not sure the adults in the
assembly were doing a whole lot better. Psychologically,
it is not wise to pray too long because people cannot or
will not listen that long. When a prayer is so long that
people lose concentration, it becomes a hindrance
rather than an aid to worship. It is better to have several
short prayers than one long one. Jesus warned, "And
when you pray, do not keep on babbling like pagans, for
they think they will be heard because of their many
words" (Matt. 6:7).

6. *Don't try to impress other worshipers.*

The story is told of a particularly impressive public
prayer which was described in a northeastern newspaper
as "the finest prayer ever offered to a Boston audience."
Leaders are not praying to the audience, but to God.
Jesus condemned those who love to pray to be seen by
men. He called them hypocrites (Matt. 6:5). Prayer must
be sincere and designed to reach the heart of God.
Although the leader is not addressing the people, he is
attempting to lead the people. Therefore he needs to
use the words "we" and "our" and "us" rather than "I"

and "me" and "my" so that the people feel they are all talking with God.

   7. *Get rid of rote prayers.*

   I didn't say get rid of *written* prayers; I said *rote* prayers. There's a big difference. In Jesus' day, most of the prayers in the synagogue had become ritual and fixed in both form and content. They were recited from memory or handed down by oral tradition. The rabbis had also developed a set of directions for every aspect of prayer, and these were followed meticulously. Leaders and people prayed the same prayers and went through the same motions week after week. It probably was this situation that caused Jesus to teach His disciples not to pray as the hypocrites who used vain repetitions (Matt. 6:5-7). Jesus wanted their prayer to be sincere, free, direct and personal. He did not want it to be a mere ritual or formality.

   8. *Get rid of clichés and hackneyed expressions.*

   Here are a few: "Guide, guard, and direct." "May we partake of this cup in a manner well pleasing unto Thee." "If we've been found faithful, give us a home with Thee." "Free of molestation." "Bless the sick and afflicted." "Thank You for this beautiful day" (when there is a tornado watch out). "Bless all of those for whom it is our duty to pray." "Bless our speaker with a ready recollection." "Forgive us of the sins we have committed since we last obtained pardon." "Forgive us our sins of commission and omission." There are others, no doubt. My intention is not to poke fun at these expressions. If a brother uses them in sincerity of heart they are as pleasing to the Father as any other prayer that could be offered. The point is that phrases such as these generally reflect a lack of forethought and planning in prayer. They often do not help us think and pray, but put our prayers to sleep. These types of expressions can be recorded and played back with almost no thought.

It is also advisable to remove prayer jargon like "just" and "really." Those words became something of a fad several years ago. It may have sounded spiritual to pepper a prayer with those words: "Lord, we *just* want to . . . ." "Lord, we *really* need to . . . ." However, jargon can be distracting, especially if it is used too frequently. Pray in a language style that is simple, straightforward, and acceptable to all.

9. *Do not treat prayer as if it were a shopping list.*

Too many times we barge before the holy throne of God with our shopping list of wants, like a child with a Christmas list going to sit on Santa's lap. "Dear Father in heaven. Give us this . . . give us that." That is not the way Jesus taught us to pray. After He addressed God, "Our Father in heaven," Jesus prayed next, "hallowed be your name" (Matt. 6:9). God wants us to make petitions and requests, but we should spend time praising and honoring and acknowledging His majesty before we start asking for His favor. Our public prayers (and our private ones, too) would be improved one hundred percent if leaders began every prayer declaring to God His greatness.

10. *Cultivate private prayer.*

Public prayers are more effective when the leader is a man of prayer privately. When you think of the great men of God throughout history, each was a man of prayer: Moses, David, Hezekiah, Isaiah, Jeremiah, Daniel, Nehemiah, Jesus, Paul, and others. Prayer was the secret of their powerful lives. When you read their prayers which have been recorded in Scripture, it is obvious they had spent a great deal of time with God in times past.

11. *Study the prayers of godly people.*

The first and best place to study great prayers is in the Bible. Use a concordance or some other Bible study aid to help you locate the prayers of Scripture. Study the ways those men of faith addressed God. Take note of the ways they praised Him. See what kind of requests they made and how those petitions were offered. Learn to pray from the "masters" of prayer.

You might also find it helpful, after having studied the prayers of Scripture first, to study the written prayers of others in more recent times. Many good Christian book stores carry books of prayer. Many religious groups have rejected the use of prayer books in worship. This rejection, which is as old as the Protestant Reformation, came as a result of the abuses made of such prayers. No prayer book should be used as a substitute for framing one's own thoughts. It is not my argument here that congregations should begin using prayer books. What I am suggesting is that individual prayer leaders would do well to see how others have composed their prayers. Those who have never read any of these prayers will likely be surprised, and pleasantly so, at the simplicity, reverence, clarity, beauty, and power of the prayers. Let us not be so arrogant and prideful as to think that we have nothing we can learn from others. To do so cuts us off from so much of the best thinking and experience of those who have gone before us.

12. *Encourage the congregation to become actively involved in prayer.*

We want the congregation to follow in their minds and hearts as the leader tries to direct the thoughts for the entire congregation. People also need to be given permission to kneel, to say "amen," even to lift their hands to God if they feel the need to express themselves to the Father in that way. Not only is this type of physical participation biblical, it also has the practical benefit of helping people keep their attention focused on the Lord.

13. *Speak up loudly and clearly.*

Admittedly, this gets into pure mechanics. It does not

make a difference whether or not a person speaks clearly or loudly when he or she is praying privately. God hears the silent words of the heart. However, when a man is attempting to lead the entire congregation in prayer, he needs to make certain that he speaks clearly and loudly enough that people do not have to strain to understand. As many distractions as possible need to be removed — one of those is unclear and inaudible speech.

14. *Restore fasting with prayer.*

This is not the place or time to conduct a thorough study of fasting, but there is no question that God's people in biblical days often combined fasting with prayer. Sometimes it accompanied times of confession and earnest repentance (1 Sam. 7:6; 2 Sam. 1:12; Neh. 1:4). At other times they were seeking God's guidance and wisdom (Ezra 8:21-23; Neh. 1:4-11; Acts 13:2-3; 14:23). Congregations would do well to restudy the role of fasting, especially as it relates to prayer. We have missed out on many of God's blessings because we have neglected this biblical practice.

15. *Plan different types of prayers for the worship service.*

We've already talked about keeping public prayers brief. It is hard to say everything to God we might want and need to say in one prayer. Occasionally it is good in planning the order of worship to focus on specific prayer concerns. Include separate prayers of adoration and praise, confession, thanksgiving, petition, dedication, and intercession. Several of these within a service may be more effective than trying to say all of those things in one prayer.

16. *Close the service with a benediction and a blessing.*

If you study the orders of service going back to Justin Martyr in the early and mid-second century and on through later centuries, they all did something very similar at the end of their services. They had a benediction and blessing.

245

A benediction is a prayer, but it is more than merely a fancy name for the closing prayer. It is not the prayer that signals the time to put away the song books, or to get your coat, or to get an early jump on the cafeteria line. The benediction commends us to God's care and announces God's blessings on His people. It should gather up the attitudes expressed in the worship service, and it should be offered to God as a commitment of the congregation to carry out God's will in the world. There are several benedictions in Scripture (2 Cor. 13:14; Eph. 3:20-21; Heb. 13:20; 1 Pet. 5:10-11). Perhaps the best known is Numbers 6:24-26: "The LORD bless you and keep you; the LORD make His face shine upon you and be gracious to you; the LORD turn His face toward you and give you peace." Another beautiful benediction is Jude 24-25, "To him who is able to keep you from falling and to present you before his glorious presence without fault and with great joy — to the only God our Savior be glory, majesty, power and authority, through Jesus Christ our Lord, before all ages, now and forevermore!"

Most of our congregations do not use benedictions and blessings in our worship partly because we don't have a theological understanding of what blessing is all about. Blessing is more than just saying a few formulated words over someone's head. People lived and died by blessing in biblical days. Blessing is the conferring of worth, dignity, value, honor, significance, and purpose on the congregation. We don't have any examples of New Testament assemblies, but we do have examples of some sermons. Essentially the epistles functioned as sermons since they were to be read in the assembly. Stop and think how almost every one of them ends — with a blessing. Second Corinthians 13:14 is an example, "May the grace of the Lord Jesus Christ, and the love of God, and the fellowship of the Holy Spirit be with you all."

Biblical worship always concluded with a blessing. In

the Old Testament, the blessing was voiced by the priests and was intended to convey to individuals the truth that the power of the worshiping assembly would go with each of them personally. In the New Testament, Christ was celebrated as the blessing. Worshipers were dismissed in His name and with assurances of His grace. Worship in the early church invariably ended with a blessing.

It would strengthen and encourage your congregation for the preacher or an elder to say to the assembly just before they dismiss, "As you go today, remember the words of Peter: 'You are a chosen people, a royal priesthood, a holy nation, a people belonging to God, that you may declare the praises of him who called you out of darkness into his wonderful light. Once you were not a people, but now you are the people of God; once you had not received mercy, but now you have received mercy'" (1 Pet. 2:9-10).

DISCUSSION QUESTIONS
ON CHAPTER TEN

1. What does God's nature (e.g., His power, holiness, majesty) have to do with prayer?

2. Why did Jesus, the very Son of God, pray so much?

3. What do the words "Abba" and "amen" mean, and why are they important in prayer?

4. In the Lord's prayer, what does "hallowed be Thy name" mean? How do we do that in prayer?

5. What is appropriate content for prayers?

6. What is intercessory prayer? What is petition?

7. What does it mean to pray in Jesus' name? Why is it important to pray in Jesus' name?

8. What physical postures are appropriate for prayer (sitting, standing, kneeling, hands lifted, lying down, head bowed, head lifted, etc.)?

9. What role does the Holy Spirit play in prayer?

11

A Supper No Christian
Should Miss

In one sense, all of life is worship. Yet, when Christians assemble to praise the Lord, something unique happens. God is in our midst; He is among us. This certainly is true when together Christians partake of the Lord's Supper. Oscar Cullmann believes that the Lord's Supper was the "basis and goal of every gathering" of first century Christians.[1] John Calvin considered the Lord's Supper the highest moment in worship.[2] By 1812 Thomas Campbell had categorically stated that "New Testament worship ceases when the Lord's Supper is not observed every Lord's day." Alexander Campbell said that the Lord's Supper "is the greatest ordinance of the day of the Resurrection."

The Lord's Supper is anchored in the historical act of Jesus' death, burial, and resurrection. In a sense, the Supper is a visual presentation, a dramatization of God's saving acts through Jesus' death on the cross. The Lord's Supper is the way we see the Word of God, just as we *hear* it when the Scriptures are read or the sermon is preached. If people do not understand the symbolism involved in the Lord's Supper, taking the bread and fruit of the vine become meaningless acts of superstition.

The nature of the Lord's Supper has been the subject of great debate throughout the centuries. The disagreements over the Supper among the leaders of the

---

[1]Oscar Cullmann, *Early Christian Worship* (London: S.C.M. Press, 1953), p. 29.

[2]Osterhaven, p. 89.

sixteenth century Protestant Reformation kept the movement from uniting more fully; it almost brought the demise of the Reformation before the Catholic Counter-Reformation.[3] Four centuries ago Christians were persecuted, exiled, tortured, and killed in the name of a "correct" understanding of the Lord's Supper.[4] No one in America today suffers such treatment for their views on the Lord's Supper. However, many believers still differ greatly in their understanding of its nature.

Old Testament Roots

The roots of the Lord's Supper are deeply intertwined in the Passover Meal which God instituted shortly before the Israelites escaped Egyptian bondage. This gives us a window into the mind of Jesus and His disciples on that night in which he was betrayed.[5] On the night of the tenth and final plague which God would bring upon Egypt, the Israelites followed the Lord's instructions that each family of Israel take a year-old male lamb without defect and slaughter it. They were to put some of the lamb's blood on the tops and sides of their doorways. They were to roast the meat and eat it along with bitter herbs and bread without yeast. On that night God passed over the land of Egypt. Everywhere He saw the blood, the Lord passed over, but on the houses without blood the Lord struck down the firstborn of both humans and animals. God instructed Israel to commemorate that day for all generations to come (Exod. 12:14-17). Parents were to explain the meaning of the Passover festival to their children throughout the generations (Exod. 12:24-27).

---

[3]Hieronymus, p. 144.
[4]Martin, *The Worship of God*, p. 145.
[5]Martin, *Worship in the Early Church*, p. 110.

There were two parts to the Passover meal. First, the head of the household would hold in his hand a loaf and recite a formula which was drawn from Deuteronomy 16:3, "This is the bread of affliction which our fathers ate when they came out of Egypt." This linked them with the life of the nation in the past. Second, the head of the household would tell the story of the Exodus, known as the *Haggadah*. The word "Haggadah" means "declaration." It was taken from the Hebrew of Exodus 13:8, "On that day tell your son, 'I do this because of what the Lord did for me when I came out of Egypt.'" This retelling of the story was a vital part of the Passover.[6] The last supper that Jesus had with His disciples before His crucifixion was in the context of the Passover meal (Matt. 26:17-30; Mark 14:12-26; Luke 22:1, 7-21).

In one way, the Lord's Supper was not new — it gave new significance to something very old. Nothing was different, and yet everything was different. Jesus gave it all a new meaning.[7] Jesus shared many religiously significant meals with his followers (Mark 7:1-8; Luke 5:29-39; 7:34-50; 9:10-17; 11:37-52; 14:1-24), but the meal He shared with them that night was special. Jesus said, "How I have longed to eat this Passover with you before my death!" (Luke 22:15, NEB). Our knowledge of exactly how the Lord's Supper was observed in the first-century is limited.[8] However, we are able to deduce enough of its nature from biblical accounts that we can observe it in a scriptural fashion.

---

[6]*Ibid.*, pp. 114-15.

[7]Burkhart, p. 89.

[8]James F. White, *Introduction to Christian Worship* (Nashville: Abingdon, 1980), p. 210.

New Testament Terms

The Lord's Supper

Although the Passover helps us understand the Lord's Supper, it is Jesus who is the foundation of the Lord's Supper. What Jesus instituted the night before His death did not grow out of the synagogue service, but came directly from Him. In that Supper He gave Himself to and for His disciples. Paul called it "the *Lord's* Supper" (1 Cor. 11:20). Participating in the Lord's Supper is a way Christians acknowledge what God has done, is doing, and will do in Christ. We are not acknowledging anything we do, but what God does. We are invited guests at the *Lord's* table. We bring nothing which we can give to Him. It is the Lord's hospitality, His food, and His grace.[9] It can be argued that the Lord's Supper is the most unique feature of Christian worship.[10]

The Breaking of Bread

The names and descriptive terms given to the Supper provide insights into its meaning. One term used to describe it is "breaking of bread." The earliest believers "devoted themselves to the apostles' teaching and to the fellowship, to the breaking of bread and to prayer" (Acts 2:42). Acts 2:46 says the Christians broke bread in their homes daily. The Jews had long held to a custom of eating together as a religious rite.[11] Christians celebrated a full common meal with prayers of blessing patterned after the Jewish table blessings and prayed before and after the meal.[12]

Many New Testament scholars believe that this meal

[9]Burkhart, p. 92.
[10]Willis, p. 37.
[11]Webber, *Worship is a Verb*, p. 80.
[12]Willimon, *Word, Water, Wine and Bread*, p. 24.

was the *agape* feast. Robert Webber maintains that the daily breaking of bread described in Acts 2:46 was the agape meal. It is likely that the Lord's Supper was celebrated in the context of the agape meal.[13] The meal described in 1 Cor. 11:17-34 seems to bear this out. By the end of the second century, the agape meal was detached from the Lord's Supper. There is no evidence that they were separated in the first century. However, the Apostle Paul indicated that there were some abuses connected with the meal in Corinth (1 Cor. 11:17-34).

Two other factors contributed to the discontinuation of the agape meal besides the abuses which were evident. One, it became impractical to have such a meal with large numbers of people. Two, some Roman governmental authorities, such as the Bithynian governor Pliny, ordered the meal stopped in his own jurisdiction. Jones says, "The wisdom of attempting to use this type of meal [agape] in connection with formal worship is questionable, as the early Christians learned by bitter experience. But the social values of such a gathering, especially for small groups, are obvious."[14]

A Memorial Feast

The Supper is sometimes called a memorial feast. Memorials are important to us. If you visit Washington D.C. you will see national memorials that remind you of the great contributions made by fellow Americans in times past. There is the Washington Monument, the Jefferson Memorial, the Lincoln Memorial, the Tomb of the Unknown Soldier, and the Vietnam Veterans Memorial, to name but a few. Memorials come in all types: trees are planted as memorials, buildings are constructed and named as memorials, scholarships are

---

[13]Webber, *Worship, Old and New*, p. 48.
[14]Ilion T. Jones, pp. 79-80.

COME LET US ADORE HIM

established as memorials, even streets are named as memorials. Each one assists us in remembering some great person, place, or event. The most marvelous memorial of all, however, is the simplest of all — a loaf of unleavened bread and the fruit of the vine. Simple, yet powerful because of what it helps us remember.

The term "memorial" comes from Jesus' command that as often as we eat the bread and drink the cup we are to "do this in *remembrance*" of Him (Luke 22:19; 1 Cor. 11:23-24). "Remembrance" comes from the word *anamnesis*. It does not mean simply to recollect some remote date or event in bygone history. Rather, it means remembering in such a way that we see our participation in the past event, and we see that our destiny and future is bound up in it. It is like the remembering the Jews do when they observe the passover and the exodus. Jews do not remember those events as some irretrievable date from 3,000 years ago. Rather, they see those events in such a way that they confess "we are the people whom God brought out of the land of Egypt, for we were Pharaoh's bondsmen."

When we remember Jesus in the Lord's Supper, the past is rendered present, and therefore, it is a re-*present*-ation of the past so that it lives again in the present time.[15] "Remembrance" in the biblical sense is not to focus on the dead past, but to proclaim it presently manifested with power and in present reality.[16] As we remember Jesus' death, burial, and resurrection in the Lord's Supper, we are not simply recalling some event that happened more than 1900 years ago. We are remembering it in such a way that we know that we are

---

[15]James B. Torrance, "The Place of Jesus Christ in Worship," in *Theological Foundations for Ministry*, ed. Ray S. Anderson, (Grand Rapids: William B. Eerdmans Company, 1979), pp. 355-56.

[16]Willimon, *Word, Water, Wine and Bread*, pp. 37-38.

the people for whom Jesus died and rose again. We are the people whose sins Jesus died to forgive. We are the people for whom God has made a new covenant in the blood of Jesus (Exod. 24:3-11; Jer. 31:31-34; Luke 22:20; 1 Cor. 11:25). God saved us by His grace through the sacrifice of Jesus long ago on the cross. Some people speak of the Lord's Supper as a sacrifice which believers offer to God, but that is incorrect. The Lord's Supper is not our sacrifice; rather, it is a remembrance of Christ's sacrifice for us. "This work of memory, of realizing our participation and fellowship in the sufferings of Christ is the work of the Holy Spirit who brings these things to our remembrance, interpreting to us the meaning of these events."[17]

The possible danger in the word *memorial* is that it may lead some to think of the Lord's Supper as being like a funeral service or wake. The church does not hold a funeral service for Christ. Jesus is not dead — He is alive! He is risen! We make a mistake to turn the Lord's Supper into something sad. The resurrection has come, and we know that the risen Lord is in the breaking of the bread. Wendell Willis writes:

> As the Jew reenacts the flight from Egypt, the Christian makes present again his freedom from bondage to sin. As the Jew thinks of the lamb slain in the place of his firstborn son, the Christian remembers Christ as his paschal lamb (1 Cor. 5:7). As the Jew remembers the covenant in the wilderness, the Christian drinks the emblem of the New Covenant. With the eye of faith Christians recall and participate in the last supper, the agony of Gethsemane and Calvary, and the triumph of the resurrection.[18]

Communion

Another term for the Lord's Supper is *communion*. It

---

[17]Torrance, p. 356.
[18]Willis, pp. 41-42.

comes from 1 Cor. 10:16-17: "Is not the cup of thanks-giving for which we give thanks a participation [*koinonia*] in the blood of Christ? And is not the bread that we break a participation [*koinonia*] in the body of Christ? Because there is one loaf, we, who are many, are one body, for we all partake of the one loaf." Paul often drew upon the concept that the church is like a human body. The one loaf becomes a sign of the unity of those who partake.[19]

Something happens to people at a table. Jesus knew this and often met and talked with people around a common meal. Sharing a table is to acknowledge another person; to refuse to share a meal is to repudiate another person. Meals help create new relationships and strengthen established ones. Like it or not, we are some-how bound to someone who sits at our table. So it should be at the Lord's Table.[20]

In the Lord's Supper, individual Christians come together. We join together to form one body. We share our lives, beliefs, and commitment to the Lord and to one another. Together, we remember Jesus' death and resurrection. *Koinonia* (koinonia), the word found in 1 Corinthians 10:16, is the Greek word translated by the English word *fellowship*. The New International Version and the Revised Standard Version translate *koinonia* "participation." The King James translates *koinonia* "communion." The New American Standard Version uses the word "sharing" for *koinonia*.

Oscar Cullmann states that one of the purposes of the Lord's Supper is fellowship. As supporting evidence of this claim, Cullmann cites a prayer found in the second century *Didache*: "As the broken bread was scat-tered upon the mountains, but was brought together

---

[19]White, *Introduction to Christian Worship*, p. 223.
[20]Burkhart, pp. 92-93.

and became one, so let thy Church be gathered together from the ends of the earth into thy Kingdom."[21]

The emphasis of 1 Corinthians 10:16 falls upon the mystical union that we have with Christ through communing with Him in bread and fruit of the vine. God enters into union with believers through faith. Not only do we have communion with the Lord, but also with fellow believers in Christ (1 Cor. 10:17). Willis writes, "The Christian communion is not the mystic retreat to the inner sanctuary of the mind in a personal ecstasy with a private Lord. It is the concrete fellowship created by a common participation of an assembled church."[22] Martin says it this way, "The meal character of the Eucharist delivers it from a too ethereal and too other-worldly status, and grounds its significance in the nature of the church as a fellowship of believers who together make up the [family of God]."[23]

The Eucharist

The Supper is also called the *Eucharist*, a word which means *thanksgiving* (1 Cor. 14:16). In the modern Greek language the word still means "I thank you." The Christian assembly was a place where believers gave thanks. The Lord's Supper was the church's great moment of thanksgiving.[24] Jesus always seems to have given thanks when he took food (John 6:11). During the Lord's last supper with His disciples before His death, He offered thanks for the bread and the cup (Matt. 26:26; Mark 14:22-23; Luke 22:17-19). This follows the ancient Jewish practice of beginning a feast by pronouncing a blessing, by giving thanks, and showing

---

[21]Cullmann, pp. 18-19.
[22]Willis, p. 40.
[23]Martin, *The Worship of God*, p. 149.
[24]Ferguson, *Early Christians Speak*, pp. 95-96.

gratitude. Jesus instituted the Lord's Supper, in part, as a thanksgiving service. Darryl Tippins said:

> Today we have almost lost the sense of the assembly as *eucharista*. The early church knew the assembly was a eucharist — a thanksgiving service. Our gratitude, unfortunately, is depleted. We are largely thankless people. We are in fact afraid to make the service a Eucharist service. It sounds foreign to us. How un-Restoration-like. The great irony is that it is the most fundamentally biblical concept you can find about worship in the Bible.[25]

The noted Reformation leader, John Calvin, rejected the eucharistic element of the Supper (the thanksgiving) in favor of a personal examination of faith. This was a significant shift in meaning. The ancient church emphasized the objective work of Christ who was the perfect sacrifice. Calvin, Zwingli, and the majority of Protestants after them rejected the corrupted practices of the medieval church which had turned the Lord's Supper into a resacrifice. Dropping the entire prayer of thanksgiving, they shifted the emphasis of the Supper from God's objective action in Christ to man's faith, self-examination, and pursuit of good works.[26]

D.R. Dungan, a preacher in the Restoration Movement around the turn of the twentieth century, objected to the word *Eucharist* to describe the Lord's Supper because it contains but the single thought of giving thanks.[27] He insisted there was more to the Supper than giving thanks. Calvin was right in teaching that Christians should examine themselves when they partake the Lord's Supper (1 Cor. 11:28). Dungan was correct in recognizing that the Lord's Supper is broader

---

[25]Tippins, "Called to Worship."
[26]Webber, *Worship, Old and New*, p. 141.
[27]D.R. Dungan, "The Lord's Supper," in Hudson, John Allen, *The Pioneers on Worship* (Kansas City: The Old Paths Book Club, 1947), p. 93.

in meaning than merely thanksgiving. However, Calvin and others were wrong in discarding the element of thanksgiving from the Supper, and Dungan was wrong to downplay the importance of thanksgiving in the Lord's Supper. Whether we ever use the term *Eucharist* or not is unimportant. What is important is that in the Lord's Supper we give God thanks for what He has accomplished for us through the cross of Jesus.

New Covenant

When Jesus instituted the Lord's Supper, He said to His disciples, "This cup is the new covenant in my blood; do this, whenever you drink it, in remembrance of me." (1 Cor. 11:25; see also Matt. 26:28; Mark 14:24; Luke 22:20). God had made one covenant with Israel, but with the shedding of Jesus' blood, a new covenant was established, thus making the first one old and inferior (Heb. 8:6).

Covenant is a significant word in Scripture. When God made a covenant with anyone, He bound Himself to do or not do a specified thing. Covenants differ from contracts. Contracts are based on mutual distrust. We aren't sure that other people will keep their agreements, so we write and sign contracts binding us to a set of consequences should we break the agreements. Covenants are built on mutual trust and a personal relationship. If a covenant is broken the relationship is broken. As you read the Old Testament you will discover that God made a number of covenants with people. Men sometimes broke the covenant by their own rebellion, but God never broke the covenant. God is always faithful to His covenants.

That is why the new covenant in Christ's blood is so marvelously reassuring and powerful. God covenants to forgive us when we are washed in the blood of Jesus (Heb. 9:11-28; 10:1-23). That's the Lord's promise —

always! It is His pledge — forever! Under no circumstances will He break His word — ever! Like the Israelites, we may turn our backs on the light and walk in darkness; we may refuse to confess our sins. If we make that horrible mistake and persist in rebellion, we will have broken the covenant and forfeited God's forgiveness (Heb. 6:6). But make no mistake about it; it will not be God who has failed, but us. John, the Apostle, makes this wonderful promise: "But if we walk in the light, as he is in the light, we have fellowship with one another, and the blood of Jesus, his Son, purifies us from all sin" (1 John 1:7). Every time we partake of the cup we are proclaiming and claiming the promise of forgiveness in the new covenant.

The Mystery of the Lord's Supper

There is a great deal of mystery in the Lord's Supper. To say that Christ is present in the bread and wine is to say something which is true (John 6:51), but which at the same time is beyond our comprehension. When Jesus broke the bread and gave it to His disciples He said, "Take and eat; this is my body" (Matt. 26:26; Mark 14:22; Luke 22:19). Handing them the cup, Jesus said, "This is my blood . . . ." (Matt. 26:28; Mark 14:24).

During the Reformation period there was great controversy over the meaning of those words. Beginning in the fourth century, the Roman Catholic Church began teaching that the elements of bread and wine were changed into the literal body and blood of Jesus, even though the properties of taste and appearance remained those of bread and wine. This doctrine, which eventually became known as *transubstantiation*, made it essential to define the actual moment this change supposedly occurred. The interpretation that became accepted in the West was that the change took place when the priest repeated Jesus' words, "This is my body. Take this, this is my blood."

Among the churches in the East there was a more mystical understanding of the change.[28] Martin Luther and other reformers rejected this teaching. They viewed the doctrine of transubstantiation as a form of magic or superstition or even pagan idolatry.[29] Luther condemned transubstantiation as "apishness and buffoonery" of the papacy.[30] Luther and Calvin believed that there was a real presence of Christ in the Supper — not in a literal sense, but in a spiritual and transcendent sense. Zwingli rejected the idea of Christ's presence in the Supper, saying that the bread and wine were *mere symbols* and not the real presence of Christ. Luther thought that Zwingli, and those who agreed with him, meant to reduce the Supper to nothing but the bare signs without their spiritual substance. Luther resisted them to their faces and called them heretics.[31] Calvin never claimed to understand exactly how Christ was present in the Supper. He wrote:

> Although I distinguish between the sign and the thing signified, I do not teach that there is only a bare and shadowy figure, but distinctly declare that the bread is a sure pledge of that communion with the flesh and blood of Christ which it figures. For Christ . . . in reality performs what he promises by an external symbol. Hence I conclude that the bread which we break is truly the communion of the body of Christ. But as this connection of Christ with His members depends on His incomprehensible energy, I am not ashamed to admit this mystery which I feel and acknowledge to transcend the reach of my mind.[32]

---

[28]Ferguson, *Early Christians Speak*, pp. 111,116.
[29]Ilion T. Jones, p. 184.
[30]Osterhaven, p. 85.
[31]*Ibid.*, p. 84.
[32]*Ibid.*

Again, Calvin unashamedly confessed his inability to penetrate the mystery of Christians' communion with Christ. He wrote:

> Now if anyone should ask me how this takes place, I shall not be ashamed to confess that it is a secret too lofty for either my mind to comprehend or my words to declare. And, to speak more plainly, I rather experience than understand it. Therefore, I here embrace without controversy the truth of God in which I may safely rest. He declares His flesh the food of my soul, His blood its drink (John 6:53f). I offer my soul to Him to be fed with food. In His Sacred Supper He bids me take, eat, and drink His body and blood under the symbols of bread and wine. I do not doubt that He Himself truly presents them and that I receive them.[33]

Calvin looked to the Holy Spirit as the One who enables Christians to participate in the body and blood of Jesus in the Lord's Supper. The Holy Spirit, according to Calvin, used the Lord's Supper as an instrument to meet our need for spiritual food and drink.[34] Some writers refer to this as the *epiclesis*, which the *Catholic Encyclopedia* defines as the prayer "in which the celebrant prays that God may send down His Holy Spirit to change this bread and wine into the Body and Blood of His Son." This has no biblical foundation, and the Reformers were right to reject it. The Holy Spirit comes upon people, not upon things, although He may use things as His instruments. Originally the *epiclesis* was a prayer for the coming of the Holy Spirit on the worshipers, not the elements. In light of all the misunderstanding tied to this term, it is probably best for us not to use the word.[35]

The explanation lies partly in the truth that God has promised to be in the midst of His people when they

---

[33]Osterhaven, p. 86.
[34]*Ibid.*, pp. 87-88.
[35]Ilion T. Jones, p. 191.

assemble to worship and when they commune with the Lord and each other around the Lord's Table. As we partake of the Lord's Supper, and as we remember all that God did for us through Calvary, the death of Christ is again made vivid in our own lives. It is not enough for Christians to take the Lord's Supper every week simply because first century Christians did so. We commune together around the Table because we are called to remember, to re-experience the very presence of Christ. Hebrews 10:19-23 assures us that we who have been washed and cleansed in the blood of Jesus have confidence to enter into the very presence of God. When we assemble and when we partake the Lord's Supper, not only do we encourage and spur one another on to love and good works (Heb. 10:24-25), but we are built up knowing that God has allowed us to come into His very presence.[36]

Explanations Concerning the Lord's Supper

The most important passage in the New Testament epistles concerning the Lord's Supper is 1 Corinthians 11:17-34. Paul wanted to be certain that when those Christians came to commune that they had their eyes trained to look in the right directions. Some thoughtful student of Scripture has come up with a helpful way of assisting us in understanding the meaning of the Lord's Supper. Based on 1 Corinthians 11:17-34, we need to look in five directions: backward, outward, forward, inward, and upward.

The *backward* look has to do with the remembrance, or memorial, which we discussed earlier. The Lord's Supper involves an *outward* look in the sense of a proclamation to the world that Jesus gave His life for all people. First

---

[36]Reese, "Called to Worship."

Corinthians 11:26 says, "For whenever you eat this bread and drink this cup, you *proclaim* the Lord's death . . . ." The word translated "proclaim" means "publish" or "preach." The Lord's Supper, therefore, is a form of preaching about the death, burial and resurrection of Christ and the salvation achieved through it. There is an *outward* look also in the sense that Christians are called to "[recognize] the body of the Lord" (1 Cor. 11:29). This admonition is not, as some have taught, a command to think about the physical body of Jesus as it hung on the cross. Rather, the instruction to recognize the body is an admonition to show concern for individuals who make up the body of Christ (1 Cor. 10:17; 12:12-13).

The Supper is a *forward* look in that it anticipates Jesus' return. First Corinthians 11:26 ends with the words "until He comes." "Come, O Lord!" Paul wrote (1 Cor. 16:22). We are not to think of Jesus being absent, for He is present even in the Supper (John 6:53-58; Matt. 18:20; 28:20; Rev. 3:20). But on that day when Jesus returns, we shall know Him fully, and we shall go to be with Him forever (1 Thess. 4:16-18).

There is an *inward* look in the sense of self-examination. It was because of sin — my sin and your sin — that Jesus died. Paul warns us of the need to take the Lord's Supper in a "worthy manner" (1 Cor. 11:27). There should be repentance and a pursuit of godliness. This does not mean that we must be sinlessly perfect. The Supper ought to arouse within us the desire to seek forgiveness and to be grateful to God for that forgiveness available in the blood of Jesus.[37] Finally, there is the *upward* look — upward in thanksgiving to God for the One who gave Himself for us. Upward to God in praise of Jesus Christ for our salvation through Him. Upward in joy, knowing that we do not serve a departed hero,

---

[37]Osterhaven, p. 90.

but a resurrected and reigning Lord.[38]

Within churches in the Restoration Movement, discussions concerning the Lord's Supper have not been so much on the nature of the Supper itself, but on the frequency of observance. How often should Christians observe the Lord's Supper? The Bible and church history bear testimony to weekly celebration of the Lord's Supper. As far as second century sources go, the Lord's Supper was celebrated only on Sundays. There is no second century evidence for the celebration of a daily Eucharist.[39] Although their views did not win the day, Luther and Calvin wanted to establish weekly communion.[40] Calvin condemned the practice of taking the Lord's Supper once a year as "a veritable invention of the Devil." Apparently, Calvin was not opposed to taking it even more frequently than every Lord's day. He quoted Augustine, saying that some of the ancient church celebrated the Supper daily.[41]

Alexander Campbell expressed his views on this subject in the October 3 and the November 7, 1825 issues of *The Christian Baptist* (Vol. III, Numbers 3 and 4). Campbell cited sources which indicated that weekly communion was preserved in the Greek church until the seventh century, and that one of the canons of the Greek Church called for excommunication of any member who neglected the Supper three weeks in a row.[42] In a particularly interesting passage, Campbell wrote:

---

[38]Willimon, *Word, Water, Wine and Bread*, p. 125.

[39]Ferguson, *Early Christians Speak*, pp. 86, 96-97.

[40]William H. Willimon, *The Service of God: Christian Work and Worship* (Nashville: Abingdon Press, 1983), p. 123.

[41]Osterhaven, p. 91.

[42]Alexander Campbell, "On the Breaking of Bread" (No. IV), *The Christian Baptist* 3, No. 4 (Nov. 7, 1825), p. 77.

Since the commencement of the present century, many
congregations in England, Scotland, Ireland, and some in the
United States and Canada, both Independents and Baptists,
have attended upon the supper every Lord's day, and the practice is every day gaining ground. These historical notices may
be of some use to those who are ever and anon crying out
Innovation! Innovation! [Italics were Campbell's.] But we advocate the principle and the practice on apostolic grounds alone.[43]

In sarcastic fashion, Campbell answered the objection
that weekly observance of the Lord's Supper would
make it too common and cause it to lose its solemnity.
He wrote, "Well, then, the seldomer the better. If we
observe it only once in twenty years, it will be the more
uncommon and solemn. And, on the same principle, the
seldomer we pray the better. We shall pray with more
solemnity if we pray once in twenty years."[44] It should be
clear that weekly observance of the Lord's Supper on
the Lord's Day is proper. This is attested not only by
church history, but also clearly was the practice of the
early church (Acts 20:7).

Making The Lord's Supper More Meaningful

How can we improve our efforts around the Lord's
Table? Here are some practical suggestions:
1) *Take enough time.*
We must be sure we take enough time to commune
with the Lord and with our fellow Christians. To rush
through the Lord's Supper is a sacrilege. Some congregations spend more time on announcements and the
collection than on the Lord's Supper. It takes time to
look backward, inward, outward, forward, and upward.
Why should we rush through a meal with our Lord?

---

[43]*Ibid.*, p. 78.
[44]Alexander Campbell, "On the Breaking of Bread" (No. III), *The
Christian Baptist* 3, No. 3 (Oct. 3, 1825), p. 54.

2) *Help Christians discern the body.*

Paul wrote, "For anyone who eats and drinks without recognizing the body of the Lord eats and drinks judgment on himself" (1 Cor. 11:29). I do not believe that this passage instructs us to think about the suffering of the physical body of Jesus. There is the "memorial" aspect of the Lord's Supper which encourages us to look back in remembrance of all the events surrounding Jesus' crucifixion. That certainly includes His false arrest, the mockery of His trial, the cruel beating, the crown of thorns, the nails, the humiliation, the taunts and jeers, and the piercing spear. We need to remember those things during the Lord's Supper. However, Paul's admonition to recognize (or as the King James Version says, "discern") the body of the Lord is a reference to the church, the body of Christ (1 Cor. 10:17; 12:12-13). That means that we are to be concerned about our brothers and sisters as we eat the Supper. We are to recognize that they, like us, have sins which need forgiveness. They, like us, need mercy. They, too, have been saved by the grace of God and the blood of Jesus.

It was a great loss to the church when Christians no longer were able to partake of the Lord's Supper within the context of the Agape Meal. Now, as then, it is in the sharing of a meal with others that we get to know them better. The more often we share meals with friends, the more we come to know their fears and concerns, their needs and burdens, their joys and victories.

There is a measure of fellowship that is possible at a table that is rarely found anywhere else. There were abuses with this type of setting in the Corinthian church, and there probably would be similar abuses today. Certainly, in large churches, it is almost impossible to observe the Lord's Supper in the larger context of a fellowship meal. But the need for such fellowship and concern is not diminished. Perhaps the best we can do on a regular basis is to remind people during the Supper of their responsibility to their fellow Christians — to love each other and to demonstrate concern for each other.

3) *Give more attention to prayers.*

Many men need encouragement and help in leading better and more appropriate prayers at the table. Prayers at the Table are often so trite and rote: "Bless this loaf; bless this cup. May we partake of this in a manner which is well pleasing in thy sight. . . ." Technically, it is not correct to ask God to bless the loaf and the fruit of the vine. A Jew does not say, "Bless this food," but, rather, "Blessed be God who gave this food."[45] The Lord's Supper can be much more meaningful if men will give careful forethought to the prayers they lead at the Table.

4) *Stress the meaning of the Lord's Supper.*

As with any activity that we repeat regularly, we tend to forget the significance and meaning of our actions. There is the distinct danger of doing this with the Lord's Supper. One good way to emphasize its meaning is to read some portion of Scripture that highlights the sacrifice of Jesus, or His resurrection, or His coming. This is similar to the practice of the Jews in Passover when the leader of the household retold the story of the Exodus — it was their way of remembering the meaning of the meal.

5) *Sing appropriate songs.*

It is helpful to sing a song(s) as a part of the Lord's Supper. Appropriate songs before, during, and after the Supper help focus minds on what God has done through Jesus. Some of the songs may be reflective and somber, like "Night With Ebon Pinion." Others may be happy and energetic, like "I Stand Amazed." No Scripture demands a quiet, almost "death-like" atmosphere during the Lord's Supper. Whichever is in keeping with the

---

[45]Willimon, *Word, Water, Wine and Bread*, p. 36.

mood and power of worship and the orderliness of 1 Corinthians 14:40 would be appropriate. It is a man-made rule that says, "You cannot engage in two acts of worship at once." Some of our songs are prayer-songs. Utilize the power of musical expression to help people focus on the death, burial, and resurrection of Jesus.

6) *Teach regularly about the Lord's Supper.*

Preachers need to teach regularly concerning the Lord's Supper, covering principles like those discussed in this chapter. There are always new people who have never heard the gospel before. New Christians need to learn about the Supper. Even older, mature Christians need regular reminders. The Lord's Supper is too important not to teach on it periodically.

7) *Select leaders carefully.*

Carefully pick the men who will lead the communion service. Most congregations look for places in worship to use men in leadership. The approach sometimes is, "We haven't used Brother So and So in the service in a while. He gets his feelings hurt if we don't call on him. Go ask him if he'll lead the prayers for communion this morning." It may not matter that he has voiced exactly the same clichés the last fifty years or that he mumbles and speaks so softly that no one can hear him. The misplaced goal becomes *using* him so his feelings will not be hurt. The Lord's Supper deserves better than that. Men who lead at the Table should be capable of directing the congregation in ways that help people focus on the wonderful meaning of the Supper.

8) *Focus an entire service on the Lord's Supper.*

Congregations might occasionally focus an entire period of worship on the Lord's Supper. The songs, readings, prayers, and sermon can all center on the Table. This draws special emphasis to the Supper and makes it more meaningful to Christians as they remember their Lord.

DISCUSSION QUESTIONS
ON CHAPTER ELEVEN

1. What relationship does the Lord's Supper have to the Jewish Passover (Exod. 12:14-17; Matt. 26:17-30)?

2. The Lord's Supper is referred to in a number of different ways. What is the meaning and significance of each of the following terms?

   a. "breaking of bread" (Acts 2:42, 46; 1 Cor. 11:17-34)

   b. "memorial" (Luke 22:19; 1 Cor. 11:24)

   c. "communion" (1 Cor. 10:16-17)

   d. "thanksgiving" (Matt. 26:26; 1 Cor. 14:16)

3. How is the bread the "body" and the fruit of the vine the "blood" of Jesus (Matt. 26:26, 28; Mark 14:22, 24)?

4. How do we "proclaim the Lord's death" when we partake of the Lord's Supper (1 Cor. 11:26)?

5. What does it mean to recognize the body of the Lord (1 Cor. 11:29)?

6. Why did Jesus want us to partake of the Lord's Supper in a worthy manner (1 Cor. 11:27)?

7. What does it mean to take of the Lord's Supper in a worthy manner?

8. How can we make the Lord's Supper more meaningful?

12
Worship Is a Verb

One of the sad realities about worship is the sheer boredom many people experience in the weekly worship assembly. Some people crack jokes about the mental gymnastics they go through to stay awake. They count the number of bricks in the wall, or find the longest and shortest songs in the hymnal — anything to stay awake. Several years ago someone gave me a little book of cartoons with the title, *One Hundred Exciting Things to Do During a Dull Sermon* (I hope they were not dropping me a not-so-subtle hint). I will have to admit, the cartoons were funny. However, the more I have reflected on that little book, the less humorous it has become. To put a twist on an old expression, "If it weren't so funny, it would be sad."

Worship should be a celebration, but many people respond as if they are at a funeral. People who are bored feel as if they are engaged in an endurance race rather than a positive encounter with God. While many people attend worship services they consider boring and unrelated to life, many more express their dissatisfaction by staying away. For them, Sunday morning is a time to run errands, sleep late, or head to the beach or the mountains. The reasons for such feelings are many. Certainly, one of the reasons many people find worship boring is that they are not personally involved in it. They attend worship, but they do so more as passive observers than as active participants. They feel like bystanders, watching as the minister, and perhaps a few other leaders, get a good workout.

Medieval and pre-Reformation worship was clergy-centered. The Reformers returned worship to the people — they wanted worship to be congregational, following the biblical pattern of participation. It seems, however, that much of modern worship has drifted back into the clergy-centered pattern of the medieval church. In a world mesmerized by electronic media, too many of us are conditioned to be uninvolved spectators.[1] We have become what Ralph Martin describes as "passive, motionless recipients, . . . an inert body of passive auditors."[2]

The Danish philosopher Søren Kierkegaard described the way many people conceive worship. They see worship as a dramatic production in which God is the prompter, the worship leaders are the performers, and the people are the audience. If worship is ever to become what God intended it to be, those roles must be rearranged. Kierkegaard insisted that worshipers are the performers, worship leaders are the prompters, and God is the audience. His point is that worship is directed to God. Human beings are not onlookers, but are to be active participants in worship. Even worship leaders themselves must be worshipers.

Webber is absolutely correct when he writes, "Worship is a verb. It is not something done to us or for us, but by us."[3] Worship is active, requiring people to get involved, to participate. Often people say, "I didn't get anything out of worship today." Such a statement belies the mistaken belief that worshipers come primarily to receive rather than give. Worshipers should be uplifted and encouraged, but as a by-product, not as an end in itself. Our primary role in worship is to offer something to the Lord. Worship primarily is a response to God, to

---

[1]Webber, *Worship is a Verb*, p. 131.
[2]Martin, *The Worship of God*, pp. 6-7.
[3]Webber, *Worship is a Verb*, p. 12.

all that He has done and is doing in us through Jesus Christ. The theological code word for our offering to God is sacrifice — not a bloody animal sacrifice, but a sacrifice of praise (Heb. 13:15).[4]

Perhaps we need to stop calling our places of assembly "auditoriums," for that word implies a place where people gather as passive listeners, not as active participants. Worship will not be rejuvenated in our day until we end the passivity that characterizes many of our worship assemblies.[5] Although many congregations within the Restoration Movement shun the word "sanctuary," it seems like a good alternative for "auditorium." It means "a holy or sacred place." The bricks, mortar, and carpet themselves are no more sacred than a shopping mall. However, when the saints assemble in that room to worship, the activity in which they are engaged is holy and sacred.

Dr. Robert Richardson, a personal friend and biographer of Alexander Campbell, published a series of talks between 1847 and 1850 in Campbell's *Millennial Harbinger*. The series was titled *Communings in the Sanctuary*. Later, at the urging of the noted scholar and commentator J. W. McGarvey, he collected 24 of those talks into a small book of the same title. The important thing is not what we call our assembly room. The point is that we need to get rid of the notion that worship is something people observe passively.

Worship which actively involves people cannot help but engage their bodies as well as their minds. However, in many churches, there is a resistance to physical involvement in worship. Many Christians are such rationalists that they approach all of religion, and worship in particular, almost totally from a cerebral perspective. They are so afraid of the uncontrolled emotional expres-

---

[4]Martin, *The Worship of God*, p. 6.
[5]Tippins, "Called to Worship."

COME LET US ADORE HIM

sions in some Pentecostal worship services that they run
to the opposite extreme, shunning any expression of
emotion or physical motion in worship. This misunderstanding and fear is unfortunate and incorrect. People
are not merely spirit beings with a soul. We also are
physical bodies made of flesh and bone and blood. We
who worship God in spirit worship Him with our bodies
as well.[6] A human being does not merely have a body, he
or she *is* a body. The tendency we have to deny the physical in worship is at least as old as the early Christian
heresy of Gnosticism which taught that the flesh was
inherently evil.[7] C.S. Lewis wrote:

> There is no good trying to be more spiritual than God. God
> never meant man to be a purely spiritual creature. That's why
> He used material things like bread and wine to put new life
> into us. We may think this rather crude and unspiritual. God
> does not. He invented eating. He likes matter. He invented it.[8]

That which most clearly validates God's approval of
the physical body is the incarnation, for all the fullness
of God inhabited the human, physical body of Christ
(Col. 1:19). God gave us our bodies and our senses.
Therefore, we do not need to be afraid of expressions of
worship that actively use our bodies and senses. Martin
Luther is reported to have said that God gave us five
senses with which to worship Him, and that it would be
sheer ingratitude to use less.[9] Throughout the Bible we
find a variety of physical postures in connection with
worship. This simply means that God wants our bodies
involved in worship as well as our heads.[10]

---

[6]Allen and Borror, p. 132.
[7]Webber, *Worship, Old and New*, p. 19.
[8]Tippins, "Called to Worship."
[9]Frank C. Senn, *Christian Worship and Its Cultural Setting* (Philadelphia: Fortress Press, 1983), p. 75.
[10]Foster, p. 147.

We have a lot of unlearning and reeducating to do in this matter of using the body in worship. By insisting that people approach worship primarily with their heads, we have asked worshipers to be incomplete, one-dimensional beings, something different during worship than they are the rest of the week. The rest of the week people express themselves not only as rational beings, but also as physical and emotional beings. If worship only appeals to people's rational minds, we should not be surprised when they have difficulty connecting what they do in worship with what they do the rest of their week. The greatest command is: "Love the Lord your God with all your *heart* and with all your *soul* and with all your *mind* and with all your *strength*" (Mark 12:30). This greatest of all commands cannot be fulfilled by a purely rational approach to worship. It requires us to use our bodies and to engage our emotions as well as our brains.

In what physical ways does the Bible say that people participate in worship? Traditionally, we have emphasized "the five acts of worship": singing, praying, preaching, giving, and the Lord's Supper. These five are certainly important elements of worship, but it is impossible to read the Old or New Testament and limit expressions of worship to only five acts. There are many verbs related to worship. In addition to the five already mentioned, worship is chanting, shouting, hearing, remembering, sharing, kneeling, lifting, bowing, embracing, blessing, kissing, glorifying, confessing, exhorting, encouraging, declaring, meditating, and many more. Look at some of the ways worshipers are to participate actively in worship.

Verbal Expressions of Worship

We begin by exploring verbal ways of getting involved in worship. King David wrote, "I proclaim righteousness in the great assembly; I do not seal my lips" (Ps. 40:9).

Neither can we seal our lips if we intend to worship the Lord. We read in the Bible a number of ways that we are to use our lips in worship.

1) *Singing.*

Worshipers sing. We have already studied singing in an earlier chapter. No other form of worship enables more people to get involved together in verbal worship at one time than singing.

2) *Preaching, teaching, and Scripture reading.*

Worship involves preaching, teaching, and the reading of God's Word. Obviously, only one person at a time can preach or teach the Scriptures. However, when one person is preaching, teaching, or reading Scripture, others are required to listen. Good listening is hard work and requires active involvement. There are other ways to include people more actively in Scripture reading. One of those ways is to engage the congregation in unison readings.

For years, the entire congregation at the Madison Church recited the Twenty-third Psalm. Other passages lend themselves well to unison reading. Congregations can also participate in responsive readings from Scripture. In a responsive reading, one person (the reader) or a group (perhaps the people sitting in one side of the sanctuary) read one portion of the Scripture text, then the rest of the congregation reads the next portion of the Scripture text. Let me illustrate this with Psalm 118:1-4.

Reader: "Give thanks to the LORD, for he is good.
Congregation: His love endures forever.
Reader: Let Israel say:
Congregation: His love endures forever.
Reader: Let the house of Aaron say:
Congregation: His love endures forever.
Reader: Let those who fear the LORD say:
Congregation: His love endures forever."

Psalm 136 follows this same pattern. There are many other texts which are well suited for responsive readings.

3) *Praying.*

Worshipers pray. Again, only one person at a time can pray audibly in the assembly, but those being led are asked to participate in the prayer. There are ways the congregation can become more actively involved in the prayers. A prayer leader might suggest an area of concern, and then give people in the assembly time to express silently their own thoughts. For example, the leader might say, "Now let us pray for our missionary family in Eastern Europe," or "let us now offer thanks to God for the ways He has provided our needs this week." The leader can instruct people to offer individual prayers that are inaudible, or he may allow men to stand one at a time and voice a prayer.

4) *Speaking Out.*

Worshipers may speak out at appropriate times in worship. One of the most frequent verbal responses in Scripture is the "Amen." In the Old Testament (and in the synagogue which developed during the intertestamental period) the "amen" was the people's full-hearted and full-throated response to and endorsement of the words of another. Evidence of this is clear in Psalm 106:48, "Praise be to the LORD, the God of Israel, from everlasting to everlasting. Let all the people say, 'Amen!' Praise the LORD." The word literally means "to be firm, true," and is connected with the verb "to believe."[11] "Amen" is a Hebrew word found in both Testaments. Basically it means "let it be," or "so be it." It is saying "yes" to God.[12] Nehemiah 8:4-6 describes the scene when Ezra opened the book of the Law before the people who had assembled to hear from the Lord. When

---

[11]Martin, *Worship in the Early Church*, pp. 36-37.
[12]Allen and Borror, p. 111.

Ezra praised the Lord, "all the people lifted their hands
and responded, 'Amen! Amen!'" (Neh. 8:6). Many of the
psalms express praise to God with a resounding and
enthusiastic "Amen and Amen" (Ps. 41:13; 72:19; 89:52).

Although the great prayers of the Old Testament do
not end with "amen," the practice of saying "amen" at
the conclusion of prayers apparently was well established
before the birth of Christianity. The "amen" at the
conclusion of prayers can be traced to the synagogue,
where saying "amen" at the end of prayers was the
congregation's way of making the prayer their own.[13]
What the Apostle John saw and heard in his visions of
heaven is instructive and inspiring:

> Then I heard every creature in heaven and on earth and under
> the earth and on the sea, and all that is in them, singing:
> > "To Him who sits on the throne and to the Lamb
> > be praise and honor and glory and power,
> > > forever and ever!"
> The four living creatures said, "Amen," and the elders fell
> down and worshiped   (Rev. 5:13-14).

> All the angels were standing around the throne and around
> the elders and the four living creatures. They fell down on
> their faces before the throne and worshiped God, saying:
> > "Amen!
> > Praise and glory
> > and wisdom and thanks and honor
> > and power and strength
> > be to our God for ever and ever.
> > Amen!"   (Rev. 7:11-12).

"Amen" was a liturgical word from the original Jewish
heritage of the church which survived in later worship of
the second century and beyond. It appears everywhere
in early Christian accounts of worship.[14] There is no

---

[13]Rowley, p. 235.
[14]Ferguson, *Early Christians Speak*, p. 101.

good reason why Christians today should not utter a resounding "amen" or a "yes" in worship, both at the conclusion of a prayer, and also as a way of expressing support and belief that what another has said or done in worship is good and right. Alexander Campbell insisted that at the close of all public prayer the whole congregation should unite, as did the primitive Christians, with an audible and clear "Amen."[15]

Another word audibly expressed in worship is "hallelujah" or "alleluia." Incidentally, the difference between these two words is the result of transliteration from Hebrew (which has an "h" letter) to Greek (which has no "h" letter).[16] "Hallelujah" is a transliterated word, meaning that it is pronounced essentially the same as it was in the original. This word is found in its transliterated form in many different languages.

The word "hallelujah" is found 24 times in the Old Testament, all of them occurring between Psalm 104 and 150. "Hallelujah" is found four times in the New Testament, all in the book of Revelation (19:1-6). The word is derived from the Hebrew root "*halal*" (הלל). There are several different shades of meaning which come from this root word. One of those meanings is "to make a noise." Another meaning is "to praise." Another shade of meaning is "to boast, to brag on, to laud, to make a show, even to the point of looking foolish."[17] "*Halal*" is the first part of the word; "*Jah*" is the second part. "*Jah*" (יה) is the abbreviated form of a name for God (יהוה). Therefore, "hallelujah" means "praise be to God."

---

[15]Cartwright, p. 37.

[16]Ronald B. Allen, "When the Psalmists Say, 'Praise the Lord!'" *Worship Leader*, (October/November 1992): p. 8.

[17]Jack Taylor, *The Hallelujah Factor* (Nashville: Broadman Press, 1983), p. 71.

The Old Testament scholar, Ronald B. Allen, writes:

The verb is an imperative, a command. When the psalmists say, "Praise the Lord!," they were not giving an interjection, or a comment — they were giving a command. They were saying "Do it!" That is, "PRAISE Him!" Further, the particular nuance of this word for praise in the Bible is that of "joyful boasting." . . . By "praise," the psalmists have in mind a specific type of response to God that is *vocal* and *public* in nature. In the mind of the psalmists, there was no thought of "silent praise" or of "quiet, personal praise." . . . There are a score of words in the Psalms that may each be translated by "praise," but they all have these two things in common: Biblical praise is done aloud, and is done in the presence of others.[18]

Jack Taylor writes, "Thus *hallelujah* became the spontaneous outcry of one excited about God, the exclamation of one upon whose consciousness part of the majesty of God has dawned."[19] We must not squelch the joyful exclamations of those who voice them. Perhaps you heard about the visitor who exclaimed in a rather staid congregation, "Praise the Lord." When he did that a second time, one of the ushers tapped him on the shoulder, and with a disapproving frown on his face said, "We don't do that 'Praise the Lord' stuff here."

Read Revelation 19:1-6, and pay careful attention to the sounds and the volume associated with the voicing of "amen" and "hallelujah" in praise. John, the author of Revelation, recorded what sounded like "the *roar* of a great multitude," and "*shouting*," and "a great multitude like the *roar* of rushing waters," and "like *loud* peals of thunder" (emphasis added). It is easy to see that at times heaven is a noisy place. Revelation 5:11-12 tells about thousands upon thousands of angels singing in a *loud* voice. Revelation 7:10 records an uncountable multitude crying out with a *loud* voice. Revelation 12:10 announces

---

[18]Allen, "When the Psalmists Say," p. 8.
[19]Taylor, p. 71.

the salvation of Christ in a *loud* voice. Numerous Old Testament passages speak of *"shouting"* in the context of worship and praise.

Joy is that which often motivated the people to shout. God's people were instructed to "Shout to God with cries of joy" (Ps. 47:1). "Shout with joy to God, all the earth!" (Ps. 66:1; 100:1). The Lord declared through the prophet Zechariah, "Shout and be glad, O Daughter of Zion. For I am coming, and I will live among you" (Zech. 2:10). Announcing the coming of the Messiah, the same prophet wrote, "Rejoice greatly, O Daughter of Zion! Shout, daughter of Jerusalem! See, your king comes to you, righteous and having salvation" (Zech. 9:9).

Not only did God's people shout for joy, but even nature itself joins in the joyful shout of praise (Ps. 65:13; 66:1; 71:23). Psalm 98:4 says, "Shout for joy to the LORD, *all the earth*, burst into jubilant song with music." Isaiah 49:13 reads, "Shout for joy, O heavens; rejoice, O earth; burst into song, O mountains! For the Lord comforts his people." Other passages call on God's people to "shout aloud to the God of Jacob!" (Ps. 81:1), or "Shout *aloud* to the Rock of our salvation" (Ps. 95:1), or "Shout *aloud* and sing for joy, people of Zion, for great is the Holy One of Israel among you" (Isa. 12:6).

It is hard to read certain passages and not get caught up in the uninhibited sense of joy and celebration and rejoicing: "Sing for joy, O heavens, for the LORD has done this; shout aloud, O earth beneath. Burst into song, you mountains, you forests and all your trees, for the LORD has redeemed Jacob, he displays his glory in Israel" (Isa. 44:23). After the Hebrew exiles returned to Jerusalem from Babylonian bondage, the people relaid the foundations of the temple which had been destroyed by the forces of Nebuchadnezzar. Ezra records the spontaneous response of many of the people, "With praise and thanksgiving they sang to the LORD: 'He is good; his love to Israel endures forever.' And all the people gave a great shout of praise to the LORD, because the foundation of the house of the LORD was laid" (Ezra 3:11).

Other Expressions

Christian writings from the early church testify to the fact that Christians voiced other expressions in worship: "Lord be with you," "peace to you," "Lord have mercy," "thanks be to God." Such short exclamations show how a sense of the presence of God permeated their worship. Early Christians actively participated in the congregational prayers by their responses and acclamations. Tertullian (c. A.D. 165-220) implies that the raising of hands to God, the uttering of "amen," and the shouting of the doxology "Forever" were all expressions of the whole congregation.[20]

A Place For Silence

This does not mean that worship services should be loud and boisterous, and that there is not a time and place for silence. We need times of silence in worship. In worship, silence is far more than an absence of sound. It makes up an important part of the dialogue between God and His worshipers. Habakkuk was told, "The LORD is in his holy temple; let all the earth be silent before him" (Hab. 2:20). Elijah heard the voice of God not amid dramatic turbulence but in stark silence — in the "still small voice" (1 Kgs. 19:12).

Silence gives people opportunity and encourages them to center on God, to confess their sins to the Father, and to pray. There are times when silence and quiet meditation are appropriate, as it was in heaven when Christ opened the seventh seal, when there was silence in heaven for about half an hour (Rev. 8:1).

---

[20]Ferguson, *Early Christians Speak*, pp. 144-145.

There is a richness and blessing in quietly reflecting and contemplating during worship what God has done for us. Silence in worship slows the frantic pace of life and allows us time for individual prayer and reflection. The Psalmist recorded the very sentiments of God, "Be still, and know that I am God" (Ps. 46:10).

However, we may have stressed the silence and stillness so much that we are not sure it is appropriate to be loud or to move physically in worship. When I was a little boy I had trouble sitting still in the assembly. When I would fidget and talk and wiggle, my mother would stare me into motionless silence. If that didn't get my attention, she would pop me on the leg and say, "Be still, we're in worship." For a while I thought God was no fun at all. A God who did not want little boys to move in church was someone I could not understand.

We know the problem with trying to keep little children still in worship. However, many adults still live with those powerful messages they received when they were children. It is like a tape playing continuously: "Be still, you're in church! Don't talk, you're in church!" We may think the only way God will accept our worship is if we are completely still and very quiet. What a distortion of true worship! Just as there are times for quietness and stillness, there are also times when Christians ought to voice their praise loudly and without shame.

Physical Expressions of Worship

Worship can be expressed non-verbally as well as verbally. The Bible informs us that people worshiped God with physical expressions of praise. Let us consider some of them.

1) *Standing.*

Sometimes it is appropriate for worshipers to stand in worship. When the people assembled to hear Ezra read from the Law, they stood up, and did so for hours (Neh. 8:5-8). Standing for the reading of Scripture probably can be credited to Ezra, the priest.[21] Jews in the synagogue stood to hear the reading of Scripture. It was also a common practice to stand when listening to a king or ruler. Since God is the creator of the universe and has declared His Son, Jesus, the King of kings and Lord of lords, it is most appropriate to stand in His presence. Alexander Campbell said, "Standing up in the celebration of praise is more rational and scriptural than sitting."[22] Standing shows respect for God.

2) *Bowing.*

Just as there are times when we should stand, there are also times when we should bow before the Lord. Bowing indicates reverence, awe, humility, and submission to the great and majestic God. When the Israelites realized that God was at work to deliver them from Egyptian bondage they bowed down and worshiped (Exod. 4:31, 12:27). After the Lord passed in front of Moses on Mt. Sinai, "Moses bowed to the ground at once and worshiped" (Exod. 34:8). Just before his death, Moses said to the Lord, "At your feet they [Israel] all bow down, . . ." (Deut. 33:3). The writer of Kings reminded Israel, "To him [God] you shall bow down and to him offer sacrifices" (2 Kgs. 17:36).

The Psalmist declared, ". . . in reverence will I bow down toward your holy temple" (Ps. 5:7); ". . . all the families of the nations will bow down before him, . . ." (Ps. 22:27); "All the earth bows down to you" (Ps. 66:4); "Come, let us bow down in worship, . . ." (Ps. 95:6). God Himself declared, "Before me every knee will bow . . . ." (Isa. 45:23; Rom. 14:11) and ". . . all mankind will come and bow down before me, . . ." (Isa 66:23).

---

[21]Millgram, p. 70.
[22]Phillips, p. 148.

The devil knew that bowing was essential for worship. During the temptation of Jesus before our Lord began His public ministry, Satan took Jesus to a very high mountain and offered Him all the splendors of the earth's kingdoms if Jesus would bow down and worship him. Jesus knew that to bow before the devil would be an act of worship, therefore He said to Satan, "Away from me, Satan! For it is written: 'Worship the Lord your God, and serve him only'" (Matt. 4:8-10).

Worship is a humbling experience. Sometimes a person will pray, "Lord, humble me." Actually, we would never want God to humble us. Besides that, it is not a scriptural prayer. Five times the New Testament commands us to humble ourselves. It is true, God will humble us if we do not humble ourselves, but the command is for us to humble ourselves. If we are too proud to bow before Almighty God, we will never be able to worship Him acceptably.

The apostle Paul wrote it most beautifully, when referring to Jesus in Philippians 2:9-11:

> Therefore God exalted him to the highest place
>   and gave him the name that is above every name,
> that at the name of Jesus every knee should bow,
>   in heaven and on earth and under the earth,
> and every tongue confess that Jesus Christ is Lord,
>   to the glory of God the Father.

3) *Kneeling.*

It is appropriate for worshipers to kneel in worship to God. Almost all Christians bow their heads in prayer. However, shamefully few people in our congregations kneel — at least not in public worship.

Given passages like the ones above (Isa. 45:23; Rom. 14:11; Phil. 2:9-11), why do so few of us kneel in public worship? Are we afraid of the things people would say? Do we fear that they would question our motives? Is it simply a matter of custom? Is it merely a matter of our modern culture?

All the early Restoration leaders agreed that people should pray on their knees. Barton W. Stone was upset to observe that in some congregations some people were standing, others were kneeling, and others were sitting. He felt that some did not kneel for fear of "sullying their fine garments by kneeling." He caustically observed that if the members would keep the floors clean, this "would be no problem."

Walter Scott criticized those who were more interested in proper form than in real substance. He said that sometimes those who were standing during prayer did not really believe in prayer, but rather were, as he put it, "gazing around upon all present as if they stood in a menagerie of wild beasts."[23] Strong words, but they indicate how passionately the early Restoration leaders felt about kneeling in worship.

A few decades ago, it was common for people, especially the men in our churches, to kneel in public worship. Why did we stop? Could it be that we are no longer impressed with God? In our humanistic, self-sufficient society, have we made God too small? Have we caved in to those who fuel fear by raising the question, "If we let people start doing this, what will it lead to? — as if encouraging people to engage in biblical practices will cause the church to drop off the spiritual "deep end." Have we stopped because we do not want to look like Catholics or Pentecostals? Could it be that we have become too sophisticated and proud to humble ourselves before God by getting down on our knees in public worship? Are we more concerned about what others might think about us than we are about what God thinks about us?

We cannot ignore what Scripture says on this matter.

---

[23]Cartwright, p. 274.

"Come, let us bow down in worship, let us kneel before the LORD our Maker" (Ps. 95:6). When Solomon was dedicating the temple, "he stood on the platform and then knelt down before the whole assembly of Israel and spread out his hands toward heaven" (2 Chr. 6:13) and prayed. After Solomon's prayer, God sent fire down from heaven and consumed the offerings and sacrifices and filled the temple with His glory. Second Chronicles 7:3 records, "When all the Israelites saw the fire coming down and the glory of the LORD above the temple, they knelt on the pavement with their faces to the ground, and they worshiped and gave thanks to the LORD, saying, 'He is good; his love endures forever.'" Years later, after King Hezekiah purified the temple and "the offerings were finished, the king and everyone present with him knelt down and worshiped" (2 Chr. 29:29).

When people came to Jesus for help, often they knelt before Him (Matt. 8:2; 9:18; 15:25; 17:14; 20:20). Jesus Himself knelt in the garden of Gethsemane as He prayed to His Father (Luke 22:41). As Paul was about to leave the elders of the church in Ephesus, they all knelt down and prayed (Acts 20:36), as did the believers when Paul left the city of Tyre (Acts 21:5). Writing to the Ephesians, Paul said, "For this reason I kneel before the Father, from whom his whole family in heaven and on earth derives its name" (Eph. 3:14).

There are other positions for prayer and submission, but kneeling is a fitting outward symbol of gratitude, humility, vulnerability, and dependence.[24] It was customary for peoples in the Orient to bow and kneel to show respect. However, kneeling transcends time and place; it is not restricted to times long ago in lands far, far away.

The real question is not "shall we or shall we not kneel in our worship services?" Rather, the question is,

[24]Allen and Borror, p. 131.

"Shall we who *will* someday bow the knee in God's presence kneel *now* as well?" Does it not make sense that those who will kneel as we worship God in heaven get plenty of practice as we worship the Lord on earth?

Alexander Campbell said, "Kneeling in prayer is always to be preferred, if it can be made convenient."[25] Obviously, there are some who cannot kneel because of physical weakness or infirmity. However, God is able to detect a bowed and kneeling heart just as easily as He sees a kneeling knee. It is also true that some of our buildings and the arrangements of pews make kneeling almost impossible. Those difficulties notwithstanding, we should not only permit people to kneel in worship, but encourage them to do so by teaching them the place it holds in Scripture. If anyone needs biblical examples for the practice, both the Old Testament and New Testament provide an abundance.

4) *With the hands.*

It is appropriate for worshipers to express praise to God with their hands. Raising hands to God serves primarily two purposes. First, in prayer a petitioner raises hands to God expecting the Father to respond. This is evident in a number of biblical passages. Moses lifted his hands to God when he prayed that the hail would stop falling on Egypt (Exod. 9:29, 33). Psalm 28:2, "Hear my cry for mercy as I call to you for help, as I lift up my hands toward your Most Holy Place" (note how this blends heart and hands and voice). Lamentations 2:19, "Arise, cry out in the night, . . . pour out your heart like water in the presence of the Lord. Lift up your hands to Him for the lives of your children." Psalm 88:9, ". . . my eyes are dim with grief. I call to you, O LORD, every day; I spread out my hands to you." Psalm 143:6, "I spread out my hands to you; my soul thirsts for you like a parched

---

[25]Phillips, p. 148.

land." Sometimes the request with uplifted hands was for forgiveness (Lam. 3:41f.; Ezra 9:5-6).

The second purpose for lifting hands to God is simply to praise Him. Psalm 63:4, "I will praise you as long as I live, and in your name I will lift up my hands." Psalm 119:48, "I lift up my hands to your commands, which I love, and I meditate on your decrees." Psalm 134:2, "Lift up your hands in the sanctuary and praise the LORD." Nehemiah 8:6, "Ezra praised the LORD, the great God; and all the people lifted their hands and responded, 'Amen! Amen!' Then they bowed down and worshiped the LORD with their faces to the ground." When Solomon dedicated the temple he worshiped and prayed "with his hands spread out toward heaven" (1 Kgs. 8:54; 2 Chr. 6:12-13). Moving into the New Testament, Paul instructed Timothy, "I want men everywhere to lift up holy hands in prayer, without anger or disputing" (1 Tim. 2:8).

The lifting of hands often followed intercessory prayer offered in worship. The people would stand, lifting their hands towards heaven. The leader would "collect" the prayers as he offered a final, summary prayer. Peter Gillquist writes:

> The lifting up of hands signified both the position of intercession, which the priesthood of God has always assumed, and the lifting up of the collected prayers to the Lord by His earthly priesthood. The symbolism here is magnificent. The praying church is not one where everyone prays by himself or herself and hopes that the Lord hears. True intercession is where the people of God *agree together* concerning that which is to be interceded for and *agree together* that the Lord will hear and answer. For the Scriptures teach, 'If two of you agree on earth about anything that they may ask, it shall be done for them by My Father who is in heaven.' Thus, as one person they lift these prayers, or collect them, and present them to the Lord as an incense to Him.[26]

---

[26]Peter E. Gillquist, *The Physical Side of Being Spiritual* (Grand Rapids: Zondervan Publishing House, 1979), p. 119.

This kind of physical involvement in prayer bolsters our faith as we pray. Lifting hands to the Lord in prayer and in praise is not a new phenomenon developed by the Pentecostals, nor is it a holdover from the pre-Christian era. Raising hands to the Lord is thoroughly biblical, having been practiced in the worship patterns of the Old Testament period, and carried on into the New Testament era — and therefore into the Christian era.[27]

Why should it seem out of place or unusual to use our hands to express ourselves? We do it all the time in other settings to express almost every response and emotion. Our hands often give us away. They are extensions of our personalities. When we feel embarrassment, we do not know what to do with our hands. We use them in walking, working, and communicating. An angry man clenches his hands into a fist. A worried person wrings his hands. We extend our hand to welcome others. We hold up and open our hand to receive from another person. We throw up our hands when we are exasperated or when we are happy. We clap our hands when we are appreciative and joyous. Why should we not use our hands in worship to express our praise and need?

There are times when my joy overflows, and everything in me longs to lift my hands to the Lord in worship. There are other times when I long to lift my arms up to God like a small, helpless child lifts his or her arms up to a loving parent. There are times when I am afraid and feel alone when I want God to hold me and comfort me. There are times when I feel so near to God that I envision in my heart and mind's eye that God is holding me secure in his arms close to His warm, strong chest. There are times when I feel so much in need of help and protection that I lift my arms to Him. I do those

---

[27]Allen and Borror, p. 124.

things — literally and physically — but usually in private.

I am quite certain that there are some who think my sentiments are nothing more than silliness or cheap emotionalism. Some may even think that what I am saying is unbiblical. I challenge you to search the Scriptures again. I am convinced I will bow and kneel and raise my hands to the Lord in heaven, and I do not want to wait until I get there to start expressing my adoration and reverence in those ways. After you reexamine Scripture, you may continue to feel uncomfortable with the verbal and physical expressions of praise presented in this chapter. In spite of your personal discomfort, I think you will be forced to admit that these practices are found in Scripture in the form of commands, necessary inferences, and examples. Whether you ever lift your hands in public worship, please give others the freedom to express their praise in these biblical ways if they long to do so.

While we are discussing the issue of using our hands, let me address another way the Bible says praise is expressed to God. There are times when it is appropriate for worshipers to clap their hands to God. Again, I appeal to Scripture for support. Isaiah 55:12, "You will go out in joy and be led forth in peace; the mountains and hills will burst into song before you, and all the trees of the field will clap their hands." Psalm 98:7-9, "Let the sea resound, and everything in it, the world, and all who live in it. Let the rivers clap their hands, let the mountains sing together for joy; let them sing before the LORD." Psalm 47:1-2, "Clap your hands, all you nations; shout to God with cries of joy. How awesome is the LORD Most High, the great King over all the earth."

Even with those passages to support the clapping of hands, there are those who feel that it is inappropriate to clap hands in worship. Many of us associate hand clapping with performance, as a way of showing appreciation for someone who has done something to entertain us. People object to the possibility of making any connection between worship and entertainment, and rightly so. Laurence A. Wagley insists that congregations are not audiences, and leaders of worship are not performers. Wagley fears that "applause is like a wet puppy — once let in the house it is difficult to control."[28] Wagley has a good point. Should we applaud the preacher when he finishes his sermon or the song leader when he concludes his singing? Can we applaud when someone is baptized or repents and returns to the Lord? Do we applaud every Sunday, every event, every person? Is there some other way to express approval? (Perhaps a hearty "amen" would take the place of applause.) Might applause degenerate into nothing but a meaningless ritual?

These are good questions and should be addressed. However, do the biblical passages cited above talk about the issue of entertainment, performance and applause, or do they mean something altogether different by the "clap" of hands to God? Is it not natural to clap your hands (or pat your feet) when you are singing a song you love? Is it not a natural response to clap your hands when you feel joyful? This is what is indicated in the biblical passages cited above. If we did not feel so inhibited, many of us would clap our hands in rhythm with the songs we sing, and we would clap our hands when we felt overjoyed in the presence of the Lord or at the good things which occur in the lives of our brothers and sisters. We may not feel comfortable with it, but it is impossible to discredit hand clapping with Scripture when that hand clapping is a genuine expression of joy, praise, and thanksgiving to God.

---

[28]Laurence A. Wagley, *The Christian Century* 103 (Dec. 3, 1986): pp. 1087-1088.

5) *Greeting one another with a holy kiss.*

It is appropriate in worship to "greet one another with a holy kiss." We are commanded to do so (Rom. 16:16; 1 Cor. 16:20; 2 Cor. 13:12; 1 Thess. 5:26). The apostle Peter commands, "Greet one another with a kiss of love" (1 Pet. 5:14). The idea seems to be that we dare not come before God in worship while we are at odds with one another. Cyril of Jerusalem wrote these words in the fourth century:

> Then the Deacon cries aloud, "Receive ye one another; and let us kiss one another. Think not that this kiss ranks with those given in public with common friends. It is not such: this kiss blends souls one with another, and solicits for them entire forgiveness. Therefore this kiss is the sign that our souls are mingled together and have banished all remembrance of wrong. For this cause Christ said, 'If thou bring thy gift to the altar, and there remembereth that thy brother hath ought against thee; leave there thy gift upon the altar and go thy way; first be reconciled to thy brother, then come and offer the gift.' The kiss therefore is reconciliation, and for this reason his Epistles urge, 'greet ye one another with a holy kiss'; and Peter, 'with a kiss of charity.' "[29]

It is not altogether unusual to see people in American churches kiss one another when they meet. Usually it is on the cheek, and an exchange more commonly practiced between women than men. However, the common form of greeting in our culture is the handshake. Less frequently than the handshake, but more frequently than the kiss, is a hug. Congregations would be much healthier today if Christians' hearts were knit together in reconciliation, forgiveness, and love. Whatever form the "holy kiss" takes, we would do well to subscribe to the explanation given by Cyril of Jerusalem some 1,600 years ago.

---

[29]Gillquist, p. 122.

These five ways of expressing worship, making use of our physical bodies, do not exhaust the possibilities mentioned in Scripture. Two more are the Lord's Supper and baptism. We have already discussed the place of the Lord's Supper and the importance of our participation in it. We have not discussed baptism. Space does not allow me to develop a full treatment on baptism. I simply want to say here that baptism is an extremely important way that believers express their faith and obedience. When one repents of sin, confesses his or her faith in Jesus as the Son of God, and is immersed in water for the forgiveness of sins, he or she participates in a visible, physical act. It demonstrates one's faith, obedience, submission, death to sin, burial of the old person, and spiritual resurrection to a new life.

Dealing With Objections

Before concluding this chapter, let me deal briefly with some objections which are likely to be leveled at what I have written concerning the physical side of worship. Some will say, "I just don't feel like doing those things." "We simply haven't done this in the past." "It's not my temperament to be demonstrative. I don't feel comfortable showing my emotions. Besides, all of this doesn't meet my needs."

Those who raise such objections must understand that the important questions are not: what will make me feel comfortable, what fits into my traditions, or what will meet my needs? Rather, the important questions are: What kind of worship does God call for? What kind of worship pleases Him? How does God prefer to be worshiped? What does Scripture say about what the Lord wants? God wants whole-hearted worship, and it is reasonable to expect that He wants our bodies as well as our minds. Richard Foster writes, "Often our reserved temperament is little more than fear of what others will think of us, or perhaps unwillingness to humble ourselves before God and others."[30]

Psychologists assure us that our physical actions affect our emotions far more than our emotions affect our actions. We can seldom *will* ourselves to *feel* a certain way, but we can *will* ourselves to *act* a certain way, and those repeated actions can change our feelings.[31] In other words, if some of us wait for our emotions to prompt us to say "amen," or to kneel or lift our hands in worship, we may never do any of them. However, if we simply *do* what is biblical, even if we do not *feel* like it at first, in time our emotional response to those behaviors will likely be positive.[32]

There have always been those who have objected to biblical praise. When Jesus was riding into Jerusalem in what some have called His "triumphal entry," the whole crowd of disciples began joyfully praising God in loud voices for all they had seen Jesus do. They cried out, "Blessed is the king who comes in the name of the Lord! Peace in heaven and glory in the highest!" (Luke 19:37-38). Some of the Pharisees in the crowd did not like what the people were shouting, so they demanded that Jesus tell them to stop. Jesus replied, "I tell you, if they keep quiet, the stones will cry out" (Luke 19:40). Must we wait for the stones to cry out because we have been so silent? I pray not! May God help us and free us to shout His praises like those disciples in Luke 19.

What will it take to get us there? Public worship is a group activity which requires worshipers to know what is going on in the service and to understand their roles in worship. That means that worship must be learned, which implies that worship must be taught.

---

[30]Foster, pp. 147-48.
[31]Senn, p. 77.
[32]Allen and Borror, p. 132.

Some of what I have presented in this chapter is frightening to a lot of believers. Although these types of verbal and physical expressions of praise have biblical foundation, they still are outside the comfort zones for many of us. We are not accustomed to doing these things. Even if we agree that these are scriptural practices, we may be too timid to try them in public worship. That is why it is essential that church leaders teach worship. Even more important, it is essential that church leaders model these biblical practices if people are going to learn how and if they are going to overcome their fear. It will take courage from elders and preachers to lead the way in restoring biblical practices of praise, for a great deal of criticism will come when we begin worshiping more actively. The degree of criticism may be an indicator of the opposition Satan is able to muster. May God help us praise Him as He longs to be worshiped!

DISCUSSION QUESTIONS
ON CHAPTER TWELVE

1. Why do some people find worship boring?

2. Are worshipers supposed to be actively involved or merely be spectators in worship? Support your answer.

3. What is wrong with the concept that in worship God is the prompter, the worship leaders are the performers, and the people are the audience?

4. How much physical involvement and what kind should be a part of Christian worship?

5. Is it appropriate for people to say "amen" or "hallelujah" in worship? Support your answer.

6. Is it appropriate for worshipers to express worship with their hands? In what ways? Support your answer.

7. When you see someone kneel in prayer or lift their hands in worship, what is your response? Is your response biblical?

8. Why are so many worshipers fearful of worship that is physically and verbally expressive?

9. How open or closed is your congregation to the things discussed in this chapter? Why is this the case?

10. In your congregation two groups of Christians disagree over the appropriateness of the things discussed in this chapter. How would you moderate between those two opposing opinions?

BIBLIOGRAPHY

Allen, C. Leonard. *The Cruciform Church*. Abilene, TX: ACU Press, 1990.

_____. "Holy Mysteries." *Wineskins* 1, no. 5 (1992): 10-11.

Allen, C. Leonard and Richard T. Hughes. *Discovering Our Roots: The Ancestry of Churches of Christ*. Abilene, TX: ACU Press, 1988.

Allen, Ronald B. "When the Psalmists Say, 'Praise the Lord!': *Worship Leader* (October/November 1992): 8.

Allen, Ronald and Gordon Borror. *Worship: Rediscovering The Missing Jewel*. Portland: Multnomah Press, 1982.

Anderson, Leith. *Dying For Change*. Minneapolis: Bethany House Publishers, 1990.

Anderson, Lynn. *Connecting Seminar*. Lectures delivered at Preston Road Church of Christ.

Anderson, Ray S., ed. *Theological Foundations for Ministry*. Grand Rapids: William B. Eerdmans Publishing Company, 1979.

Bailey, Robert W. "Preaching in the Context of Worship." In *Preaching in Today's World*, ed. James C. Barry, 179-192. Nashville: Broadman Press, 1984.

Bales, Norman. "How to Initiate Worship Renewal." *Image Magazine* 9, no. 2 (March/April 1993): 18-19.

Barth, Karl. "The Event of Divine Worship." In *Theological Foundations for Ministry*, ed. Ray S. Anderson, 330-347. Grand Rapids: William B. Eerdmans Company, 1979.

Baumann, J. Daniel. "Worship: The Missing Jewel." *Christianity Today* (1981): 27-29.

Beckelhymer, Hunter. "The Place of Preaching in Worship: A Theological Rationale." *Encounter* 44, no. 3 (1983): 277-289.

Benson, Louis F. *The Hymnody of the Christian Church.* Richmond, VA: John Knox Press, 1956.

Bishop, Ervin. "The Assembly." *Restoration Quarterly* 18, no. 4 (1975-76): 219-228.

Blackwood, Andrew. *The Fine Art of Public Worship.* New York: Abingdon-Cokesbury Press, 1939.

Brasler, Mark. "Sensitive to the Senses." *Leadership* 7, no. 2 (1986): 21.

Brewer, G.C. *The Model Church.* Nashville: Gospel Advocate Company, 1957.

Burkhart, John E. *Worship: A Searching Examination of the Liturgical Experience.* Philadelphia: The Westminster Press, 1982.

Butterfield, George E. "Worship Integration or Getting Our 'Word and Act' Together." *Mission Journal* (1983): 9-11.

Callahan, Kennon L. *Effective Church Leadership.* San Francisco: Harper & Row, Publishers, 1990.

Campbell, Alexander. "On the Breaking of Bread" (No. III). *The Christian Baptist* 3, No. 3 (October 3, 1825): 52-55.

_____. "On the Breaking of Bread" (No. IV). *The Christian Baptist* 3, No. 4 (November 7, 1825): 76-78.

Carroll, Jackson W., Carl S. Dudley, and William McKinney, eds. *Handbook for Congregational Studies.* Nashville: Abingdon Press, 1986.

Cartwright, Colbert S. "Disciples Worship: A Rich and Relevant Heritage." *Mid-Stream* 28, no. 3 (1989): 263-274.

Clouse, Robert G. "Pietism." *The New International Dictionary of the Christian Church,* p. 780.

_____. "Wycliffe, John." *The New International Dictionary of the Christian Church*, pp. 1064-1065.

Coleman, Michael and Ed Lindquist. *Come and Worship*. Old Tappan, NJ: Fleming H. Revell Co., 1989.

Costas, Orlando E. *The Church and Its Mission: A Shattering Critique From the Third World*. Wheaton: Tyndale House, 1974.

Cullmann, Oscar. *Early Christian Worship*. London: S.C.M. Press, Ltd., 1953.

Dale, Robert D. *To Dream Again*. Nashville: The Broadman Press, 1981.

Davies, Horton. *Christian Worship: Its History and Meaning*. New York: Abingdon Press, 1957.

Davis, Kenneth, Jr. "The Need for Higher Quality Music in Worship." In *Harding College Lectures*, 150-163 Austin, TX: Firm Foundation Publishing Company, 1978.

DeGruchy, John W. *Theology and Ministry in Context and Crisis*. Grand Rapids: William B. Eerdmans Publishing Company, 1986.

Devan, S. Arthur. *Ascent to Zion*. New York: The Macmillan Company, 1942.

Dudley, Carl S. "Using Church Images For Commitment, Conflict, and Renewal." In *Congregations: Their Power to Form and Transform*, ed. C. Ellis Nelson, 89-113. Atlanta: John Knox Press, 1988.

Dulles, Avery. *Models of the Church*. New York: Doubleday, 1987.

Dungan, D.R. "The Lord's Supper," In *The Pioneers on Worship*, ed. John Allen Hudson. Kansas City: The Old Paths Book Club, 1947: 93-114.

Epperley, Bruce. "Exploring the New Frontiers of Disciples of Christ Spirituality." *Mid-Stream* 28, no. 3 (1989): 275-285.

Feeley-Harnik. *The Lord's Table*. Philadelphia: University of Pennsylvania Press, 1981.

Ferguson, Everett. *Early Christians Speak*. Austin, TX: Sweet Publishing House, 1972.

_____. "The Case for Acappella Music in the Christian Assembly." In *Harding College Lectures*, 197-201. Austin, TX: Firm Foundation Publishing Company, 1978.

_____. "The Theology of Singing." In *Harding College Lectures*, 77-81. Austin, TX: Firm Foundation Publishing House, 1978.

Foster, Richard J. *Celebration of Discipline*. San Francisco: Harper & Row, Publisher, 1978.

Gaddy, C. Welton. *The Gift of Worship*. Nashville: Broadman Press, 1992.

Gillquist, Peter E. *The Physical Side of Being Spiritual*. Grand Rapids: Zondervan Publishing House, 1979.

Goldtrap, George. *The Madison Story*. Nashville: Gospel Advocate Co., 1987.

Hageman, Howard G. "Changing Understandings of Reformed Corporate Worship." *Reformed Liturgy in Music* 18 no. 2 (1984): 155-158.

Hart, Larry. "Some Theological Observations on Ministry." *Restoration Quarterly* 27, no. 2 (1984): 93-94.

Harvill, J. "Worship: A Theological Introduction." *Restoration Quarterly* 19, no. 2 (1976): 75-83.

Havens, Bruce. "Celebration." *Mission Journal* 16, no. 11 (1983): 14-15.

Herbert, A. S. *Worship in Ancient Israel*. Richmond, VA: John Knox Press, 1959.

Hieronymus, Lynn. *What the Bible Says About Worship*. Joplin, MO: College Press Publishing Company, 1984.

Hollenbach, Debbie May, and Larry Hostetler. "The Creative Necessity of Worship." *Christian Standard* 121, no. 49 (1986): 11-13.

Hopewell, James F. *Congregations: Stories and Structures.* Philadelphia: Fortress Press, 1987.

Horst, Mark. "Worship's Focus: Seeking the Face of God." *The Christian Century* 140 (November 11, 1987): 991-992.

Howard, Alton. "The Contributions of Modern Church Music to Worship." In *Harding College Lectures*, 165-166. Austin, TX: Firm Foundation Publishing House, 1978.

Hudson, John Allen, ed. *The Pioneers on Worship.* Kansas City: The Old Paths Book Club, 1947.

Hustad, Donald P. *Jubilate!* Carol Stream, IL: Hope Publishing Company, 1981.

Irwin, Joyce. "Music and Theology: A Systematic Approach." In *Sacred Sound: Music in Religious Thought and Practice*, 1-19. Chico, CA: Scholars Press, 1983.

Jarvis, Cynthia A. "Worship and the Stranger." *Reformed Liturgy in Music* 20, no. 2 (1986): 787-790.

Jones, Cheslyn, Geoffrey Wainwright, and Edward Yarnold, eds. *The Study of Liturgy.* New York: Oxford University Press, 1978.

Jones, E. Stanley. *A Song of Ascents.* Nashville: Abingdon Press, 1968.

Jones, Ilion T. *A Historical Approach to Evangelical Worship.* New York: Abingdon Press, 1954.

Jungmann, Josef A. *The Early Liturgy to the Time of Gregory the Great.* South Bend: University of Notre Dame Press, 1959.

Killinger, John. *Fundamentals of Preaching.* Philadelphia: Fortress Press, 1985.

_____. "Reviving the Rites of Worship." *Leadership* 10, no. 4 (1989): 82-86.

Kohler, Ludwig. *Old Testament Theology*. Philadelphia: Westminster Press, 1957.

Leafblad, Bruce. "The Psalms in Christian Worship." *Southwestern Journal of Theology* 27, no. 1 (1984): 40-53.

Mankin, Jimmie Moore. "The Role of Social Service in the Life and Growth of the Madison Church of Christ." D.Min. thesis, Fuller Theological Seminary, 1986.

Marini, Stephen A. "Rehearsal for Revival: Sacred Singing in the Great Awakening in America." In *Sacred Sound: Music in Religious Thought and Practice*, 71-92. Chico, CA: Scholars Press, 1983.

Martin, Philip W., John M. McMillan, and Edward A. Robson, eds. *The Biblical Doctrine of Worship*. The Reformed Presbyterian Church of North America, 1974.

Martin, Ralph P. "New Testament Hymns: Background and Development." *The Expository Times* 94, no. 3 (1983): 132-136.

_____. *The Worship of God*. Grand Rapids: William B. Eerdmans Publishing Company, 1982.

_____. *Worship in the Early Church*. Westwood, NJ: Fleming H. Revell Co., 1964.

Maston, T.B. *Why Live the Christian Life?* Nashville: Broadman Press, 1974.

Maxwell, William D. *An Outline of Christian Worship: Its Developments and Forms*. London: Oxford University Press, 1936.

McArthur, John. *The Ultimate Priority*. Chicago: Moody Press, 1983.

McGuiggan, Jim. "Worship in the Old Testament Prophets." In *Harding College Lectures*, 107-112. Austin, TX: Firm Foundation Publishing House, 1978.

Meador, Prentice A. "Keep Silent Before Him." In *Harding College Lectures*, 92-97. Austin, TX: Firm Foundation Publishing House, 1978.

Millgram, Abraham. *Jewish Worship*. Philadelphia: The Jewish Publication Society of America, 1971.

Moule, C.F.D. *Worship in the New Testament*. Richmond, VA: John Knox Press, 1961.

_____. *Worship in the Early Church*. Grand Rapids: William B. Eerdmans Publishing Company, 1964.

Nelson, C. Ellis, ed. *Congregations: Their Power to Form and Transform*. Atlanta: John Knox Press, 1988.

Newman, David R. *Worship As Praise and Empowerment*. New York: The Pilgrim Press, 1988.

Norman, J.G.G. "Moravian Brethren." *The New International Dictionary of the Christian Church*, p. 676.

North, Ira. *Balance: A Tried and Tested Formula For Church Growth*. Nashville: Gospel Advocate Company, 1983.

Norton, Howard. "Church Needs Doctrinal Balance." *Christian Chronicle* 47 (1990): 22.

Noyes, Morgan Phelps. *Prayers For Services*. New York: Charles Scribner's Sons, 1934.

Oden, Thomas C. *Pastoral Theology: Essentials of Ministry*. San Francisco: Harper and Row, Publishers, 1983.

Ortlund, Anne. *Up With Worship*. Ventura, CA: Regal Books, 1975.

Osterhaven, M. Eugene. "The Lord's Supper as an Act of Worship in the Theology and Practice of Calvin." *The Reformed Review* 37, no. 2 (1984): 83-93.

Patterson, Ben. "Worship as Performance." *Leadership* 2, no. 3 (1981): 49-52.

Peterson, David G. "Further Reflections on Worship in the New Testament." *The Reformed Theological Review* 44, no. 3 (1985): 34-41.

_____. "Towards a New Testament Theology of Worship." *The Reformed Theological Review* 43, no. 2 (1984): 65-73.

Phillips, Dabney. "Worship in the Early Restoration Churches." In *Harding College Lectures*, 141-149. Austin, TX: Firm Foundation Publishing House, 1978.

Reese, Jack. "Called to Worship: The Assembly as Encounter." Lectures delivered at Abilene Christian University, Abilene, TX. Audiocassette, 1991.

Rempel, John. "Christian Worship: Surely the Lord is in This Place." *Conrad Gregel Review* 6 no. 2 (1988): 101-117.

Richards, Lawrence O. and Gib Martin. *A Personal Theology Ministry*. Grand Rapids: Zondervan Publishing House, 1981.

Robinson, Haddon W. *Biblical Praching*. Grand Rapids: Baker Book House, 1980.

Rowley, H.H. *Worship in Ancient Israel: Its Forms and Meaning*. Philadelphia: Fortress Press, 1967.

Saliers, Don E. *Worship and Spirituality*. Philadelphia: Westminster Press, 1984.

Schilling, S. D. "Theology in Hymnody." *Reformed Liturgy in Music* 21, no. 3 (1987): 145-146.

Schilling, S. Paul. *The Faith We Sing*. Philadelphia: The Westminster Press, 1983.

Segler, Franklin M. *Christian Worship: Its Theology and Practice*. Nashville: Broadman Press, 1967.

Senn, Frank C. *Christian Worship and Its Cultural Setting*. Philadelphia: Fortress Press, 1983.

Seymore, Robert E. "Liturgy and the Shape of Your Life." *Mission Journal* 21, no. 5 & 6 (1988): 26-27.

Shelly, Rubel and Randall J. Harris. *The Second Incarnation.* West Monroe, LA: Howard Publishing Company, 1992.

Shepherd, Massey H., Jr., ed. *Worship in Scripture and Tradition.* New York: Oxford University Press, 1963.

Siburt, Charles. "Worship — The Real World." *Gospel Advocate* 133, no. 2 (1991): 23.

Simmons, Morgan. "Hymnody: Reflections on Our Faith." *Reformed Liturgy and Music* 21, (Summer 1987): 139-144.

Squire, Russel N. *Church Music.* St. Louis: The Bethany Press, 1962.

Stott, John R.W. *Between Two Worlds.* Grand Rapids: William B. Eerdmans Publishing Company, 1982.

Swindoll, Charles. *Three Steps Forward, Two Steps Back.* Nashville: Thomas Nelson Publishers, 1980.

Sytter, A. Pugh. "On Innovation in Worship." *Christian Standard* (April 26, 1987): 4.

Taylor, Jack. *The Hallelujah Factor.* Nashville: Broadman Press, 1983.

Temple, William. *Reading in St. John's Gospel*, First Series. London: Macmillan and Co., 1939.

Tippins, Darryl. "Called to Worship: The Assembly as Encounter." Lectures delivered at Abilene Christian University, Abilene, TX. Audiocassette, 1991.

_____. "Rediscovering Christian Worship." *21st Century Christian Magazine* (December 1991): 19.

Toon, Peter. "Waldenses." *The New International Dictionary of the Christian Church*, pp. 1025-1026.

Torrance, James B. "The Place of Jesus Christ in Worship." In *Theological Foundations for Ministry*, ed. Ray S. Anderson, 338-369. Grand Rapids: William B. Eerdmans Company, 1979.

Tozer, A.W. *Worship: The Missing Jewel of the Evangelical Church.* Harrisburg, PA: Christian Productions, Inc., n.d. (Pamphlet)

Von Allmen, J.J. *Worship: Its Theology and Practice.* New York: Oxford University Press, 1965.

Van Beeck, Frans Jozef. "The Worship of Christians in Pliny's Letter." *Studia Liturgica* 18, no. 2 (1988): 121-131.

Wagley, Laurence A. "What's Wrong With Applauding in Church?" *The Christian Century* 103 (Dec. 3, 1986): 1087-1088.

Wainwright, Geoffrey. *Doxology: The Praise of God in Worship, Doctrine, and Life.* New York: Oxford University Press, 1980.

Webber, Robert E. *Evangelicals on the Canterbury Trail.* Wilton, CT: Morehouse-Barlow, 1985.

_____. *Signs of Wonder.* Nashville: Abbott Martyn, 1992.

_____. *Worship Old and New.* Grand Rapids: The Zondervan Corporation, 1982.

_____. *Worship is a Verb.* Dallas: Word Publishing, 1985.

Webber, Robert E. and Rodney Clapp. *People of the Truth: the Power of the Worshiping Community in the Modern World.* San Francisco: Harper and Row, Publishers, 1988.

Weed, Michael. "Junk Food Worship." *Christian Chronicle* 44, no. 23 (1987): 24.

White, James F. "A Protestant Worship Manifesto." *The Christian Century* 99, no. 3 (1982): 82-86.

_____. *Christian Worship in Transition*. Nashville: Abingdon, 1976.

_____. *Introduction to Christian Worship*. Nashville: Abingdon, 1980.

_____. *Protestant Worship: Traditions in Transition*. Louisville: Westminster/John Knox Press, 1989.

_____. "The Missing Jewel of the Evangelical Church." *The Reformed Journal* 26, no. 6 (1986): 11-16.

_____. "Where the Reformation Was Wrong on Worship." *The Christian Century* 99, no. 32 (1982): 1074-1077.

Whitehead, Alfred North. *Science and the Modern World*. New York: The Free Press, 1967.

Wiersbe, Warren W. *Real Worship: It Will Transform Your Life*. Nashville: Oliver-Nelson Books, 1986.

Willimon, William H. *The Service of God*: Christian Work and Worship. Nashville: Abingdon Press, 1983.

_____. *Word, Water, Wine and Bread*. Valley Forge: Judson Press, 1980.

Willis, Wendell. *Worship: A Definitive Study of the History, Methods and Intent of Christian Worship*. Austin, TX: Sweet Publishing Co., 1973.

Wolterstorff, Nicholas. "Worship and Justice." *Reformed Liturgy in Music* 19, no. 2 (1985): 67-71.

Wright, Jim. "The Place of Singing in Worship." In *Harding College Lectures*, 125-130. Austin, TX: Firm Foundation Publishing Company, 1978.

About the Author

Daniel A. Dozier, D.Min. is the associate minister at Madison Church of Christ, Madison, Tennessee. He received his B.A. from David Lipscomb University, his M.A. in Religion from Harding Graduate School of Religion, his M.Div. from Midwestern Baptist Theological Seminary, and his D.Min. from Abilene Christian University. He has authored several articles for *Power for Today, 20th Century Christian, Gospel Advocate, Image Magazine,* and *Up Reach.*